BLACK WIDOW

MARION COLLINS

St. Martin's Paperbacks

BLACK WIDOW

ISBN: 0-312-93946-9
EAN: 9780312-93946-5

Printed in the United States of America

St. Martin's Paperbacks edition / June 2007

St. Martin's Paperbacks are published by St. Martin's Press, 175 Fifth Avenue, New York, NY 10010.

10 9 8 7 6 5 4 3 2 1

ACKNOWLEDGMENTS

Many thanks to Janet Midwinter for her invaluable help with research; to Linda Hardy and James Turner, Donald Cawthon, Mike Archer, David Dunkerton, Stacey Messex, and to everyone who shared their memories of Glenn and Randy. And a special thank you to two courageous ladies, Kathy Turner and Nita Thompson.

CHAPTER ONE:
Death in the Afternoon

At 2:00 P.M. on Thursday, March 2, 1995, 911 operator Lynn Turner and her policeman husband, Glenn, arrived at the door of the emergency room at the Kennestone Hospital in Marietta, Georgia. Glenn was doubled over, clutching his stomach and moaning. He told the attending doctor that he had been throwing up for days. He'd also had blinding headaches and nosebleeds, and was dizzy when he stood up. It hadn't been Lynn's idea to have him seek help, she was sure that all that was wrong with him was a flu bug that would simply run its course; she wanted someone in the E.R. to take a look at a bump on her head. When Glenn heard she was going, he had come along for the ride.

He'd been ill for most of that week. On Tuesday, the motorcycle cop had called into the East Cobb 4th Precinct where he worked the 3:00-to-11:00 P.M. shift and said he would not be reporting for duty. His shift supervisor, Sergeant Mike Archer, took the call. "He got on the phone, and he was just moaning, saying he was throwing up, had diarrhea and cramps. He said, 'Man, I've never been this sick. I feel like I'm about to die. I've been like this for days and I can't shake it. I've never hurt this bad,' and I'm like, 'Dang!'

"I said, 'You going to be all right?' He said, 'Man, I don't know. I ain't never hurt like this. I'll let you know if I'm going to work tomorrow or not.' He called in sick three days, and the last day he called in sick, you could hear it in his voice, he was shaking as he was talking on the phone."

Glenn sounded so bad that for a fleeting second, Archer wondered if his strapping friend was really as ill as he claimed. "He'd never been that sick before and I'm thinking, when you call in sick to work you have to act sick, you know, and so I wasn't sure, and then I called in the schedule to radio. The lady there said, 'Well, that's funny, because Lynn called in sick the last three days, too.' Red lights started going up."

When his lieutenant came in, he shared his misgivings. "I told him and he said, 'Something isn't right, someone's got to go out there, something's going on. Why don't you ride out there and check? Go to the house.' Well, that Thursday we got busy, and I really didn't want to go out and check on Glenn because I didn't want him to think I wasn't trusting him, but we just got so busy I never got the chance."

After checking him out, the doctor at Kennestone agreed with Lynn's diagnosis that Glenn had come down with a powerful and debilitating virus. Vomiting and diarrhea had left him dehydrated and his heart was racing. Alarming though it was for him, dehydration was easily treated. Stretched out on the hospital gurney and attached to an IV that pumped fluids into his body, he was expected to bounce back fairly quickly. When the first bag emptied out, his vital signs were checked again. The doctor frowned: the patient was not perking up as he should have. "Give him another one," he instructed a nurse.

As the second dose of lifesaving liquids finished dripping into his vein, his wife, whose knock on the head had required no treatment, stood impassively at his side while the doctor discharged Glenn with medication to alleviate the nausea. Four and a half hours after they'd checked in, the Turners were on their way back to their home at 881 Old Farm Walk, Marietta. Glenn felt much better.

Later that same night, his partner David Dunkerton rang. "I was working at another precinct when I heard he'd called in sick, so I called him to bust his chops over it. Nobody answered and then I found out he had gone to the hospital."

Donald Cawthon also called after hearing that his friend had been rushed to the E.R. Glenn was a strapping, 6'3", 200 plus–pound workhorse; Donald had never known him to take time off the job, never mind call in sick for days, and decided to call and razz him about it. "Hey, Fat Boy, what's up with you? What'd you do, eat too many doughnuts?" he teased. "Nah, I got flu," Glenn told him. "Then I started getting these nosebleeds and thought I should get checked out. They gave me some stuff and I feel okay now. See you tomorrow." Donald hung up, reassured.

Glenn called his sister, Linda Hardy, between 8:00 and 9:00 P.M. He told her the same thing: his belly felt as if he'd been kicked in the gut; one minute he'd be shivering all over, the next he'd break out in a drenching sweat. But he'd gone to the hospital earlier that day and been taken care of. "I feel really good now," he told her. "What did they do for you?" Linda had wanted to know. He told her about being hooked up to the IV and added that the doctor had given him a suppository to stop the vomiting. He told her not to worry, he felt good enough to suck on the frozen treat that Lynn had just given him. "I think I'm going to be all right. I am going to go back to work tomorrow, or the next day," he said before hanging up. She was very relieved. "I thought everything was great. He was great. He was eating a Popsicle while he was talking to me."

He also called Mike Archer, who had heard from another officer that Glenn had been at the E.R. "I was leaving the precinct that night when he called and said, 'Hey, I went to the hospital and got some IVs in me. I'm feeling a lot better and I'll call you tomorrow and let you know if I'm going to work.' I said, 'Okay, let me know.' I was in a hurry to get out of there and I forgot I was off Friday."

Only one person alive really knows what happened that night, what agonies Glenn Turner endured. By the afternoon of the following day, Friday, March 3, he was dead. When the EMT workers arrived at the house they found him in the front bedroom, lying on his left side on a carved wooden four-poster bed. He was on top of the patchwork quilt his grandmother had made him for Christmas, dressed in nothing but Jockey shorts and wrapped in blankets. On the floor were his pants and sneakers, crumpled in a heap just where he'd struggled out of them. Beside him on the nightstand were his police radio, four plastic containers of drugs and a picture of his mother. Glenn Turner was just 31.

Mike Archer was at his apartment when his pager went off around one o'clock. He called the precinct and spoke to Judith Fannon, the other sergeant on his shift. Her voice sounded flat and dull, as though she had been sucker punched. "They found Glenn Turner dead in his bed this afternoon," she told him.

Mike couldn't believe what he was hearing. Glenn dead? How could that be? If anyone was larger than life itself it was Glenn Turner. He was a big teddy bear of a man, one of the most popular guys on the force. Half a dozen of the cops he worked with called him their best buddy. They'd josh him about his fluctuating girth—although he was never fat, he carried twenty pounds of yo-yo weight, and when he stepped on the scales, the pointer could hit anywhere between 220 and 240 on any given day. But he was in good shape. He turned up at the station house early nearly every shift. He loved being a cop and was never happier than when he was astride his police hog. "He's gone," the sergeant continued, and it had been Lynn who'd called with the news.

A rush of adrenaline went through Mike's body as an appalling notion took hold of him. "I was walking back and forth saying to myself, 'F***ing b****, f***ing b****, f***ing b****, she f***ing killed him.' That was my first instinct, I thought she had done something to him. I called Donald right after that and said, 'Hey, get over here.' I told him what happened. I called over the radio and Major Harold Turner [no relation to Glenn] of the Crimes Against Persons Unit phoned me. I immediately told Major Turner I suspected that she had done something to him. I said I'd be right over, and was told, 'Don't come to the house, we're already thinking that, we are going to look into that. Don't come over here.' "

Donald Cawthon was driving on Route 575 when Mike paged him. "We didn't have cell phones at that time, and I looked at the pager and saw it was a nine-one-one signal sixty-three, which was code for an officer down. I called Archer and he yelled, 'Where the hell are you at? Glenn's dead, Glenn's dead!' "

Donald shook his head, then said, "Don't be funny, Archer, who's down?"

"No, Glenn's dead."

Donald immediately thought his pal had been hit in the line of duty. "Did he get shot? Did he roll up on something?" he fired at Mike. He looked at his watch; Glenn didn't start work until three. It was only two thirty, so that couldn't be it. "No. Get over here right away," Mike told him.

"Did she kill him?" Donald blurted out.

"I don't know what's going on," Mike said. "Just get over here."

As he drove, Donald churned the unthinkable over in his mind: she killed him, she killed him, she killed him. Lynn had done something to him. Like Mike, he was aware that Glenn's marriage had been on the rocks—it was no secret. Half the precinct knew, and anyone who claimed not to hadn't been listening to the young officer who, for the last few weeks, had admitted it to any pal with a sympathetic ear and five minutes to spare. Donald dialed Glenn's sister and left a message: "Linda, you need to call me."

As the news spread among Glenn's friends on the force, the emergency services swarmed all over his pale gray two-story house. Major Lee Moss, Harold Turner and Detective Charlie Mazariegos had answered Lynn's call. When they got there, she told them that Glenn had been sick and that she'd taken him to the emergency room the day before. He'd felt better after being treated and they'd driven home. During the night he had been restless. She had woken up, checked the room where he had been sleeping, and found his bed empty. When she'd glanced at the clock, it was 3:00 A.M.

She had gone downstairs, but couldn't find him. Then she'd heard noises coming from the basement and had gingerly climbed down to find her husband ranting and raving. He was hallucinating, she said. He had lifted a plastic container of gasoline and nearly had the top off to drink it before she snatched it away. Back upstairs he'd told her he could fly. He had gone out on the second-floor deck and nearly succeeded in propelling himself off the top of the railing before she managed to haul him down. Eventually, she had talked him into returning to his bed.

In the morning he had seemed all right. She had told him she needed to go to the store and asked if she could fix him anything to eat before she left. He had wanted Jell-O. When she got back around two in the afternoon, she had gone into his bedroom and saw him under the covers, very still. As she drew near, she could see the sheet that covered him wasn't moving up and down as he breathed. Creeping closer, she pulled back the quilt, and she could see that his face was blotchy and turning purple. She knew he was dead.

She had dialed 911, acutely aware how often she'd been on the receiving end of many similar desperate calls. Within minutes, an ambulance and police cars, lights flashing and sirens blaring, came roaring down the drive. The EMT guys had checked Glenn's vital signs, hoping for something, anything that would signal he could be revived. But the man they were looking at had been dead for a while. They had turned to Lynn, shaking their heads. "There's nothing we can do for him," one of them told her gently.

Right from that moment, Glenn's fellow cops had been skeptical. Goddamn it, healthy 31-year-olds don't just die of the flu, they said to each other back at the precinct, where they milled around trying to make sense of this tragedy. But though they talked about little else to each other, they knew that publicly they would have to keep their doubts to themselves and wait for the medical examiner's report to determine the real cause of death.

Donald and Mike had no such reservations. "The afternoon he died, within an hour of finding Glenn's body, and while his body was still at the house, we talked to the people at the police department. They told us to stay away, don't point fingers at anybody. We were still talking [to them] the next day when they still had his body down there doing the autopsy, and they assured us that everything was being done. He was a police officer, they would check into it," says Donald. A post-mortem would uncover the truth.

For the department, it was a double tragedy. Not only had they lost a veteran officer, a guy without an enemy in the world, but his young wife, now his widow, who had made the shocking discovery, was also one of their own. As a 911 operator, she worked with them every day.

The officers on the scene had been amazed how Lynn was in control, stoic even, despite her dreadful loss. There were no tears. They saw nothing suspicious about her calm exterior, since, if their experience with the bereaved had taught them anything, it was that people react to the deaths of loved ones in many different ways. Some become hysterical, others are too overwhelmed to even cry, yet others go into denial. There was no concrete reason for believing anything was amiss; the medics were leaning towards a finding of heart attack, and a cursory look around the premises revealed no sign of foul play.

They asked Lynn how they should get in touch with Glenn's family, since a search of his belongings had failed to uncover a phone book. She shrugged and shook her head; she said she couldn't help, as she wasn't in touch with any of them. The sympathetic investigators put this down to shock. They asked if there was anywhere they could take her, anyone they could call to come over to be with her. She told them her mother and a friend were on their way.

"The major called Archer and asked if anyone knew how to get in touch with the family," recalls Donald. "Archer says, 'Yes, Cawthon's standing right here, he does.' They had done some change with phone numbers and they couldn't find Glenn's book. They later found it with his motorcycle. The major said, 'Tell them we apologize.'"

Linda was dumbfounded when she was told her sister-in-law didn't know how to contact her. "She told them she didn't know any of our phone numbers or where any of us lived even though she had been to my house on numerous occasions," she says. "She knew where we lived,

she knew everything, and she told them nothing. It was
the biggest crock. Captain Green tried to hunt us down.
[The cops] were out on the road trying to find us because
they didn't want to tell us on the phone."

Donald kept ringing Linda until he finally reached
her. She and her husband Jimmy Hardy had a drywall-
finishing business and as they usually did at the end of
the working week, they had gone out for a bite to eat.
"Most Friday nights we went to a Chinese restaurant up
in Cartersville. I was sitting having dinner with Jimmy
and he wanted us to go to Tennessee for the weekend.
Sometimes we did that, we'd go to dinner, then drive
somewhere and take a hotel room for the night. I didn't
want to go. I remember I was adamant. Jimmy kept asking me why I didn't want to go, and I didn't have a reason, I just didn't want to," she says.

When they got home it was after nine and the light on
their answering machine was flashing. She flicked it on
and heard Donald's urgent voice: "Linda, you need to call
me." The next call was from Mike Archer. His message
also sounded serious: "Linda, you have to call me," he
said. As she was going through the rest of her messages,
the phone rang.

"It was Donald," she remembers. "He said, 'Linda,
Glenn's dead.'

" 'No!' I said.

" 'He's gone.'

" 'No!' " I said again.

" 'He's gone.'

"I screamed at him, 'What did she do? Did she kill
him?' I just lost it. Jimmy started freaking out. He got in
the car and left to tell Dad. I was in the house alone trying
to make sense of it. How could this have happened? I had
talked to him last night and he was perfectly fine. How
could he be dead? She must have killed him," Linda remembers thinking.

Glenn's mother had called him on the morning he died. She was leaving for a family reunion in Jacksonville, Florida, and was concerned because the nasty bug that had put him on his back earlier in the week showed no signs of quitting. She had just wanted to make sure he was okay before heading south. When she got no answer she decided that if there was no one home, then Glenn must have recovered to the point where both he and his wife had gone back to work.

Linda frantically began trying to find her mother. Kathy Turner hadn't left the number where she'd be staying, she had promised to get in touch when she arrived in Jacksonville. "I called someone in the church trying to figure out how to find my mom, and I got her friend, Mrs. Tryon," says Linda. "She said, 'I'll make some calls to figure out where she's at.' She called back and said they had found her. 'Do you want to tell your momma or would you like Doctor Tryon to do it?' she asked me. I remember thinking that her husband had experience doing this kind of thing and maybe it would be better coming from him. I said, 'I don't think I could tell my mother that.' She said, 'I'll have Bill tell her, he'll know what to say.'

"I also called the house trying to get ahold of Lynn, to find out what happened, but there was no answer. Then I tried to find her mother. I called directory assistance and got nowhere. And I didn't have her cell phone number."

That night, with Glenn's body lying in the city examiner's office and an autopsy scheduled for the next morning, his family kept trying unsuccessfully to talk to his wife. His brother James, his Aunt Becky and his father all called her. Linda rang twice. The first time Lynn picked up and said, "I have to call you back." The second time she told her, "I can't talk to you right now."

Linda's house in Acworth began to fill up. "Jimmy came back from Dad's, then Bubba [James] came over, Scotty and Becky Halter came in [Scott was also a cop at the 4th Precinct] and then Donald and Mike arrived. Friends, people from the church, they were coming and going—that Friday night was unreal. Donald was with us the whole time."

A few hours after her husband's body had been removed to the morgue, Lynn finally contacted her sister-in-law. "She called me after eleven that night to give me her side of the story," says Linda. "She told me she was in her car driving very fast and talking on her cell phone. 'I don't know where the hell I am going,' she said. I couldn't take it in. It's eleven and she's driving around? She wasn't crying, she wasn't upset . . ."

Quite the opposite, Lynn was all business. She matter-of-factly launched into a lengthy account of what had happened since Glenn returned from the hospital. Linda was numbed into silence as her sister-in-law recounted her brother's nighttime ramblings. He had been fine in the morning. He'd asked for some Jell-O and crackers and she'd left him nibbling on them when she'd gone out around 9:30 A.M. When she'd returned at 2:30 P.M., Glenn was dead. "While she was talking, I took notes. I wrote down what she was saying. I don't really know why," Linda says.

She was dumbfounded by how calm Lynn was, how glibly the details tripped off her tongue. But the story just didn't wash. Linda kept thinking: Glenn was so sick he had dragged himself to the hospital the day before, then during the night he'd suddenly become unhinged, and first thing in the morning his wife leaves him alone to go shopping? When she hung up the phone, Linda repeated the tale to the family and friends gathered in her living room.

It was met with snorts of derision. "Wouldn't you have said, 'Wait a minute, maybe he's having an allergic reaction'? You can die from that," says Donald. "As a trained 911 officer, Lynn was well aware of that. They had just come back from the hospital, yet she didn't pick up the phone, doesn't call anybody. But six hours later she takes her ass out of there and goes to the store. Now, your husband's deathly ill and you go to run errands?"

Robert Tressell, an investigator for the Cobb County medical examiner's office, spoke to the new widow. She told him Glenn had been sick for three days and had gone to the emergency room because his nose had started bleeding. She said the nursing staff had been concerned about Glenn's fluctuating blood vessels. But he had been discharged when he'd shown signs of improvement. When they got back from the hospital he'd tried to eat a Popsicle, but it had upset his stomach.

She repeated her story of being wakened in the middle of the night by Glenn stumbling around, knocking things over, acting irrationally, convinced there was someone in the house. She said she'd calmed him momentarily by promising to search for the intruder. Then she'd heard him go down to the basement and followed him. He began to complain about being thirsty and reached for a small container of what she thought was gasoline. Lynn told Tressell she'd removed it from his grasp and persuaded him to go back upstairs with her. She'd helped him into bed and brought him a large glass of water.

The autopsy, carried out the next day, failed to uncover anything that would suggest a crime had been committed. That winter a particularly virulent strain of flu had swept the area, and all signs pointed to Glenn being its tragic victim. He'd been fighting textbook symptoms all week. His blood and urine were put through routine drug-screening tests and revealed nothing suspicious, but Cobb County medical examiner Dr. Brian Frist did find something totally unexpected—Glenn's big, generous heart was just that: too big. The enlarged organ had simply given out. He ruled that Glenn died of natural causes.

To his devastated friends and family Glenn's death was

anything but natural. Linda describes her nagging unease: "Rigor mortis had already set in when they found him. The time of death was approximately between nine and nine fifteen in the morning, and according to Lynn, she ran her errands at nine thirty. She left when she knew there was no recovery. He was dead when she left."

CHAPTER TWO:
A Date With Destiny

Glenn Turner's death left his family stunned. The middle child of five siblings, he had been their anchor. He was born in Atlanta on September 25, 1963, to Dillard C. Turner and his wife, the former Kathryn Rilea, who'd named their second son Maurice Glenn Turner before deciding the newborn would be known as Glenn. Tim and Linda had arrived before him, Margie followed a year later and James didn't show up for another decade.

"I got married in nineteen sixty and had four kids in four years," says Kathy. That winter was a cold one in Atlanta. "I remember slipping on ice with him in my arms and falling. I saved him, but I was all bruises." While he was still a baby, the Turners moved fifteen miles northwest of the city to Smyrna where they'd bought a house. "He was a very, very happy, very go-lucky little guy," she says. "One time when we were living in Smyrna I sent a picture of him and Tim to the TV station—they wanted pictures of happy kids. Glenn had this big old smile on his face, and when they showed it they said, 'Now there's a happy guy!' He was just four or five then and he got a kick out of seeing himself on television." When he wasn't smiling, he'd have a thumb in his mouth. It didn't matter which, he'd suck on both. "He told us one thumb was 'milk' the other was 'water.' "

Less than two years later, the house was sold and for a while they lived with Dillard's folks in the tiny town of Ball Ground, where a couple of centuries ago the Cherokee played a version of lacrosse. But the sudden influx of two more adults and four boisterous tots proved too much for their paternal grandparents to handle and Dillard and Kathy soon went on the hunt for a home with a bit of breathing room for their kids. They found the ideal place in Alpharetta.

"It was small, but we had three bedrooms and a little room James occupied after he was born. That's where the kids really grew up," says Kathy. "The house was surrounded by about two hundred acres of woods. I had a garden and there was a creek and a lake behind the woods. There was a little hill where the children could slide down on their fannies and just enjoy themselves. Dillard raised pigs and he had hunting dogs. There was also a baby goat they carried around—it was really Margie's 'baby.'

"We just loved that place. The kids made their own entertainment. We grew vegetables and I had them gardening with me. Later, when we moved to Acworth we planted apple and pear trees and we had blueberry bushes." A stay-at-home mom, Kathy used time spent on walks in the woods and indoor games to make sure her kids grew up smart. "We would play table games for hours. We'd play Monopoly to help with their counting, and Scrabble to help with spelling and words," she says. And while she immersed herself in her young family, Dillard commuted to his job as a roto press operator in an Atlanta paper company that supplied packaging for the food and beverage industry.

The family dynamic changed with the birth of young James. Glenn was 10 at the time and did not greet the event with unalloyed joy. "He loved things to be neat-looking and then James came along and was into everything, and he hated it, he hated having James around," Kathy recalls. "I had played ball with the older kids and I remember they'd say, 'Momma, you are not playing with us anymore,' and I'd tell them, 'I have to take care of the baby.'"

Kathy readily admits that she too was dismayed when she found out she was pregnant again, but she was determined that it wouldn't stop her still being active in all of her children's lives. "The kids were in a club called Pathfinders where they'd ride their bicycles, fly kites, do just normal kid stuff. It was always outdoors. It was like Boy Scouts and Girl Scouts, and I joined with them. I took James everywhere. He went camping with us at age four."

His arrival brought more changes in the older kids' lives. They had started Marietta Seventh-day Adventist Church School and after they moved to Alpharetta, Kathy drove them there every morning. "When James came along Dillard told me I couldn't travel that far with the baby—it was a thirty-minute trip by car—so I put the kids in public school there in Alpharetta. They liked their rural school, but they didn't stay too long because we moved back to Marietta again—there was a lot of moving," she remembers. When the baby grew old enough to be easily portable, she put the kids back in church school, and as soon as he turned 5, she enrolled him with his siblings. Her life was so hectic that keeping track of her youngsters was a logistical headache. "I left James at the church a couple of times by mistake," she says.

Because Dillard's working hours were anything but ideal for a family man, the brunt of raising the five kids fell on Kathy's slim shoulders. "He was a good daddy when he was home, but he slept all day and worked nights. I had to be a mom and a dad," she says. "My dad was on the third shift with Mead Packaging in Atlanta for most of his life and retired after thirty years," explains Linda. "He was an absent parent most of the time. Mom was the one who was always there and was the core of the family."

Although Dillard earned a decent wage, stretching his paycheck to support the seven of them wasn't easy. To make ends meet, the enterprising Kathy figured she should start a cleaning business. "We were always dead poor," she says. "My life was spent picking up after my kids anyway, so I thought I might as well clean up for other folks and get paid for it." The job had the advantage of letting her choose her own hours, so she could be home for her kids when she had to be; the downside was that it didn't pay too well. When James was old enough to go to the Atlanta Adventist Academy, she drove a school bus to pay his fees.

With her husband away much of the time coupled with her growing independence, it was almost inevitable that their relationship would develop more than a few cracks. As her marriage sailed into troubled waters and the four older children began challenging her authority, Kathy found solace in her youngest one. "James was beginning to be my comfort because I could be loving to him when the other kids were treating me like trash," she says. "I have been telling him all his life that I didn't want him, but he's been the best thing that ever happened to me." According to Linda, the baby of the family got away with practically anything. "He was always getting into trouble and never got punished for it. But me and James were very close. I tried to keep him out of scrapes."

Kathy had been raised as a Seventh-day Adventist and she turned to her church for support in raising and educating her lively brood. It did not let her down.

"I took the children to church by myself. Dillard joined the church around nineteen sixty-four when Margie was a baby, and he really liked the pastor. When the pastor left, he left." Saturday is the holiest day of the week for Seventh-day Adventists, and when Glenn and the older kids rebelled at having to sit in Bible class when their friends were out having fun, Kathy often found herself in the family pew with only James for company.

When he was in 10th grade, Kathy sent 16-year-old Glenn to boarding school in Gordon County, about seventy-five miles from home. The Georgia–Cumberland Academy was run by the Church, which made scholarships available to financially challenged parishioners. As she and Glenn drove up there with his suitcase, they were greeted at the town line by the sign: "Welcome to Calhoun, Georgia—Land of the Cherokee." Situated an hour up I-75 north of Atlanta and forty-five minutes south of Chattanooga, the little town is steeped in Native American history. A restored museum trumpets the New Echota Historic Site, headquarters of the Cherokee Nation in the early 1800s, and traces the infamous Trail of Tears taken by the tribe when the burgeoning settler population, armed with rifles and government-issued property deeds, forced its members off their ancestral land.

Although it was the first time Glenn had been away from his family, he wasn't totally surrounded by strangers. Linda was a senior and had already been at the academy for a year when her brother joined her. Also enrolling that semester was his closest buddy from his old public school, Jerry Lee McMichael, whose family also attended the Church. The two boys were inseparable despite the marked differences in their personalities. Glenn was steady and placid, J.L.'s hotheadedness often landed him in scrapes. The two boys roomed together throughout their junior year and like every other student, they wore the mandatory uniform of CAA logo shirts with khaki pants or shorts.

The school's mission mirrored that of its parent body: to broadcast the everlasting gospel from the Three Angels' messages of Revelations, chapter 14, verses 6–12, with the aim of encouraging people to accept Jesus as their savior and prepare for His second coming. The Church's leader was William Miller, a New York farmer. He divined that the end of the world and Christ's "rebirth" would occur sometime between the spring equinoxes of 1843 and 1844.

When the planet outlasted his prophecy and another doomsday prediction for the fall of 1844, many believers bailed out. Those who kept the faith formed the Seventh-day Adventist Church in New Hampshire in 1863.

The students at GCA spent part of each day at religion class and on Wednesday and Friday nights and for most of the day on Saturday, they were required to attend the chapel on the school grounds. Any free time was taken up with allotted chores, particularly for scholarship recipients. Glenn and his pal were assigned to build and sell outdoor furniture.

It was a tough life, according to J.L. "Most of the students were rich kids, but Glenn and I weren't, we had to work. We were put in a redwood factory on the school grounds where picnic tables were made and sold. It was hard, we worked from eight in the morning until midday, when we'd shower and go to the cafeteria for lunch, then we were in class for the next four or five hours."

"It was hard, but Glenn said he enjoyed it," says Kathy. "He made things he would have never learned to make before. It made him feel good about himself. He came home with a redwood outdoor stool he had made."

"It was a Christian school and there were probably fifty people in the class," J.L. remembers. "We were both poor and I was always trying to beat the seniors at everything. We were always together." They were picked on until the two of them got into a marathon wrestling match that started in the dorm and continued all down the stairs. "We wrestled for about two hours and eventually Glenn got me in a scissors hold and I had to give because he was bigger and stronger than me. But from that day, nobody ever messed with us again," says J.L.

"When Christmas break came you could leave or stay and work until Christmas Eve. The people we worked for . . . brought a bottle of Wild Turkey for one of our supervisors for Christmas. I got drunk and Glenn took care of me until my dad came for me. I don't think Glenn was involved, although he might have been, because we were raising all kind of hell, and when my dad arrived, I got in trouble."

According to Linda, boarders went home about once a month. "That depended if your mom or dad had enough gas to come pick you up," she says. J.L. recalls he and Glenn were sprung most weekends. "My dad would come up there and get us and we'd go to his house. He had a boat, and we'd go waterskiing on Lake Allatoona."

With a solid Christian education behind him, Glenn graduated at 18 and tried various jobs in landscaping and construction, building houses and log cabins. He did a stint with United Parcel Service. Then he and J.L. began working as landscapers at Smyrna Adventist Hospital (now Emory-Adventist Hospital). When his pal moved on, Glenn stayed on in security and took to it like a duck to water. His mother says he briefly contemplated life in the army. "He came to church one Saturday with J.L. They had shaved their heads and he said, 'Mom, we are joining the Marines.' I said, 'Okay,' and he never mentioned it again," she recalls.

On weekends they hit the bars. "We got in trouble with Glenn's mom when we got out of high school," says J.L. "We'd go out partying. We didn't do the religious things anymore, and every Sunday morning Glenn's mom would be fixing breakfast and we'd be passed out in the living room, and she'd do a little preaching at us—we did that for a long time until I ended up getting married. After that we'd get together once in a while and go out somewhere on Friday or Saturday nights, to wrestling or to rock concerts. Glenn liked country music and rock 'n' roll. We went and saw Prince once, and that was kinda fun.

"I was always getting into fights. Glenn would never fight unless I was getting badly beaten up, and then he'd wade in to rescue me. One time, we were riding up and down Highway Forty-one and got into it with two guys in another car. They thought they could outrun us, and they did. When we pulled over they came after me. They started punching me in the car and wouldn't let me get out. Glenn just sat there, and I am yelling at him, 'Get them off me!' Then I got hold of one of them and the guy grabbed the liner in the car. Glenn just calmly walked around and slings him off. 'Now you've touched my car,' he said. Then he told me to get out. 'Kick his ass,' he said, and I did."

It was no surprise to his friend that Glenn got steamed over the threat to his wheels. "Just out of high school he drove a big ol' Dodge Dart, a grandma-looking car, but he cleaned that thing up—we thought we were big shots in it. Then he had a Chevy truck he just loved," remembers J.L.

At 21 Glenn announced that he wanted to be a cop. "When he told me he was going to join the police, I wasn't too happy about that. I was afraid what would happen to him," remembers Kathy. "A friend of ours who is a dentist gave a recommendation for him. When they sent him the form, he didn't recognize the name. He said, 'I don't know a Maurice Glenn Turner.' They said, 'What about a Glenn Turner?' He said, 'Oh yes, I know a Glenn Turner, I used to take care of his teeth.' When he died, Dr. Larsen felt so guilty. He said, 'I am so sorry I let him become a police officer,' and I told him, 'That had nothing to do with him being a police officer.' "

In 1984 he was accepted at the North Central Georgia Law Enforcement Academy at Marietta. Linda readily suggested that he live with her and Jimmy at their place at the East Lake apartments while he was training. He graduated at the end of 1985 and was assigned to Cobb County's 4th Precinct.

"Glenn wasn't a real aggressive go-getter. He was more of a laid-back police officer," says his former sergeant, Mike Archer. "When something was in front of him he handled it, but he wasn't one of those kick-ass-and-take-names–type police officers. But he wasn't lazy either. He went with the flow."

It wasn't just the Chevy truck that young Glenn loved. He was also crazy about a girl named Stacey Suzanne Abbott who he had met in the spring of 1986. She went to school with James, and the two families attended the same church. At first, he paid little attention to her. Sparks did not begin to fly until they both went to a Pathfinder camp-out arranged by the church. "He had driven up there in his brown Silverado truck and I thought he was so handsome. He exuded this wonderful confidence. He was so sweet and his smile just drew me in. I was smitten," says Stacey. "That entire weekend we spent talking, laughing and having a great time. He was absolutely the best guy I had ever met and he was interested in me! WOW!"

She knew that her mother would not let her date Glenn, who has seven years older than Stacey, and over the next few weeks, their friendship was confined to phone calls. But despite the restrictions laid down by her mom, it was deepening into something more serious. "I became more and more enamored with him. I would see him at church and sneak over to hold his hand during the service. He was my first love. As time went by, my mother let me see more and more of him. She really liked him and had a lot of respect for him, so the age difference did not seem like such a big deal."

After a couple of years as a patrolman, he was reassigned to the motorcycle unit. Glenn was in heaven—hog heaven. He was partnered with David Dunkerton. The two men, who were born just six months apart, were both motorcycle crazy and quickly became buddies. A permanent reminder of their friendship is the tattoo of the Archangel Gabriel on David's left bicep. Glenn's police ID number, 0116, is etched into the picture, and David proudly displays it.

They started riding together on the afternoon shift. "It was a great job, especially if you have motorcycles in your blood and love police work," he told reporter Janet Midwinter. "We rode huge Harley-Davidson FXRP bikes and if you were the kind of guy who didn't want to be in an air-conditioned car, it was great, although not everyone wants to do it. You can melt under that helmet in summer. We dealt with mostly traffic-related incidents, and whenever we stopped kids for speeding in that area, inevitably the first words out of their mouths would be, 'My dad's an attorney,' as if that made any difference."

David says it would take an awful lot for someone to press Glenn's buttons, but he rarely needed to be harsh with anyone—his size was intimidating enough. "We would eat together, and for the most part we rode together for the entire shift. I didn't have to tell him what I was thinking when we were dealing with the public. All we had to do was glance at each other to know what to do next."

It was a matchup that nearly never happened. On Mother's Day of 1986, just as he'd joined the bike unit, Glenn bought a new motorcycle. He called Stacey to see if she could go for a ride. Her mother wasn't thrilled at the idea, but after a little persuasion, she relented. It was a beautiful day and everything seemed perfect to Stacey as she pulled on the denim overalls that Glenn loved her to wear.

They rode past Kennestone Hospital and stopped at a red light on Church Street. "There weren't many people on the road that day, and we were the only ones stopped at the light," she remembers. "A blue Ford Escort pulled up

beside us in the right lane. The windows were down and
we could hear yelling coming out of the car. Two large
men got out of the back. The man closest to us was carrying a bat and waving it around in the air while yelling.
Glenn kept focused on him.

"I looked behind us and saw a large brown van barreling down the street. It was coming at a speed where I knew
he was not going to be able to stop. I had my arms wrapped
around Glenn's waist and started hitting him and yelling,
'Go, go!' " There was no way they could have moved in
time. It slammed into them with such a great force that
Stacey flew off the bike and into the grille of the van.

The impact took but a split second, but to Stacey it
transpired in slow motion. "I remember every detail,
every scream, the tires on the motorcycle and van squeal-
ing," she says. "Because the van was still traveling forward I had slumped over the back tire of the motorcycle
and started to slip under the wheel. Glenn was so strong
that he held up the bike with one arm long enough to
reach back and grab the back of my overalls with his left
hand and throw me out of harm's way."

When she regained consciousness, Stacey could hear
Glenn screaming, but she couldn't see him. Her helmet
had protected her head, but she could barely move her
neck. She hauled herself onto her hands and knees and
began crawling down the street in the direction of his
howls, fighting bystanders who tried to stop her.

"The next thing I remember was paramedics over me.
I was told that I was being taken to Kennestone and
Glenn would be right behind me. I just cried. I have
never heard a man yell in pain like I heard Glenn."

Stacey later found out that the van had dragged him
for several blocks until a car pulled out in front, forcing
the driver to stop. "The bike flipped out the side, but
Glenn's chest got caught on the rear axle and his leg was
mangled." When he arrived at the hospital, he was still

screaming. Sedated in the room next door, she heard everything through the fog of the drugs. The doctor assured her that Glenn would probably not remember much about it.

Before her mother took her home she was allowed a few minutes with him. "They said they were going to keep him for observation and release him within the next few days. When I went in to see him he cried and apologized over and over. It broke my heart," she says.

Some time during the night, she heard the phone ring and her mother answering it. Glenn's condition had deteriorated to being critical; a fatty embolism from the break in his leg had leaked into his lungs. He was in intensive care and not expected to last twenty-four hours. J. L. McMichael recalls the spine-chilling call he got from someone who told him, "You better come down here quick, your friend's about to die."

It was no exaggeration. At first, when Glenn came around from the anesthetic, he seemed fine. His mother remembers arriving at his bedside. "His femur was shattered, the skin was just hanging on. But he was joking and laughing," she says. "I asked if I could stay with him that night and the nurse said I had to ask his roommate first, since they were both men. About two in the morning she came in and asked Glenn to wake up, but he didn't move. She slapped his face and blew in it and did all kinds of things, then went out and came back with someone else who tried, and also got no response.

"I don't know why it took so long to do something, but the next morning Linda came to relieve me—I had a house to clean and I needed the money. She called to say they were sending him to the Intensive Care Unit because he was still not responding." For the next week Glenn was kept in an induced coma in the ICU with a battery of machines providing sustenance, monitoring him and helping him breathe.

"He was all swollen up and the doctor said they were going to take him off the ventilator because he could stay on it only so long." Kathy says when she began to question taking out his breathing tube, she was told, "Mrs. Turner, you do not understand, he might not make it."

Once again she turned to her church for help. "I called the pastor to come and anoint Glenn, for I believed that God was in control of his life. We had the anointing with oil and a prayer of God's healing. I went home that night and his daddy and the kids stayed, they spent every night in the waiting room. The next morning I went back to the hospital and they were all smiles. 'Guess what happened?' they said. 'Glenn woke up about two in the morning and was a different person.' I couldn't wait to see him. Soon after, they took him off the ventilator and he started improving. The doctor didn't know why and said it was a miracle. I knew it was God's healing and a miracle."

The devoted Stacey also visited him every day, sometimes sleeping on the floor of the ICU waiting area, just to stay close to him. He remained hospitalized for thirty days, and faced at least six to eight months of grueling physical therapy before he could even think about going back to work. In fact, few people, including his doctors, thought returning to his job as a policeman was an option.

Stacey helped Kathy take care of him. "He was not extremely mobile, so my mother let me stay with him to help out, get his food, help him out of bed, etc. . . . We grew closer every day we spent together. I felt so needed and loved by him. It was wonderful."

Once Glenn got back on his feet, he went back to his sister and brother-in-law's home at the East Lake apartments. When he was back on his feet he'd happily tag along while Linda went shopping, helping her pick out things for her house without so much as a whimper of complaint.

"They said he would never be able to walk again," remembers Donald Cawthon. He was running a data voice tracking business at the time and got to know Glenn some months after the accident, when he was looking for someone to fix up a car his stepdaughter had just wrecked. "There was a body shop just up the road [from the police station] and one of the cops was the painter there. He introduced me to Glenn, who had just returned to work and was still limping." The two hit it off immediately.

As Glenn regained his strength he moved into another unit in the same complex, rooming with Scott Halter. Like several other Cobb County officers, they worked security at East Lake in exchange for a hefty discount in rent. Despite his terrifying brush with death, he couldn't wait to get back on his bike. He hated being on desk duty, although Linda says he was a good sport about it. He wasn't giving up. The only thing that still bothered him was the angry scar on his arm.

"He made a perfect recovery. Otherwise he wouldn't have been accepted for the police motorcycle safety course we went through together in nineteen ninety-two. It was physically very demanding," says David Dunkerton. Back on his hog, back at the job he loved, Glenn was on top of the world when 22-year-old Lynn Womack walked into his life.

CHAPTER THREE:
In Walks Lynn

Lynn was born in Marietta on July 16, 1968. As she was fighting her way into the world, the Beatles were bickering over the recording of what became known as the "White Album" in London, students in Paris streets were tearing up the cobblestones to hurl them at the French police, or Les Flics as the rioters contemptuously referred to them, and the Braves were beating the Astros 6–2 at the Houston Astrodome. She shares her birthday with legendary movie bad girl Barbara Stanwyck and toe-tapping glamor-puss Ginger Rogers.

She never knew her birth parents, who were divorced when she was 2 on account of her father's womanizing. When she was 5, she was adopted by Helen Womack, who named her new daughter Julia Lynn. Quickly the *Julia* was dropped, and she was known simply as Lynn.

Her new parents' marriage turned out to be no more stable than that of her natural kin: the Womacks separated when Lynn was 2, and divorced soon afterwards. Helen packed up her toddler and moved from Marietta to Cumming, where she got a job as a secretary at the now-defunct law offices of Jones & Jones. With her mother at work for most of the day, the little girl was looked after by her maternal grandmother, who loved to spoil her and whom she in turn adored.

Her life changed again when, just before she turned 6, her mom married a man named D. L. Gregory and she found herself not only with a stepfather, but also with a stepsister nearly fifteen years older than her. The new family was comfortably well off; they lived in a spacious home with a swimming pool and there was enough money left over for riding lessons. According to what little she has ever divulged about her past, even to the man who became her husband, Lynn grew up free from any kind of physical or sexual abuse in the midst of an extended family with plenty of cousins, aunts and uncles around.

Helen indulged her only child's every whim, a course of action that came back to bite her. Growing up, Lynn displayed a willful streak and by the time she was a teenager, the typical mother–daughter conflict threatened to get out of hand. There were blazing rows followed by slamming doors and buckets of tears. Her grandmother seemed to be able to handle her better than Helen, who later admitted that Lynn was always "strange." She also did not get along with her stepfather. After they were married, Glenn told his mother that Lynn and D.L. did not have a good relationship and that she flat-out didn't like him. He told Linda that D.L. was "just a grumpy old man."

When she was 17, the atmosphere in the home grew so acrid that Helen felt she was losing control of her daughter and carted her off to the Charter Peachford Hospital in Atlanta. She told the admitting staff that she suspected the girl was using drugs, but after a short stay and evaluation, the doctors assured her that Lynn was clean.

Her period of rebellion behind her, Lynn graduated from Forsyth County High School on Peachtree Parkway in Cumming in 1986. She enrolled in community col-

lege, where she earned a two-year associate degree before following her mom into the court system, working at
first as an administrative assistant and later as a secretary
to a lawyer. She became fascinated with law enforcement
and in particular, was drawn to the young men on the police force. One way to meet them was to cruise up to a
parked patrol car, roll down the window and strike up a
conversation with the often-bored cops inside.

When their shifts were over, the young officers from
the 4th Precinct met at the stationhouse or the Amoco
across the street to get changed for a night out. Or they
gathered at someone's apartment before hitting favorite
bars like Confetti, the Crystal Chandelier and another one
on Franklin Road that had six-feet-tall speakers strong
enough to support the weight of three revelers.

With a wife at home who was older than him and had
the sense to keep him on a long leash, Donald Cawthon
would join Glenn and his buddies Scott (Stumpy) Halter
and Jeff Mack when they went out nights carousing.
They went everywhere together in those days. The hell-
raising foursome dubbed themselves "the Rat Pack" and
displayed the same unflinching dedication to partying
and chasing women as their screen heroes. Their rallying
cry was "Let's go hunt" whenever they felt starved of
feminine company.

After drinking and dancing and flirting, the Rat Pack's
next favorite hobby was organizing cookouts. Everyone
was invited. Donald remembers Glenn hosting one in the
summer of 1990 and inviting his mom. He recalls Glenn
telling him about an embarrassing moment when she
came across a stash of girlie magazines in the apartment.
She had looked at her son quizzically. "They're Donald's," Glenn assured her with a straight face. "He came
by today, they must be his." When he gleefully recounted
the episode later, Donald was horrified. "You didn't tell

her that?" he asked. "Yep," replied Glenn, grinning from
ear to ear, "I said they're all yours."

Linda first met the woman who would become her
sister-in-law at the barbecue her brother and Stumpy threw
at their East Lake digs. With several cops living rent-free or
paying nominal rents at the complex where they moon-
lighted as security guards, there were always plenty of like-
minded guys ready to roll out a keg and crank up the music.
On weekends the night air would reverberate with din from
the rowdy get-togethers, which attracted pals with wives or
girlfriends in tow, as well as a healthy number of single and
still-looking buddies. Unattached females were always
welcome.

In 1991 Lynn applied and was accepted for training
to become a 911 operator with the Cobb County Police
Department. She started as a report writer, taking com-
plaints about petty crime from folks who called the
emergency services complaining they'd had garden furniture stolen from their yard or a kid had thrown a rock at
their car. Her ambition was to become a police officer,
and she saw the job as her foot in the door. Dispatchers
were supposed to wear a regulation uniform consisting
of black pants and white or light blue shirts decorated with
official patches. The outfit concealed Lynn's shape a little
more than she liked, and most days, she'd squeeze instead
into snug-fitting blue jeans, twirling a couple of times in
front of the mirror to check that they flattered her curves.

Soon she was hanging out with cops kicking back and
relaxing after work. To the guys in the 4th Precinct, it
soon became well known that the pretty Lynn Womack
never saw a man in uniform she didn't like. In fact, many
of her colleagues believed it was her desire to get close to
the police fraternity that had prompted her to go after the
dispatch job in the first place. Others were less kind. In
their opinion, she was a cop groupie.

One of the men who had come under her thrall was
Paul Rushing, who had joined the Cobb County Police
Department the year before. She had met him when she
was scheduled for some on-the-job instruction. "She was
a radio operator at the time and was assigned to my shift
to ride along with a uniformed officer to experience what
we see on the road. It gives everybody a better understanding of what each other's jobs are. She rode in my
car for probably six or seven hours of an eight-hour
shift," he later recalled.

Their friendly relationship gave him a useful ally on
the 911 team. "Because of that ride-along, there were
times we'd have to call the radio room, and she gave me
a great deal of help with working the GCIC [the police
database] and things like that as I came along," he said.
Although they became close, Paul was hardly potential
boyfriend material. For a start, he'd been married to his
wife Melinda since 1987, and in 1991 he'd become a father for the first time. Instead, Lynn started dating a Cobb
County cop named Boyd Garrett.

She also had her eye on another cop who Paul knew
from a stint in the motor unit. After completing the field
training officer program, Paul had drawn the shift where
Glenn Turner was one of the senior officers. He wasn't
surprised when Lynn targeted Glenn. "He was one of the
more outgoing and approachable officers, a great guy,"
he said.

On that, everyone agreed. Known as "Buddha" by his
pals on the force, Glenn Turner's unflappable nature and
courteous manner made children love him and old ladies
trust him. He was the obvious go-to guy when the Cobb
County Police Department needed someone to make
classroom visits and lecture the kids about wearing helmets when they rode their bikes and warn them never to
get in a car with a stranger. "He loved children," says
David Dunkerton. "He loved talking to them and playing

with them. He would say how nice it would be to have kids of his own."

The four-year romance with Stacey was petering out. Recently it had been more off than on, and with no special girl waiting for him at home, Glenn was single and on the prowl. A sweltering day had given way to a hot summer night, the beer was flowing and the jukebox belting out heart-tugging country songs when Lynn caught his eye. As soon as she saw him looking, she gave him the full-on flirt, leaving him in no doubt that if he was interested, he could be making breakfast for two in the morning.

From the minute she had first spotted him, Lynn liked what she saw. He was hard to miss: at 6'3", he towered over most of his buddies. He was no Brad Pitt, but he was tan with cropped dark blond hair, gentle blue eyes and flashing white teeth. Comfortable in his own skin, he was also easy to be around. "Glenn was the kind of guy who never had a bad day, and if he had, it lasted about a minute. He was always in a good mood," says Donald.

Donald met Lynn at Glenn's apartment where the Rat Pack and friends were assembling before a night out. "We were all going over to meet up with a couple of pals who were also courtesy officers at this place, and she came out the back bedroom down the hallway. She had on a short blue dress with no sleeves. She had some figure and she had two pistols in her hands." Donald was so busy checking out her physical attractions that he wasn't fazed by the fact she was armed. "I thought nothing of it, we all had guns," he says.

By the end of the evening, it was clear to everyone there that Lynn was something of a pistol herself. She was happiest when she was putting on a show, dancing and strutting her stuff in the middle of the room. She was a party girl. And she always seemed to have something else going on. In the days before people had cell phones permanently plastered to their ears, Lynn had a pager and it buzzed continually.

After that first night when she'd initially honed in on him, Lynn pursued Glenn doggedly. In the months that followed she'd turn up with a gaggle of girlfriends at all the Rat Pack's haunts. When she'd catch a glimpse of him, admiring her from across the room, she'd gravitate towards him. Everyone in the joint would notice the striking-looking brunette who always seemed to be circling him, hanging on his every word, laughing uproariously at his jokes.

Donald didn't make too much of it at first, since his pal attracted women like flypaper attracts flies. His old-fashioned courtesy and the cop uniform made for a dynamite combination. "Glenn treated women with respect, like ladies. You never saw him pawing at them," Donald says. "But he was a stud. At parties or when we were just hanging out at bars, there were all these women around him. Half of them were just friends, but Lynn was seeing it like he was a challenge."

Whatever her plans for Glenn, and his undeniable sexual feelings for her, love didn't blossom overnight. This was due in part to the fact that the more Glenn got to know her, the less Donald could stand her. "It was about a year before they became a couple," he says. "Lynn and I always went at it, she cussed me like a dog and I would cuss her like a dog. I was cocky, she was cocky. She would tell you flat out it's her way or no way, and then one time Glenn told me, 'You gotta cut that out, she's my girl.' I said, 'Okay.'"

Mike Archer first became aware of Lynn Womack when she was seeing a cop named Boyd Garrett. "There were a lot of bad rumors about Lynn around. She was kinda loose, she was into a police groupie–type of thing and she was just kind of shady, not somebody you would

want to really trust," he says. "Then I found out that Glenn
was dating her. She had a reputation, but Glenn was so
gullible and so nice, and she was attracted to that. She
knew she could walk all over him, she could be in control."

"Right off the bat you knew she was a bitch," says Donald. "But we all dropped our guard when it came to the
women." And though none of his friends were surprised
that Lynn targeted the amiable Buddha, they could see
where he'd be flattered too. Vivacious, her smiling face
framed by a halo of dark brown curls, she had startling
blue eyes that held men riveted. With an hourglass figure,
at 5'4", her 130 pounds were well distributed and her as-
sets never went unnoticed in a room full of testosterone.

What was just as alluring for Glenn was that she
talked his language. She loved high-powered and flashy
automobiles with the same passion that he did. She could
talk knowledgeably about his beloved Harley. They compared notes; he told her about the Monte Carlo he'd
owned—*Boy could that thing run*, he'd said—and about
the burgundy Mustang that was his pride and joy.

She was also heavily into stock car racing and
NASCAR, spending frequent weekends at the track, partying late into the night with the grease monkeys and race
fans long after the checkered flag had waved in the win-
ner. And it wasn't just hanging out with the drivers and
the smell of gasoline that turned Lynn Womack on—she
knew everything there was to know about the combustion
engine. If anyone had car trouble, she'd throw up the
hood, pinpoint the problem and reach for a wrench. "She
could be a mechanic," Glenn boasted proudly to pals.

She even bought herself a motorcycle, something that
cemented her fascination for Glenn. In the early days of
their romance, they'd tear along country roads side by
side. Glenn was nonplussed to find out that his new girlfriend had a more extensive arsenal of bike tricks at her

fingertips than he had. She could pop wheelies like a pro
and leave him in the dust. She was the perfect date, almost like one of the guys, except for her drop-dead gor-
geous body.

According to Donald, Lynn lured Glenn with sheer animal magnetism that had him panting, and after she had
him drooling, she made her move. His friends and family
agree that he had no chance. Fun-loving and unattached,
he had told his buddies that he had no intention of walking down the aisle anytime soon. That was a challenge
Lynn Womack couldn't resist.

Once she made up her mind to have him, she set about
seducing him—and not only with sex. She dropped a
small fortune reeling him in. She'd turn up with gifts,
a camera, a radio, high-priced accessories for his car like
Mag wheels, the magnesium alloy wheels used on racing
cars. As the romance progressed, Linda remembers Lynn
revamping Glenn's wardrobe. Suddenly he was sporting
$1,000 snakeskin cowboy boots and matching Western-
style belts. She plied him with tickets to Atlanta Braves
games and pricey bottles of liquor. Glenn was thrilled—
a cop's salary didn't stretch to such luxuries even if he
was living virtually rent-free. Neither did a 911 operator's
paycheck, for that matter. Heaven only knows what she'd
told him about the costly price tags, but whatever tale
she had concocted, Glenn had swallowed her explanation and he proudly showed off his new gear to his pals.
"Look what Lynn bought me. Look at this cool thing,"
he'd tell them.

Former police officer Terry Lee, who worked with
Glenn at the 4th Precinct, was also struck by Lynn's single-
minded pursuit of him. She was convinced that Lynn was
so determined to marry Glenn that she'd sat down and calculated the odds of winning him over. Restocking his
closet with the expensive clothes she chose for him and
showering him with presents was an investment in a future

where she would be Mrs. Glenn Turner. Terry also said that at the time she knew her, Lynn also worked for an attorney, and when he threw a party, she would pilfer twenty to thirty bottles of his liquor to impress Glenn and his cop buddies, who had no idea the booze they were quaffing was stolen.

Her largesse also extended to his family, who figured she must really love him to shower him with such lavish items. Yet despite her freehanded generosity, she still seemed to have plenty of money to spare. In 1993 she bought a three-bedroom house at 881 Old Farm Walk in an upscale area of Marietta.

To begin with, Linda Hardy liked her. She knew Lynn augmented her dispatcher's salary by doing bookkeeping for the same lawyer Helen Gregory worked for, and offered to get her a job at First Southern, the collection agency where Linda was a manager. "Lynn did data entry work part-time. She was good, she worked hard." Linda also recalls that her brother's sexy girlfriend seemed to have come out of nowhere. Nobody knew anything about her. "She was very secretive. We only knew she went to school in Cumming and she said she was an only child."

Linda wasn't the only one who had questions, but somehow nobody ever pinned Lynn down about her background. "We never knew anything about her past. We were all busy running from dawn to sundown and all we were thinking about was our next party," says Donald. "There [were] so many girls around, we never talked to her for more than five minutes." Not that Lynn was eager to shoot the breeze about her family anyway. "She'd never hang around. She'd pop in and pop out. If we were going somewhere and she found out that she wasn't going to be in total control, she was bored, she was gone," says Linda.

But in the extended family of hard-partying cops and their pals, it wasn't always possible to run the show, even for a hot number like Lynn. "She tried that, but it was pretty hard to do," says Donald. "We all went out in a big group, and you'd spend fifteen minutes talking to this one and then fifteen minutes talking to that one. She didn't like that. She had to be in the middle of everybody's things or she'd just leave. She would come [into the bar] and had something to do where everyone would be looking at her, and then she'd be out of there. But Glenn was head over heels in love with her."

Mike Archer was bothered by the change that came over his pal when she appeared. "Glenn was cool to hang out with when she wasn't there, but when she came over he was a totally different person. When she'd come to his apartment I would pretty much leave," he says. "Even when she was there she was just doing her own thing, it wasn't as if she was hanging all over Glenn—there wasn't a lot of affection involved in it. They weren't holding hands, or sitting on each other's lap, or hugging. It wasn't like that. I thought it was strange, but I know people like that, there's not a lot of affection.

"Glenn wasn't the best-looking guy, but he had a little bit of high taste. He wanted a girl with a nice figure and all that stuff. He was real picky. Lynn had a real nice figure and she was very pretty, and he found someone who actually [had all that]. Sure, she was walking all over him, we all knew she was walking all over him."

With the romance becoming serious, Glenn took Lynn home. "He brought her over to see me," says Kathy. "I think that was the only time she was ever in my house. He didn't tell me then they were getting married, he told me later on the phone. She didn't have anything to say to me that day, and she never did talk to me. I remember seeing her at Linda's birthday party—we had a surprise party for both of them together—and she seemed to have a good time at it, although I can't believe she had a good time when it wasn't just for her."

The party was for Linda's 30th birthday and was held at Glenn's apartment. "We had included her in it to keep the peace," remembers Linda. "She wanted me on her side and she managed that for a while. We hung out and went out to eat a few times, went shopping together. She always talked about Glenn. She was always checking his cell phone, seeing who he was calling, checking his house phone; she was insecure. But she always wanted me to respect her, and I did, for a while."

In 1993 Glenn packed up his belongings to go live with Lynn at the house on Old Farm Walk. "When he moved in she had no furniture," remembers Donald. "She had a water bed, a chair and a little old dinky table and that was it. And she had a rottweiler." It also wasn't to be the cozy twosome Glenn had in mind, as Linda found out when she dropped by. Lynn also had a lodger, Alisa Moody, who had grown up virtually next door to her in Cumming. According to Donald, the manipulative Lynn treated her like a puppet. "[Lynn] used her to go out with—whenever she was doing anything, she'd use Alisa as her excuse, whether it was shopping or just hanging out. It was like, 'I've got my girlfriend with me, I'm not doing nothing.'" The rent Alisa paid came in handy as well, says Linda. "[Lynn] needed the money to pay for that house. She also used Glenn to pay her bills."

"Donald and I helped him move all his stuff into Lynn's place," says James, who believed from the start that his brother was making a huge mistake. "As a couple, they just didn't fit." There was no doubt that Lynn was running the show, and rather than argue with her, the amiable Glenn would back off and let her have her way." We used to make jokes about it, Donald, Glenn and I. We would say, 'We know who wears the pants in that family.'"

James also remembers that Lynn was hot-tempered. "She'd fly off the handle. I'd be over at Glenn's apartment sitting watching TV with him. She'd come in, and if we didn't immediately acknowledge her or make her the center of attention, she'd throw down her stuff and go storming out of the house—for no reason. She'd never come in with a smile on her face. She had this God-awful look. At first Glenn would go running after her, but we would egg him on about it so much that he had to be more mannish about it and would let her go." And yet James says that she wasn't one-dimensional; she also had a kind and helpful side. "There were other times where I could call her up at one thirty in the morning and say, 'Hey, Lynn, I got a flat tire, would you mind picking me up?' and she'd be, 'Where you at? I'll be there in five minutes.'"

To begin with, Linda visited the couple, but the link between her and Glenn slackened when she and Jimmy moved north to Acworth, a short hop from Marietta. Although brother and sister only saw each other a couple of times a month, they still talked on the phone two or three times a week.

She was uncomfortable with the fact that even after the two started living together, when they went out, Lynn would shamelessly gravitate to other guys in the room. "I didn't like her ways, I didn't like the way she portrayed herself, showing her body to other men, hanging on other men, sitting on their knees or giving them back rubs. She disrespected not only herself but Glenn," Linda says.

But Lynn didn't seem to care if her disloyal behavior humiliated Glenn. Donald remembers a night when she sat down beside him at a party and put her head in his lap. "I wonder what it's like to kiss you," she'd murmured provocatively. With his buddy a few feet away Donald brushed her off, telling her to "Get the hell off my lap." His friends suspected that while Glenn was in a monogamous relationship, she wasn't. According to Mike Archer, she was seeing five or six other officers behind his back. But if Glenn had any inkling about this, he looked the other way—perhaps convinced that she really was irresistible to any man. He decided there was only one way to tame Lynn, and that was to marry her.

When Glenn shared his theory with his closest pals, they were appalled. He had confided to several of them that he was going to propose to her, but they didn't take him seriously. Did he really believe that Lynn Womack was wife material? None of them saw her as the domestic type. As a girlfriend she was enough of a liability, but as a wife, she'd be trouble with a capital T.

"I tried to put him off her," says Mike. "I made a comment one day, I was like, 'You've got to be kidding me' and he kinda smiled and told me, 'She's going to inherit all this money from her grandmother, she has all this land,' and he's bragging he's gonna be rich marrying Lynn. I said to him, 'Man, she's lying like hell to you, you know. She hasn't got nothing.' But Glenn had told me that he wanted to be married by the age of thirty and so I wasn't surprised by it when he told me."

James was horrified, but loyally kept his mouth shut. "I'm the younger brother, Glenn's the older brother, he's a cop and he was supposed to know what he's doing," he says. "It caught us all off guard when he started dating her. I mean, it wasn't like she was his type, she was into the real flashy stuff, a bunch of jewelry, fancy cars, spend a lot of money, and he wasn't raised that way. He enjoyed going out and having nice things and all that, but it wasn't 'Look at me, look at how much money I have or gold I have on.' The guys all assumed he was getting laid. Then the next thing we know they are engaged and they're living together and getting married and it was like, boom, boom, boom and we are all, Wait a minute! And then it's too late. Once someone's made up their mind like that, you can't change it."

One night just before Christmas 1992, Glenn drove over to Donald's house. When he heard the car, Donald went out to meet him. Glenn was already halfway to the door and buzzing with excitement. He dived into his pocket and pulled out a small package with the unmistakable shape of a ring box. "It was Christmastime and he had bought it at D. Geller, a jewelry store right over there on Highway Forty-one where cops get a discount. It was a nice ring, a solitaire diamond," he says. If Glenn hoped his pal would share his joy, he was quickly disillusioned. "He rolled into my driveway and showed me the ring and I said, 'You must have lost your damn mind. You sure you want to do this?' And he said, 'Well I didn't tell you not to marry Grandma in there.' I said, 'Yeah, you're right,' and we just laughed."

CHAPTER FOUR:
A Married Man

Ignoring the lack of enthusiasm from his friends, Glenn and Lynn set a date; they would be married the following August. Before he became smitten with her, when he was out with his buddies on the hunt, trolling the bars and clubs for females, he would joke that he'd "never be caught." He loved women, but he was not planning on trading in his freewheeling bachelor status to be a henpecked husband. Yet here he was walking into a marriage where his wife would unquestionably rule the roost, and doing it with his eyes wide open. There were only two explanations that made sense: First he'd set a nonnegotiable target for himself to be married by the time his 30th birthday rolled around, as he'd admitted to Mike and his family; or second, he really was in love.

In the months they were engaged, nothing Lynn said or did endeared her to his friends. They told him, they warned him, pleaded with him to think again. It was all going to end in tears, they cautioned. She was a tramp. But Glenn had made up his mind and would not be budged.

Kathy tried her best to be happy for her son. "They had been living together and when Glenn told me they were going to get married, and I said, 'Well yes, if you are living with her, you might as well go ahead and marry her. If that's what y'all wanna do, then that's what you need to do.' "

Linda was so upset at the idea of Lynn Womack becoming her sister-in-law, she didn't want to go to the wedding. Though his mother could not really warm to her son's bride either, she urged them all to try their best to try to like her for Glenn's sake. Meanwhile, Lynn had managed to worm her way into the heart of at least one of the Turner men. On the few occasions they had met, she and Glenn's father got along well.

The fair-minded James also tried to focus on her positive traits: her openhanded generosity and her willingness to help when needed. He remembered when Glenn first brought her home to meet them, she had arrived laden with gifts for everyone and offering to lend a hand in the kitchen. But by the time the wedding rolled around, even he was having second thoughts. "None of us really liked her, but we accepted the fact that Glenn loved her," says James. "That was all that mattered, and out of respect we accepted that." They resolved to bury their doubts long enough to be at Glenn's side on what was supposed to be the happiest day of his life.

Lynn, meanwhile, blissfully forged on with the wedding arrangements. She asked a cousin, Stacy Roaderick, Stumpy Halter's wife, Becky, and another cousin's wife to be her attendants. She made it clear it would be a fancy affair. "Lynn said Momma's church wasn't big enough for all the guests she had invited," says Linda.

The pre-wedding dinner was held at the home of one of Lynn's aunts, and it was an evening that has Glenn's family and friends scratching their heads over twelve years later. "We were sitting there and some mysterious car kept coming by," says Donald. "All of a sudden Lynn leaves the house and the car pulls way up to the end of the street so you can't see who it is, and Lynn's bent over with her head in the car talking to the driver. It kept coming by and coming by, and she's outside. We are all, 'What is this?' and Glenn just laughed and said, 'I don't care.'"

Kathy, whose own marriage to Dillard had ended in divorce in 1987 after twenty-seven years, threw a shower for the couple at her church, and Lynn's mother had one later. "Helen didn't come to the shower I had for them. I went to the one she had over at her house on Post Road in Cumming. I was invited and Glenn said, 'Come,' and I said, 'Sure, I'll go,' and so I went, but not many people talked to me," she remembers. "When Glenn walked in, Helen said, 'Well, I guess you know you lost a son.' I told her, 'No, I haven't lost a son, he's still my son.'"

With Lynn fussing over every detail of the bridesmaids' dresses and menus, Glenn began planning the honeymoon. Donald immediately pitched in: "Let's get out the brochures and see where you can go." Glenn brushed him off, "No, I'll handle it." Rebuffed, his pal shrugged and said, "Okay."

By the time August 21, 1993, arrived, it wasn't only Linda who wished her brother was marrying someone else—anyone else but Lynn Womack. Yet Glenn's family turned out in force; his sisters Linda and Margie, brothers Tim and James, his Aunts Thelma and Becky, his little niece and nephew, Tiffany and Michael. Despite Lynn's insistence that she would need a large church to accommodate her long guest list, her side of the aisle was sparsely populated.

The groom and the men in the wedding gathered in an anteroom at the church to get dressed. Checking out Donald, Glenn paled. "I had the same kind of buttons on my tux as Glenn had on his, and he looked at me and said, 'Oh God, I'd better get these things off before she sees that or we'll have all hell break loose,'" he recalls.

Glenn and Lynn may have been oblivious to the undercurrent of dismay as they stood before the altar at the Johnson Ferry Baptist Church in Marietta, but they had to have been the only ones. They undoubtedly made a handsome couple. Lynn was a beautiful bride. Her white satin and lace gown had a long train, puffy sleeves and a sweetheart neckline that showed off her cleavage. Her veil was held in place by a tiara of white flowers, and she carried a bouquet of trailing pink and white blooms.

After the couple exchanged vows they each took a taper to light the unity candle, the burning ends flickered for a few seconds, then went out. They lit another, and another with no luck. After several attempts, they had to give up. It sent a chill through the congregation. Glenn's Aunt Becky turned to Kathy and said, "These candles not being lit? There's a reason for it."

"It was like an omen," says James. "I was like, 'Okay, there's your first sign from above. Walk out, go on, walk out now,'" he silently implored his brother. Yet as Lynn held his arm and they took their first steps together as man and wife, Glenn was wearing a grin that nearly split his face in two. His childhood pal, J. L. McMichael, remembers thinking that he looked so happy.

James was Glenn's best man, a job he would have gladly weaseled out of if he hadn't been persuaded that it was his duty to stand up for him and toast his new sister-in-law. He had been press-ganged into it, a strategy that backfired when he made the mother of all wedding speeches. "They [Glenn's friends, the family] all kept pushing me to do it, 'You have to make the speech, you are his brother,' they told me. I said, 'I don't have a speech, I don't want to say nothing,' and they said, 'Well, just say what you feel.'"

He rose to his feet, a glass in his hand, calling for everyone to hush up. What came out of his mouth next astonished everyone in the room—including James. "I feel like I'm more at a funeral than a wedding," he began. To this day he still can't explain why he said what tumbled from his lips. "It just came out," he says. Everybody laughed, except Lynn, who shot him a look of sheer hatred. "Glenn laughed, but not real hard, because Lynn was standing next to him and he saw the evil look she was giving me," he says.

The mood of foreboding that had started with their engagement, persisted through the pre-wedding planning and caught on fire when the unity candle failed to light, never lifted for the rest of the afternoon. Mike Archer remembers a bunch of folks sitting around talking and there was one question on everyone's lips: "How long are they going to last?" The answer they all agreed on was, "Not long." He recalled feeling miserable for his friend. "I knew he was going to have his heart broke," he says.

His mother also has chilling memories of the day. If her son's fiancée had been cool towards her before the wedding, she was positively frigid after Glenn slipped the gold band on her finger. "She never spoke to me that day. [Apart from the one photograph in which the couple posed with his family] she didn't even have her picture taken with me. I took pictures with Glenn, but I hardly saw Lynn at the wedding.

"They were all taking bets downstairs as to how long it would last," says Kathy. "I had to accept her for Glenn, but it wasn't a good relationship and I hated it. We were all talking about the situation at the reception. Everybody was, Glenn's friends, the family and all were saying, 'Oh, this is never going to make it, why is she getting married to him?' It wasn't a pleasant day."

"It was dreadful," remembers Donald. "We were all sad and gloomy and thinking, 'This isn't right.' James was right. It looked like a funeral and it felt like one too."

After the newlyweds changed out of the wedding finery, Glenn into a short-sleeved shirt, Lynn into a sleeveless white dress with a flower pinned to her left shoulder, everyone gathered around the car to wave them off on their honeymoon. The vehicle was Lynn's pride and joy, a spanking new Chevy Camaro her mother had bought for her. It was black over the hood and the roof, white underneath, with the words OFFICIAL PACE CAR 77TH INDIANAPOLIS 500 MAY 30, 1993 on the driver's door and CAMARO across the top of the windshield, and it was polished to a shine where a girl could look into it and put on her lipstick. "It was a pace car—it wasn't just your regular showroom Z28 Camaro, it was a special edition, they didn't make a whole bunch of them, and they cost about ten grand more than the regular edition," says J.L.

As they got ready to leave, several of the guests threw birdseed at them. Lynn didn't like that. "Don't let it get too near the car," she warned. Glenn climbed in behind the wheel. As his mom leaned down to kiss her son and his bride good-bye, her brand-new daughter-in-law hissed at her, "Get away from my car." Kathy stopped in her tracks as if struck by a bullet. She said nothing. "I had my hands behind my back. I wasn't doing nothing to her car, I was looking inside it to see if anyone had decorated it and nobody had." Glenn's Aunt Becky overheard the hurtful remark and took action. "I will fix that little bitch," she said, taking aim with an entire packet of seed and scoring a bull's-eye as every morsel flew in the open window. "Glenn said it took forever to get rid of it," says Kathy.

With a roar from the high-powered engine, they were off. After they left, the reception dwindled down and people began to go home. In the confusion, Kathy says she and Becky found themselves the last ones there except for Lynn's mom. "Everyone else had gone and we had no ride. Helen drove off without asking if she could take us home or drop us off somewhere. We had to go back into the hall and call for someone to come and pick us up."

For their honeymoon, Glenn had chosen what he hoped would be an idyllic cruise. He'd handled all the travel arrangements, but made the mistake of not checking out more about the kind of trip he'd booked. Instead of enjoying romantic dinners under tropical stars and dancing cheek-to-cheek on moonlit decks, the newlyweds found themselves surrounded by hundreds of noisy vacationing families on a ship where the entertainment and everything else was geared to a G-rated crowd. Lynn was furious and let Glenn know all about it. When they returned home, she told her friends it had been a disaster.

The first time they got together after the ill-fated holiday, Glenn admitted woefully to Donald that their first week as a married couple had been neither exotic nor erotic. "Hell, did I make a mistake," he said.

"What did you do?" asked Donald.

"We went on The Big Red Boat," he moaned.

"For a honeymoon you chose a boat with a bunch of kids?" asked Donald incredulously.

"Yeah, and Lynn raised hell most of the time. She didn't like this, she didn't like that, she didn't like the food, and most of all, she couldn't be on the telephone. She was mad. She didn't like nothing about it," Glenn told him.

He didn't say anything pleasurable about his honeymoon. But Donald remembers, "We kind of laughed it off."

He also recalls that his friend had something else on his mind that day. He was trying to placate his disgruntled bride by taking care of her financial health. "It was the Monday after they got back and we were driving around going to get an insurance policy. She had to have it immediately and we were down [at the insurance office] that morning. Lynn had already got [policies], but she had forgotten one and we were supposed to go and get it. She said it had to be done that day.

"I said, 'Whoa, Fat Boy, she's worried about you getting shot, that she's not going to get any money.'

" 'I guess,' he said, 'but she wants this done right now.' "

Later, when Glenn called his mother to tell her that she

was no longer his beneficiary on a policy he'd taken out years before, it sounded to Kathy as if Lynn was standing over his shoulder. It struck her as odd that her son would make a point of phoning her to tell her about a change to an insurance policy rather than just mention it the next time they met, but she made no comment. "I didn't tell anyone because I didn't want anyone to think I was jealous or something, but they called from the office. It was as if she wanted me to know she was taking control."

Lynn handled their joint finances from the start. And since Glenn had amassed some debts of his own before they were married, he could hardly raise any objection when she made all the decisions about where their money should go. She told him she was planning for their future. They would start by clearing off his outstanding bills, and to that end, she put him on a budget of $20 a week. A month after the wedding, she convinced him to buy a life insurance policy for $100,000 and name her as the sole beneficiary.

If Glenn and Lynn's honeymoon had gotten off on the wrong foot, the marriage slid downhill just as fast. According to Glenn's friends, the relationship deteriorated into a one-sided affair just a week or two after they'd tied the knot. Within weeks of the wedding, Glenn confided to Donald that they were no longer having sex. Lynn claimed to have some female problem that she used as an excuse to avoid marital relations, and they were sleeping in separate beds.

He also told the same story to his partner. "We went to Taco Mac or some place like that to eat hot wings, have a beer and sit around and talk. He wasn't a big drinker—it just depended on his mood," says David. During one of those pit stops, he said that his wife refused to sleep with him. "According to Glenn they had sex just twice after they got married and most of the time he slept on the couch."

"I looked at him and said, 'Man, why do you stay?' Most men wouldn't put up with that, or they would step outside the marriage, maybe have an affair, but he wouldn't do that. It was upsetting for me because we were very close."

Glenn's family became aware of the change. Although Kathy went over to see the wedding pictures, Lynn didn't exactly make them welcome to visit. She wouldn't let them talk to him when they called. His brother James heard background noises every time he called. He'd ask Glenn, "What's that?" and the response would be, "It's Lynn, she wants me to get off the phone."

By the time of their three-month anniversary, Glenn had stopped hanging out with his friends, no longer turning up at the Atlanta Falcons or Braves games he used to love. It was as if he had deliberately cut his oldest friends out of his life. When they'd get on his case about it he would shrug and explain that his bachelor days were over. "He said, 'Lynn says I'm her husband now and I need to spend time with her,' " says David.

The truth was more complicated. Glenn didn't have any time to spend with anyone, let alone his new wife. The lavish spending habits she'd displayed during the months she was pursuing him continued after their marriage. It soon became obvious to him that he could not support Lynn in the manner to which she was accustomed, at least not on the money, around $30,000 a year, he earned with the police department. Despite the stringent budget she had imposed on him and despite the fact that she earned several thousand a year less than her husband, Lynn still went shopping, and when she did, it was with an open checkbook. She bought a new car and a more powerful motorcycle. She had a wallet full of credit cards and she maxed them out. As the bills flooded the mailbox, Glenn took on a second and then a third job.

As his all-work-no-play life began to take its toll, his

partner grew concerned. "It's not unusual for cops here to have a second job, but he worked more hours than anybody else, and that was unusual, especially when there are two people working in the home. People do it to pay for a few extras, but it got to the stage where he was working out of sheer necessity to pay the bills," David says. "He wasn't making it fast enough and she was spending it faster. His other job was at a Chevron gas station and convenience store on Roswell Road in Sandy Springs and he also did odd jobs at a Baptist church and a local theater." What really riled David was that when Glenn was working, Lynn would be off on some jaunt.

She also made what seemed to him unreasonable and unnecessary demands that drove them into the red. "There wasn't really a need for him to have an automobile because we were allowed to ride our bikes home. But she made him get rid of his truck and get a Camaro," says David. "It was madness on our salaries, and we were paid a little extra for riding motorcycles—it was considered hazardous duty pay.

"He did everything to please her and gave her anything she wanted." What Lynn wanted next was a new pace car, he remembers. "It was a convertible, burgundy-colored model with NASCAR graphics on it—a special edition with all the bells and whistles—that she'd set her heart on. It was expensive, but she got it anyway."

Glenn's childhood sidekick kept in touch despite his dislike for Glenn's wife. "I always give people a chance, but after I met her a few times, I could see through her, see just how mean she was. She's just mean, she's a mean person," says J.L. "She tried to dominate Glenn, that's why me and him didn't go out and do a lot of things, because she was just so dominating. Once they got married, boy, she just took over his life. I'd call him mostly on Sunday nights, like a secret sort of thing when I didn't think she was going to be there. He was my best friend, I wasn't going to let some woman get between me and my buddy."

At first Glenn didn't complain. Outside his partner and Donald, nobody really knew how bad his home life had become. Yet despite his growing misery, he remained loyal to Lynn. "When they got married, that was it. He was committed to her. He was more committed to the relationship than she was, but it was heartbreaking to see he wasn't getting anything in return either emotionally or financially," says David.

James tried to put his finger on what made Lynn tick and why she'd married his brother in the first place. "She could change at a moment's notice. She could go from being just the nicest, kindest, lovingest person to being the worst, the biggest bitch that you'd ever meet, and nothing would satisfy her. The only thing I've been able to come up with is—and I saw it then, but I didn't realize to what extent it was correct—was that to her it was a game. In her mind it was, 'Let me show you just how much I can control him,' because that's what it was, a game, between her and the other girls. Everyone wanted to go out with Glenn. He dated many women, but he didn't really settle with anybody, and she was like, 'Let me prove that I'm the one who can get him.' "

Lynn may have snared him, but what she didn't know was that another woman still had a place in her husband's heart. Although they were married to other people and she had moved to Washington, Glenn kept in touch with Stacey Abbott. "It was innocent communication," she says. "We would visit at my parents' house when I came back to Georgia to see family and friends. We never did anything that would be inappropriate." But she could see that his marriage wasn't bringing her former love any joy.

That first Christmas together Glenn and Lynn made a

stab at togetherness with family and friends when they spent the day at Linda and Jimmy's. "Stumpy and Becky and Donald all came to my apartment at East Lake with my family to open presents. They brought stockings they had made at Lynn's house. Mom still has Glenn's," Linda says.

CHAPTER FIVE:
Her Cheating Heart

While his partner shook his head over Lynn's "jaunts" and Glenn worked himself to the bone, some of the Cobb County police fraternity were beginning to say that if Lynn had gynecological problems that prevented her from sleeping with her husband, they seemed to miraculously disappear around other men. Less than six months after their wedding, she was already fooling around on Glenn.

One guy on her radar at this time was Bryan Bennett, a Regal Nissan car salesman from Roswell who said he had known Lynn for years, but maintained that the relationship had never been sexual. "I went to Six Flags with her once and we went out a couple of times to a nightclub. The majority of the dates that we had planned she stood me up." He later discovered that she was married to Glenn Turner during some of the times they'd spent together. "When I found out, I tried to distance myself from her."

Mike Archer's ears were buzzing with questions from several of his men wanting to know if Glenn and Lynn were still a couple, because they had seen her out with another cop. "We all knew she was walking all over him," he says. "They weren't married long, maybe seven or eight months, about halfway between when they got married and he passed away, when an officer called me and told me he had seen her with somebody else and asked if he was still married. I was going to say something to Glenn, but another officer [Glenn's friend Sergeant Bobby Fisher] told me. 'He ain't going to believe you,' he said. I figured it would just play its course. Then another one called me, and asked if they were still together and I said, 'Yeah, as far as I know,' and he said, 'Well, I saw her over at this other officer's apartment and it was like, twelve thirty in the day,' and I am like, 'Yeah?' I called the officer back and told him, 'You need to say something to Glenn,' but he never did.

"Then I heard she was screwing some Forsyth County deputy. Donald called me and told me that someone he knew was in a McDonald's up there and Lynn was sitting with a couple of county deputies talking bad about Glenn."

Some of his fellow cops had already heard that Lynn had begun an affair with a 25-year-old man two counties over. What made it particularly galling was that her illicit boyfriend was one of their own—or almost. Randall Thompson was a Forsyth County sheriff's deputy working on traffic control at the time. She'd met him when she and a girlfriend had been trolling for police cars and pulled up alongside him at the side of the highway. She told him she was visiting her family in Cumming and they marveled over the fact that although they had both grown up in the town, their paths had never crossed.

The resemblance between her lover and her husband was startling. Both were big men, but muscled and fit. Like Glenn, Randy liked anything that ran on wheels. Although both men worked in law enforcement, they'd never met. For his part, Randy had no idea that his pretty, vivacious girlfriend had a husband with whom she still lived; she had told him that she'd been married once but it hadn't worked out and now she was a fancy-free divorcee ready to dive headlong into a new relationship.

To Lynn's delight, Randy was as crazy about NASCAR as she was. For her, it was the perfect cover to provide a feasible excuse to slip away for surreptitious weekends with him. She'd tell Glenn she was off to a race and he would just nod, too tired from his crushing round-the-clock work schedule to complain. She'd rev up her flashy Camaro and disappear in a cloud of exhaust fumes, leaving him to contemplate another dawn start at the gas station.

He knew he was working like a hamster on a wheel, but he didn't have the energy to step off. It would be nearly midnight before he finished his eight-hour shift as a cop, and when he walked through the front door he'd fall into bed and pass out from exhaustion. Since they slept in separate bedrooms, he rarely even heard her come home.

Lynn's lover was born in Warner Robins, Georgia, on June 12, 1968. By the time he was 2, his parents had divorced, and a year later, his mom, Juanita—known as Nita—married Perry Thompson and moved to Conyers, where her new husband had taken a job at a funeral home. Perry later joined the Gwinnett County Police Department. Randy's sister Kimberly was born when he was 4, and three years later, Brandie arrived.

When he was in first grade, on the urging of Nita's best friend, who had recently relocated there, the family moved to Cumming. Perry went to work as a truck driver for Frito-Lay, the Texas-based snack food giant whose products like Lay's chips, Tostitos and Cracker Jacks have kept kids crunching for more than half a century.

Like Glenn, Randy had grown up in what was, for a kid, a rural paradise. With her husband away on long-distance trips for much of the time, Nita did most of the child rearing, staying at home with the children until the youngest started school, and then finding a position at a bank. The family had the run of 250 acres of agricultural land and lived in the big old house they rented from the farmer. There were two lakes on the property and a pond at the back where, when Perry was gone, Nita would get the poles and take Randy and the two girls to fish. There were trails for the children to race their bikes. It was a magical place for a youngster.

They also had livestock and pets all around them. "Randy loved animals—we always had cats and dogs on the farm," says Nita. "The owner of the farm, Mr. Roper, had Holstein cattle and when he was about ten or twelve, Randy began to raise the calves for him. He would get up every morning at five or six o'clock . . . and go out and feed those calves with a bucket that had a nipple on it, and when they got big enough to take to the cattle sales, Mr. Roper would take Randy with him and let him pick out any cow that he wanted and sell it. That's how Mr. Roper paid him, he would let him sell the cow."

"Randy was a character," says his mom. "He loved life, he loved outdoors, he loved football, baseball; he loved sports. He started playing football when he was a little bitty thing. Kimberly and Brandie were cheerleaders for his team at Forsyth County High School—Lynn went there too, but he didn't know her then. Sometimes he liked school and sometimes he didn't, it depended what kind of mood he was in."

She also remembers how he loved being a big brother and took his responsibilities very seriously. "When he was growing up, he was very protective of his two little sisters, more so of Kimberly, who had epilepsy, because of the seizures." Once she had one on the school bus, and 13-year-old Randy used his body to shield her from the fascinated eyes of the other kids.

Things weren't always harmonious at home, says Nita, who traces the tension to the arrival of Perry's daughter Angie from his first marriage, who came to stay with them when she was 13. "A lot of things that happened when Randy was young—he was what me and Perry fussed about most of the time. When Angie came to live with us, Perry would let her do things that he wouldn't let Randy do. And Randy was my child and I would stand up for him no matter what," she says. Yet despite any friction between his mother and his stepfather, when he was growing up, he told everyone to call him Randy Thompson, and as soon as he turned 18, he legally changed his name to his stepfather's.

After high school Randy went to work for the sheriff's department in Cumming, starting as a dispatcher before becoming a deputy. But his heart lay elsewhere. As soon as he was old enough, he became a volunteer fireman. By the time he turned 22, Randy was in love. One thing led to another and pretty soon he was telling his disappointed parents that 19-year-old Dara Taylor was pregnant. A wedding was quickly arranged. "They got married in our home," says Nita. "We had a small ceremony with mainly family and a few friends, nothing big. It wasn't what we would have chosen, but he tried to do what was right. We'd raised our children to have morals and thank God, my daughters are all very involved in their church. Randy knew right from wrong."

The couple lived with his parents to begin with, but the marriage was shaky from the start. A year later they parted, but managed to come to a workable arrangement, and Randy kept very close to little Nicholas, who was born in 1991. The little boy inherited his dad's sunny nature. "Randy's son was supposed to be a Christmas baby, but came a few days early. He's a wonderful boy and is definitely his father's son. He is just like Randy in looks, build, and personality," says Angie Bollinger. "Randy had a very infectious laugh. It was contagious! Even if he came into a function late, it always seemed to liven up more when he entered the room."

His mother maintains that, despite the failure of their

marriage, Randy always carried a torch for Dara. "When he died, he still loved her. After that he dated a few girls several times, but there was never really anyone serious until Lynn Turner came along," says Nita.

Initially, his family believed that Randy's new girl-friend had come into his life at just the right time. They were hopeful that the bubbly Lynn would put a smile back on his face. Once the life and soul of any party, he'd been depressed and miserable over the split from Dara and was struggling to meet his court-ordered alimony and child support payments for 3-year-old Nicholas. The situation left him chronically short of cash, and dating was an expensive business. There was barely enough money left after he'd cashed his paycheck to pay rent, never mind to relaunch his love life.

He was so broke he couldn't afford his own place, and was living in the basement room of a house belonging to a local electrical plumbing contractor when he met Lynn. The fact that he was financially strapped might have been off-putting to many women, but Randy's lack of ready cash was not a problem for Lynn. Although for a while she had augmented her salary with the part-time clerical work Linda Hardy had secured for her at First Southern, by the time she was in the first throes of a passionate romance with Randy, she had a husband working around the clock to take care of their credit card debt. Glenn had no idea that he was toiling every hour God gave him to help finance his wife's fling.

Just as she had done a couple of years before when she zeroed in on Glenn, she went on a mammoth splurge to woo her new object of affection. Randy soon found himself the recipient of all sorts of conspicuous gifts, like a leather coat and leather pants. When he would protest that she was spending too much on him, she would just smile and coo, "Baby, you're worth it."

Nita and Perry Thompson had never seen anything like it. They first met Lynn in the fall of 1993 at the going-away bash another deputy threw for him after he resigned from the sheriff's department. His mom insists that Randy quit when they decided to relocate. "He didn't want to live away from us," she says. But Chris Childers, a former criminal investigations officer with Forsyth County, believes his resignation came after he got into an altercation over Lynn. "He went off his rocker at a party. I remember coming in on Monday morning, I was working undercover at the time, and they said, 'Randy Thompson showed his ass over the weekend,' as we say in the South. He ended [up] leaving the department after that. I am pretty sure it happened over her."

During the weekend of Thanksgiving 1994, after fourteen years in Cumming, Perry transferred to Frito-Lay's Warner Robins depot and the Thompsons bought a new home at 802 Huntington Chase Circle in the Bonaire section of town. Nita, who had started as a cashier at the Cumming Wal-Mart, got a job in personnel at the Warner Robins branch, eventually becoming the store's training coordinator. Randy stayed on in their Cumming house until it was sold, and continued to see Lynn Turner.

"He met her after we moved. He stayed on in the house and when we finally sold it, he came down here with us," says Nita, who maintains that after just a few weeks, Randy was already souring on his new girlfriend. "He tried to get away from her. He was not serious about her for a long time. He didn't want to go with her, but she chased him and she chased him and she chased him. I think she had a thing about people in uniforms. She set her sights on Randy, and she wasn't going to give up, and she didn't. Lynn kept bothering him. After he moved in with us she was down here all the time. Of course, we thought she was divorced."

Oddly, Lynn seemed incapable of sticking to one

version of her autobiography. Although she led Randy
and his parents to believe she was divorced, she told some
of his friends that she was a widow, and with mind-
boggling audacity, she described herself to Randy's sister,
Angie Bollinger, as a police widow whose husband had
been killed in the line of duty.

Randy had found himself a job as a car salesman at the
Bill Butler Chrysler/Dodge/Jeep dealership on Watson
Boulevard. Angie, who says she and Randy were very
protective of each other through their mutual divorces, remembers her first meeting with Lynn. "She did kind of
come out of nowhere. Randy and I were pretty close
growing up, and one day, out of the blue, he tells me about
her. They had been seeing each other for a while before I
met her."

Lynn told Randy's parents she was working at the Cobb
County Police Department and gave them no reason to
suspect she was leading a double life. If they thought it
odd that she was always hanging around their house while
Randy never went to her place, they never gave it more
than a passing thought, since it was Lynn who was pursuing their son and not the other way around. It certainly
didn't enter their heads that she was already married to
someone else.

Nita couldn't help but notice that her son's new friend
seemed to have access to a fleet of very fancy autos. "She
had these nice sports cars and was running about with
Randy. I questioned her and I questioned Randy after she
bought all the expensive gifts," she says. "I knew that
with her job that she didn't make enough to afford all this
stuff, and I just wanted to know where she got her money.
She told me her grandmother had died and that's where
she got it. She said she had gotten a large inheritance."

Lynn set out to impress Randy's family from the start.
Little Nicholas' 3rd birthday was on December 21, and
the weekend before, Nita organized a party for her

grandson. "It was the first time she stayed with us. Perry was on the road. It was myself, my daughters, Brandie's boyfriend at the time, Randy and Lynn and Nicholas. We had a birthday cake. I'm not sure if it was a Friday or a Saturday night, but Lynn showed up in the Mazda. I remember the make, because she had bought Nicholas one of those electric cars, and she said she couldn't get it into either of her Camaros."

The party had been a huge success. The tot spent a gleeful evening ripping open his presents and being fussed over not only by his dad, grandma and aunts, but by this delightful new stranger who cuddled and kissed him and gave him presents. Nita was relieved that Lynn had taken to the child so easily. "She thought Nicholas was great. She was always picking him up and just acting like she really loved him. I guess Nicholas thought it was Christmas, because our decorations were up at the time and he was only three." The party was particularly special to Nita and Randy, since the little boy would be spending Christmas Day with his mother and her family.

Because it was dark outside by the time Lynn arrived, it was decided to wait until the morning before she would give the child his main gift. "It was one of those little Jeep cars that is battery-powered—you charge the battery and he can get in it and mash the gas and drive it," says Nita. Nicholas hopped around impatiently while his dad finished assembling it, and everyone trooped outside to watch the delighted youngster take it for a test run. For the rest of the day, he zoomed up and down the driveway as his doting aunts snapped away with their cameras and Brandie's dog yelped excitedly.

While the Thompsons welcomed Lynn to their home and were okay with her staying over, they'd already warned Randy that they would not tolerate any floorboards creaking in the middle of the night. Although she had told Nita and Perry she was divorced, and Randy was too, for that matter, Lynn was consigned to Kimberly's room, sharing her queen-sized bed. "Well, some people might call us old fogies, but she was not allowed to sleep with our son, so she was supposedly in the other room with Kimberly. That's where she was supposed to sleep. We did not allow them to sleep together in our home," maintained Nita.

It was a house rule neither Lynn nor Randy intended to keep, that weekend or any of the following ones that she spent under the Thompsons' roof, according to Kimberly, who said that Lynn would wait until her parents would go to bed, then slip along the hall to Randy's room.

Back in Marietta, Glenn caught up again with Stacey who was visiting with her folks. "He met my first-born daughter, several months before he died. His first words about her were, 'She's humongous!' I gave him a funny look and said, 'That's nice,' and we laughed. She was a little butterball, but adorable. Glenn held her and played with her for hours when we saw each other. I now think the feelings were still there between us, we just did not act on them because we were both married. I was in a bad marriage and he was also."

All these years later, she says he was still her knight in shining armor. "One time I was at my parents' house, alone. There was a bad storm and a door in the garage had blown open. The door knocked and banged against the wall. The power went out and I became scared. I called Glenn, who was still on evening patrol. I guess he could hear the fear in my voice, and rushed over. In the middle of the storm he rode his police motorcycle at great speed to get to me, and came right through my parents' front yard, in the rain. The ground was soaked and he slid around, tearing holes and tire marks in the grass. He laughed at me when we found it was only a blown-open door and not an intruder. The next morning my parents saw the tire marks in the grass and just shook their heads saying, 'Oh, Glenn!' "

When she was back in Marietta for Christmas, they got together again. "He spoke of Lynn. He was always respectful, though. I knew there were problems between the two of them, but he did not give me specifics. As there were problems in my marriage, also, I sometimes would dream about one day Glenn and I both getting past that time in our lives and maybe building something together again. I think he thought the same thing, but am not sure. We were just such incredible friends."

On Christmas Eve, Stacey ran into Mike Archer when he was directing traffic for a midnight mass service. She told him that she had seen Glenn several days earlier. He stared at her for a few moments and then blurted out, "Oh, Lynn's gonna love that." Stacey says she protested that it had all been completely innocent—they had just visited, and her parents had been at home at the time. "He said it wouldn't matter to Lynn, and she would be furious if she found out. I knew he was right from what I had heard about Lynn, and I hoped that she wouldn't find out, for Glenn's sake."

She decided then that it would probably be better for both of them if they didn't see each other until they were free from their respective marriages. "The funny thing about it was that both of us had considered divorce from our spouses, long before we had been in touch again. But once we both found out that each other was divorcing, that brought new hope to a situation that seemed hopeless. At least to me, it did."

Christmas 1994 was the second since Glenn and Lynn's wedding, and they were supposed to be spending the day with his family, who were taken aback when he turned up alone. "We were all at Margie's house and [Lynn] didn't show up at all," says James. Earlier, Glenn had stopped by Linda's with all the gifts. "I think he had it done at the store, but the presents were so beautifully wrapped, that I took a picture of them," she says. "I asked him where Lynn was and I can't remember what he said, but he sounded like he'd had it. He played with the kids and had a good time with them and then he left. He didn't stay for Christmas dinner."

Kathy Turner was upset. To her it wasn't natural for husband and wife to spend such an important holiday apart, and to her way of thinking it was as sure as hell a sign that this marriage was going nowhere. It tore at her that her once happy-go-lucky son yawned throughout the day, and often seemed distracted. "All he does is pay bills," she said to the others after he'd gone.

None of them knew that Glenn had woken up that morning in an empty house. Lynn had driven up to Warner Robins the night before after announcing she had plans of her own for Christmas and they didn't include hanging out with her in-laws. She had arrived at the Thompsons' house like Santa Claus, shopping bags bulging. Even though little Nicholas wasn't there, she had brought something for him too.

Perry was floored. "We received some rather expensive presents from Lynn," he later testified. "My wife and I got an expensive stereo set. It was a Kenwood component set which is just not the kind of thing I would have bought, because I couldn't have afforded it. Lynn supplied gifts for everyone in the family and she was with us Christmas morning when we opened them up."

They were awestruck by the amount she'd spent on their son. "She gave him a pair of rather expensive snakeskin boots and some leather pants and a shirt that had stars and stripes, and things like that," said Perry. "The boots still had the price tag attached, and they were in the neighborhood of eleven hundred dollars. When Randy first told me about them, I said, 'There's no pair of shoes that cost eleven hundred dollars,' and he said, 'Oh yes, Dad, there is,' and he showed me the tag. She also gave him a video camera. Both of my daughters also got gifts from Lynn that Christmas morning."

Angie knew better than anyone how much money Lynn had spent. She had been persuaded to go on one of her holiday shopping sprees, and she was there when many of the gifts for Randy had been bought. On that particular trip Lynn had also marched into Victoria's Secret, where she stocked up on lingerie for herself and for Angie, who was blown away by her extravagance. At each stop, when she found something she liked, Lynn would pull out a wallet, rifle through her stash of plastic cards as if she were a casino sharper, then whip one of them out and hand it to the salesclerk, telling her imperiously, "Charge it."

According to Angie, Lynn had so many cards that she kept them together with a thick rubber band. When she had asked Lynn where on earth she had gotten all the money, she was fobbed off with the same breezy "Oh, my grandmother left me some dough when she died" line she had spouted to Nita a few weeks before.

His mother was growing increasingly uneasy about Lynn's relentless pursuit of Randy. "She only missed one or two weekends the whole time he lived with us, and she was occasionally there during the week. She'd arrive during the day and a lot of times she would spend the night. She phoned him constantly—there were a lot of phone calls," she remembers.

While she was aware that her son was swept up in his girlfriend's flashy, extravagant lifestyle, Nita was far from sure that what she believed to be no more than a passing infatuation would ever develop into a love that would last; to her mind it was a lopsided relationship with 26-year-old Lynn doing all the running. At one point, Randy seemed almost smothered with all the attention being lavished on

him, and confided to Perry that sometimes he wished
she'd just go away and leave him alone. "Why?" Perry had
asked. "Because she's nuts and has snakes in her head,"
he'd replied.

She wasn't the only family member who had misgivings about Lynn. Angie's husband, Doug Bollinger,
didn't take to her at all. "My husband was never fooled
by Lynn. He always said from the very beginning that
something about her was just not right," she says. Kimberly also wondered what was really going on. She figured it was beyond weird that Lynn would make all these
two-hour round-trips between Marietta and Warner
Robins. When she was pretty sure she'd tumbled on to
Lynn's true motive, Kimberly tackled her.

She later recalled the conversation for *Dateline*.
"Lynn, I think you love the chase. I don't believe you are
in love with Randy." Even when Lynn emphatically assured her that her theory wasn't true, Kimberly was still
not convinced. "Well, that's not for me to say, but from
everything that I see, you know, I think once you've got
Randy, you won't want him anymore," she told Lynn.

CHAPTER SIX:
Sick as a Dog

Glenn's refusal to criticize his wife, or to admit to himself or anyone else that he was being systematically isolated from the people who cared most about him, let Lynn almost maneuver his best friend out of his life. By the fall of 1994, Donald Cawthon's marriage had foundered and he and his wife were living apart. To have a footloose and fancy-free Donald back on the prowl and exerting his rascally influence over her husband was not something Lynn was prepared to tolerate. She came up with a plan to sideline him for good.

"I was driving right by the police precinct where Glenn worked when I got called on my car phone," Donald remembers. When he picked it up, there was a detective on the other end. She told him, "We got a report that you intend to kill your ex-wife," I said, 'What kind of shit is this? Let me take a guess where that came from. If my ex-wife [who was 57 at the time] gets to hear about this and has a heart attack, I'll sue,' I told her. 'Do you want me to come back to the precinct? I'll be glad to. You have nothing on me. I haven't done anything and I'll sue you for harassment. And if she has any kind of stroke, I'll sue you.'"

He quickly confirmed that it was Lynn who had made

the complaint. "She said that I was going to blow up the boat and kill my ex-wife. I was furious. I called Lynn and called her every cuss word under the sun. I was raging and then Glenn got on the phone and him and me, we got into it. I said, 'Meet me at the Post Office.' When he showed up I told him, 'You know what? I don't get along with her, I don't like her, I think she's a bitch and she thinks I'm a bastard so we, you and I, are going to separate.' He said, 'Fine!' After that we'd speak when we ran into each other on the road, but that was it. The rift went on for ages, we hardly saw each other for six to eight months."

Linda realized that her sister-in-law's animosity towards Donald went deeper than just the clash of two strong-willed personalities. Lynn viewed the gregarious and outspoken Donald as a threat to her control. She had Glenn on a psychological leash and that's exactly where she wanted him. She was well aware that her husband still loved her and would do almost anything to please her. The last thing she needed was Donald egging him on to exhibit some resistance. "She didn't like the relationship Donald had with Glenn. They were like brothers and that was interfering with her trying to get in the little fix there. Lynn didn't like that," Linda says.

Around the 4th Precinct, Glenn's friends on the force were becoming increasingly sickened by their friend's humiliation at the hands of his wife. "I saw the way she treated him, and it was horrible," says David Dunkerton. "He showed me how a box of a dozen Krispy Kreme doughnuts could fit just so in the motorcycle's radio box, and sometimes we would go to [the] dispatch center where Lynn worked. Everyone was pleased when we turned up [with doughnuts], but she would pretty well dismiss him. That happened every time we took food there."

Cynthia McGhee (now Cynthia Mull) worked alongside Lynn at the 911 switchboard. She later testified that she thought her coworker's attitude towards her husband was downright hostile when he rolled up with dinner or welcome treats for her and the other dispatchers. "She basically ignored Glenn. She was very cold towards him. I never saw any type of intimacy, a hug or kiss or even 'Hi, how are you?' "

David knew that while Glenn was spending every minute of his spare time pumping gas, his wife would take off. "Sometimes she'd go on last-minute trips to Florida or some other place, usually to watch car racing, and she would tell him she didn't want him to go," he says. "From my point of view she was slapping him in the face without touching him. He tolerated it a lot longer than I would, or most men I know. But he used to say, 'The only way this relationship will come to an end is when I've done everything I can to make it work.' "

Although he had tried to keep his heartbreak to himself, it was inevitable that the dam would break; months of unhappiness couldn't stay bottled up forever. Without Donald to bolster him, signs of his discontent trickled down to his fellow cops. Nearly everyone in the station house had heard about the "medical problem" that kept his wife from having sex with him, and they muttered amongst themselves that it seemed to miraculously cure itself when other guys were around. Mike Archer says they began to wonder what kind of sap Glenn Turner was. He'd now told several guys they'd only made love twice since the wedding. How could he not know that Lynn was running around on him? Linda is convinced her brother was aware of the situation, but buried the knowledge deep inside. "He was humiliated, but his pride wouldn't let him admit it," she says.

By the beginning of February, Mike was unnerved when all the misery Glenn had kept to himself came bubbling to the surface. They were eating dinner at Chili's when Glenn suddenly dissolved in tears. Between sobs, he told Mike that they had argued. Lynn had told him that she didn't love him and had never loved him. Glenn didn't trust her anymore. She wasn't the same person he had married. Appalled, his supervisor told him to pull himself together—they were both in uniform and he couldn't have an officer weeping into his plate in public. As Glenn struggled to get his emotions under check, he kept repeating, "You can tell Donald he was right. I don't care, you can tell him."

Midway through February, Glenn turned up at Linda's house in Acworth with a gun he said Lynn wanted to sell to his brother-in-law. "Jimmy collected guns. He never had a gun store or even bought them to sell, he just collected them. Glenn and some of his buddies would pawn their guns to Jimmy from time to time when they needed extra cash, and they would come by later to retrieve them when they had the money," says Linda who remembers thinking that Glenn didn't seem like himself. While they were talking, he told her that Lynn was looking at a house in Cumming. "I asked him, 'Are you moving to Cumming?' He said, 'I'm not going, I am not leaving Cobb County,' and I said, 'It must be pretty bad then?' He nodded and said, 'It's over.'"

Glenn told his sister he was thinking of bunking down at his dad's place up in Woodstock. But Dillard had urged him to sort out his differences with Lynn and give their marriage another go. Maybe he would take a spare room that a friend's mother was looking to rent out, Glenn said. One thing he made plain, he didn't want any part of the home he'd shared with Lynn. "You can always stay here," Linda assured him.

"It was embarrassing for him. He had so much pride and he couldn't admit he screwed up [in marrying Lynn]. He really wanted [his marriage] to work. We were raised that when you took those vows, it was for a lifetime, and he was having a very hard time with it being over," she says.

On Wednesday, February 22, with her husband at near-breaking point, Lynn, Randy Thompson and two pals, Shane Williams and Doyle Roland, drove down to Florida for the 1995 Daytona 500 stock car race which was won that year by Sterling Marlin. They traveled in a Chevy Astro van that Lynn had borrowed from a dealership, and they stayed at Daytona Beach. "Lynn paid for the motel and we each bought our own food. We didn't have to pay for tickets for the race—there is a special gate for law enforcement officers and we entered through that gate," later testified Roland. At the end of the four-day trip, he had no doubts at all that Lynn and Randy were a couple.

"I knew that they had been dating for a little while. I didn't know what Lynn's marital status was. As a matter of fact I never knew she was married until the news broke [about Glenn's death]. I never saw her wear any wedding rings. I stayed in the same room as Lynn and Randy. They shared a bed and I slept in the other bed in the room."

By then, news of Lynn's cheating had filtered down to Glenn's brother. "We did know about Randy and a couple of more officers too. We kept hearing things like, 'I saw Lynn over at so-and-so complex and you know that's where Officer Blank lives.' She ran around the whole time. She ran with cops, then firemen. We heard there was an officer in Cumming. We all knew, and we discussed it, but we thought, Glenn is not going to want to hear it, so why make enemies?" recalls James. His mother was kept in the dark about her daughter-in-law's infidelities, as no one could bear to pass on the hurtful truth. "We didn't say anything to Kathy. Why would we have?" says Donald.

"He didn't share his heartache until the end," he adds. "The incident with Archer at Chili's was thirty days before he died. It took that to make him talk. It went all the way to the wire because he didn't want anyone to know. He wanted to work things out, he wanted to make it work."

His friends and family were worried about him. His

whole life had become centered around money: he earned it; Lynn spent it. He was also exhausted. Starting early in the morning, he put in a full day at the Chevron gas station owned by a relative of Lynn, Judith Ann Hendrix, before beginning his 3:00-to-11:00 P.M. shift with the motorcycle unit. "That was her way of keeping him busy while she was going out," says Donald. And no matter how much extra cash he made, their debts never dwindled, she kept ringing up the charges. It was a runaway train, and the only way to avoid a crash was to jump off.

The only bright spot on the horizon was that, with his marriage virtually over, the rift between Donald and Glenn had begun to heal. They had started speaking again when they bumped into each other, each feeling the other out to see if they could revert to the easy and close relationship they'd enjoyed before Lynn plunked herself firmly between them. Donald knew what his old buddy was going through. Mike Archer had kept him up to date with the horror tales of Glenn's nightmare life.

On the morning of February 23, Donald dropped by the gas station where Glenn manned the pumps for $7 an hour. The two friends swapped stories and bantered just like old times. He remembers the conversation as if it were yesterday.

"We laughed and cut up so much that day that the owner came out and asked, 'What's going on? I've never heard such laughing.' That's when Glenn said he was going to have to sort things out. He stopped laughing. It was just like a dark cloud came over him, and he said, 'She's at Daytona right now.'

"I said, 'You mean she's there and she's telling you y'all are so much in debt?'

"'No,' he said, 'I've been working three hundred and sixty-five days this year and I have thirty days left on the bills to be paid off.'

"So I asked him, 'Why are you working here for seven

bucks an hour when you could be getting twenty-five working security?'

"He says, 'This was her job and she's always got something going on.'

"'What's going on?' I asked and he tells me, 'She's at the races.'

"'The races? Why is she at the races and you are here working?' I said to him. Then he says, 'She bought a car on her credit card.'

"'What do you need to buy a brand-new car on a credit card for? What's wrong with that one you got? I thought you were trying to get out of debt?' I said.

"'I am,' he tells me. 'I'm just thirty days away from being out of debt. I've worked the whole year without missing a day. We either work it out or I am filing for divorce.' Then he shook his head and said, 'A man can only take so much. Either we are going to work this thing out, or it's over. Either I am going to straighten her out, or on Friday I'm gone.'"

But before he could walk out the door, there was one final row, a spat so bad that Glenn told his cop pal Bobby Fisher, "If anything happens to me, look at Lynn. We had a fight and she threatened to shoot me with my own weapon."

By the end of the month, Glenn had more than his lousy marriage to contend with. Normally strong as an ox, he'd been under par for days. On the morning of Tuesday, February 28, he called Mike Archer. He was shivering with chills and his voice was quavering. "I'm not going to make it in today," he told him. Then he blurted out, "I am so sick, I think I'm going to die."

The next day he called in sick again. Just the fact that he wasn't there had the whole stationhouse talking. Nobody could remember the workhorse cop being off work three days in a row. He must be really bad, they agreed. When he spoke to Mike the next morning, Glenn said he was still too sick to come in and repeated that he was dying. "I feel so bad, I'm hurting, I've never had anything like this before, I've never hurt like this before." "Look, Glenn, you've got to get yourself to the hospital," Mike had told him. "I will. Man, I hurt so bad," he'd replied.

Mike got on the phone to Donald Cawthon. "Archer kept calling and saying, 'Something is going on. Glenn's not himself, he's talking all this stuff and he's all teary-eyed and laying out of work,'" he says. He also knew that his buddy never slacked off the job, even for an hour, and dialed his number. "What's wrong with you, man?" Donald wanted to know. "I think I have the flu, I've had it for a week or more. I have cramps, I keep throwing up, I am running a temperature and one minute I am hot as hell, the next I'm freezing," Glenn replied. That sure sounds like he's got a real bad dose, Donald sympathized, the poor guy must really be suffering. Then Glenn said something that had Donald reeling. "But it's these nosebleeds, I can't stop them, the blood just pours out my nose and I am worried about it."

Whoa, that doesn't sound like flu, thought Donald, his mind racing. What's going on here? He urged Glenn to see a doctor—at once. If his nose was continually gushing blood, he'd be worried too, he told Glenn.

Later that day Glenn's mother called him. Kathy was alarmed by how sick he was, and after she'd hung up with him, she called Linda. Linda immediately phoned Glenn. "I've been ill for days. I've got the flu bug, but it isn't going away," he said. Then he told her the same thing he'd told Donald—that he felt so awful he thought he was going to die. At first Linda wasn't too concerned; the "I'm going to die" business was something all the Turner kids had said when they were growing up if they weren't feeling good. But then he described the excruciating dagger-like pains that shot through his belly, making him double over. When he wasn't vomiting, he was racing to the bathroom with diarrhea, he told her wearily. "I've never felt like this before, never had pain like this."

Around lunchtime on Thursday, March 2, the phone rang in Helen Gregory's Cumming home. It was Lynn. "Mom, can you come over right away? I've hurt my head. I might have to have it looked at."

"Hurt your head? How did that happen, what were you doing?" Helen asked.

"I was putting a fan up in the attic and I fell," she answered. "Mom, I think I'd better go to the hospital, everything looks blurry, I don't think I can drive, can you take me?"

"Sure, honey, just hold on. I'll be there as fast as I can," Helen told her.

When she arrived at 881 Old Farm Walk, the front door opened and there was Lynn, holding her head. She was showing her mother the spot where it had made contact with the floor, when Glenn appeared. He was a horrible color, his eyes were dull with pain and Helen later recalled thinking, He's had that flu for over a week, and he still has such a cold. "You know, I am just not feeling well. I think I will go with you," he said. Helen looked at him and nodded. "Well, I think that's a good idea," she told him. "C'mon," and held the car door open while he climbed in the back.

With her daughter dabbing at the egg-sized bump on her head, and her son-in-law behind her clutching his guts and moaning, Helen drove to the Kennestone Hospital on Church Street. They arrived just before two in the afternoon. Lynn told the aide at the door, "I've had an accident and hurt my head, and my husband is sick with flu. I don't think he can walk." A gurney materialized, and after Glenn sank gratefully onto it, he was wheeled into triage. Lynn was taken to another part of the E.R., where she was seen by Dr. Alan Maloon.

As he checked out the damage, she told him she had fallen and hit her head on a two-by-four plank of wood. She said her vision was blurred and she had a bad headache. Although she had no lacerations, the doctor ordered up a CAT scan that showed no injury. But just to be on the safe side, he suggested she make an appointment with a neurology specialist for the following day. It was an appointment she didn't keep.

Staff nurse Becky Russell was working the 7:00 A.M.–to–7:00 P.M. shift on the main floor of the E.R. She first saw Glenn on the gurney he'd been brought in on. There was another patient in room 6 and she closed the curtain to give Glenn some privacy as she helped him undress. "I helped him into a gown, and he was the nicest guy."

Dr. Donald Freeman came to check him out. Glenn told him he felt lightheaded, especially when he stood up. He ached all over, he'd had blinding headaches, diarrhea and had been throwing up for days. He also said he'd had a fever and his nose was congested. The doctor's examination revealed that Glenn was severely weakened from dehydration, caused in all probability by the prolonged vomiting. He displayed all the symptoms of typical stomach flu. "His pulse and blood pressure were abnormally high," said Nurse Russell. "The normal rate is somewhere between sixty and one hundred beats per minute, his standing blood pressure measurement was one hundred and forty-six. I inserted an IV and gave him two or three liters of saline to rehydrate him. Usually after a liter or two of fluids you feel a bit better and your appetite returns, but that wasn't the case with him."

For the next four hours and twenty-six minutes, Glenn lay there in a miserably weakened condition with the IV stuck in his arm. When the first bag was empty, it didn't seem to have had much effect and a second one was hooked up to the drip. Nothing was diagnosed that might have set alarm bells ringing.

Becky, who had worked at Kennestone for two years, kept a watchful eye on him. "He was treated on Level One, which deals with acute sickness, heart attacks, strokes, that sort of thing," she said. She recalls how stoic Glenn was. Even though he was plainly very ill, he didn't complain. "Whenever I went in to see him he would say, 'I'm okay,' or, 'I'm fine,' when he clearly wasn't."

She late testified that Glenn had also told them about his nosebleeds—which are never associated with flu symptoms—but since they had stopped, no further investigation was thought necessary. He was given medicine for his nausea and vomiting.

He didn't act like a dying man. Though barely able to speak, the gentle Glenn remained true to form and even in his debilitated state, he charmed those looking after him, and fretted about Lynn. "He told me he was a police officer, but he was so sick it was obvious he didn't really want to talk. I asked him standard questions and at one point he asked me to check on his wife." Lynn was in another part of the E.R. less than thirty feet away. Becky found her and saw she was doing fine, and didn't need any treatment. Becky went back and told Glenn she would be with him in a little while.

He should have been in the right place. The Kennestone Hospital is the only trauma center in the area—the next nearest is twenty-five miles away. It has its own helicopter pad, and the modern fifteen-room E.R., opened with great fanfare after a major overhaul in 1990, is rated the busiest in the state. Every day it handles between 150 and 200 cases. In 2004, its busiest year to date, it registered 110,000 visits.

That Thursday was a typically demanding day for the E.R. staff. When Glenn was admitted there were four

nurses, a charge nurse, a technician, a secretary and doctors on duty. It was an established team that had been together for a long time and according to Becky Russell,
they worked well as a unit. "There was a good relationship between doctors and nurses. When there was down-
time we had fun, just like you see on TV hospital shows,
but when it was busy we were very focused.

"When somebody arrives in [Glenn's] condition,
blood is taken when the IV goes in, and the lab work is
done while a diagnosis is being made. Usually it's done as
a standard," she also testified. "The doctor in this case did
not draw any blood. If he had, he would have gotten a red
light. But he didn't and that wasn't really normal. Maybe
it was because Glenn was young, strapping, healthy-
looking and it was presumed he had the flu."

She remembers noticing that Lynn Turner didn't seem
overly anxious about her husband. Around 6:00 P.M. she
was told she could take him home. The doctor said the IV
fluids had helped somewhat, and he was confident the
medication he was going to prescribe would take care of
the sickness and pain in time. Lynn asked no questions
and began to gather up Glenn's belongings without saying anything to him.

"There was obviously no connection between them.
When he was released at twenty after six that evening his
blood pressure between standing and sitting was still off
by about twenty points. It was a big discrepancy and
that's not usual in a dehydration case," said Becky, who
now works as a radiology nurse at St. Joseph's Hospital
in Atlanta. "He wasn't much better and usually, family
members will say, 'You haven't done anything for us.'
Here's this guy who was sick for four or five days, there's
not a real reason why he doesn't feel good, but nobody's
pressing the issue."

Becky was struck by Lynn's lack of curiosity about
her husband's illness. "Most young wives would have

said, 'He's not better after four hours in the hospital. Hey, I'm not taking him anywhere. You haven't done blood work, you haven't taken X-rays.' I just remember thinking it was so weird she was taking him home when he wasn't any better."

Becky tried to persuade Glenn to get into a wheelchair for the trip to the parking lot, but he refused. "He wanted to walk out, but when he stood up he was dizzy, unsteady on his feet. I coaxed him to sit down in the wheelchair after I convinced him that because he was a big fella, tall and broad-shouldered, his wife wouldn't be able to help him if he stumbled or collapsed. She wasn't very tall and quite slim, so she just couldn't have handled him." As Lynn went to get the car, the kindly nurse who had cared for him all afternoon reluctantly wheeled Glenn out of the one place he would have been safe, and into the care of a woman who wanted him dead.

That night he called Linda. "He told me that they had been to the emergency room and they had given him two bags of fluid, a suppository for the vomiting and that he was going to be fine." Lynn was also busy on the phone that evening, on the line to her pal Paul Rushing.

When Glenn got home, the red light was blinking on the answering machine; he flicked the switch to PLAY and grinned weakly as he heard the familiar voice. "This is Momma. I'm heading to Florida in the morning and I love you, Glenn, and I love you, Lynn." Knowing that she was about to leave early for the drive south with her brother to Jacksonville to attend the Rilea family reunion, he called her back and told her he was feeling better and would probably go to work the next day. It was the last time his mother heard his voice.

Before she left in the morning, Kathy called to check on her son again, but got no reply. She wondered if she should swing by his house before heading off, but figured that if there was nobody answering the phone, Glenn must be feeling well enough to go to back to his job. She hung up and got in the car. She'd been looking forward to this vacation weekend for ages, and even the journey would be fun, since Bob was going to share the wheel with her on the 300-mile drive.

It was nearly 9:30 at night before they pulled into the seaside motel where fifty assorted aunts, uncles, cousins, second cousins and their children had already gathered. Glenn's mother remembers how her life changed forever in an instant. "I had just gotten there and the phone rang. I thought, Who in the world is calling me down here? When I saw it was my friend Bertie Tryon I was like, What does she want? My kids didn't even know where I was staying and she had called all the motels on the beach till she got me. 'Kathy,' she said, 'Bill wants to talk to you.' Then her husband, Dr. Tryon, came on the line. He said, 'Kathy, I have bad news. Glenn died.'

"At first I said to myself, This is a joke, and then I thought, He wouldn't joke about that, so I said to the family, who were sitting around, 'Glenn died,' and they all looked at me like I was out of my mind. I asked Bertie what happened and she said, 'We don't know.' So my nieces and nephews started finding me a way to get back. We just couldn't have driven back. I had to wait until the next morning to fly home. Waiting until the next day was the hardest part." Getting her mother and her uncle on the first flight was all that mattered to Linda. "She called and said, 'I can't come home tonight, I don't have a ticket.' I told her, 'Just come, Mom, I'll put it on my credit card.'"

When Donald Cawthon arrived at Mike Archer's place, Mike said, "We have to go to his house, he's at the house. All the detectives and everyone's there."

"I'm not going, there's no way I am going over there," Donald told him.

"What do you mean, you are not going?" Mike asked.

"It would be disrespectful. She killed him," Donald said.

Mike sat down and sighed, and he said, "I was thinking that too. Then what are we going to do?"

They looked at each other, momentarily stumped. Mike's phone rang. It was Rat Pack associate member Eddie Campuzano on the other end telling them that he was at the scene. He said he was standing right there in the living room, and he tells them the story Lynn has just rattled off. "This is messed up," he tells them.

"I asked him, 'Who's in charge over there?' " recalls Donald. "He tells me it's Phil Campbell or somebody and then he says, 'This is a crock of shit.' He's telling me, 'She says at three o' clock in the morning Glenn goes for his service revolver; she used that, "service revolver." Does anyone say that? She says he's out there on the deck trying to fly, saying he can fly.' "

"Eddie told me she said that Glenn tried to drink some gas, he said there was a burglar in the house, he heard somebody, and I'm saying to him, 'Tell them she murdered him!' Finally, Archer gets on the phone with the detective out there and he's yelling, 'I'm telling you, man, we know her, we know her and there's something wrong here.' The detective says, 'You calm down and stay away from here, understand? Don't come up here. We already know what's going on and we are checking into it.' "

Later that day, the body of their beloved buddy was removed to the office of the Cobb County medical examiner to await an autopsy that was to be carried out the next day.

CHAPTER SEVEN:
The Widow

Kathy and her brother arrived back from Florida on Saturday morning, the day after her son had died. Her first contact with her daughter-in-law since she got the news didn't sit well with her. "I called Lynn first and told her I was home. 'Well, when are you coming over?' she wanted to know. I said that I had to see my kids first. 'Hurry up,' she barked. I said, 'Lynn, I have to speak to my kids first.'"

After trying to console each other and make sense of what had happened, Kathy, Linda and Margie, James and his girlfriend at the time, Donald and family friend Sonya Sule went over to Old Farm Walk. In the rush to get back home Bob had left his driver's license in Florida, so Kathy asked Sonya to come over and drive them around. Lynn opened the door, stared at them for a second and then said, "Oh, the whole clan's here!" Her mother-in-law put her arms out to embrace her, but Lynn turned and walked into the living room. "She didn't hug anybody. She wouldn't even sit on the couch with us," remembers Kathy.

While they were there, Lynn repeated to Linda that she had found the delirious Glenn on Thursday night stumbling around in the basement trying to drink gasoline.

Then she complained that she was "pissed off " because the police had raked through the nightstand in the bedroom where Glenn had died and taken away pills she said had been prescribed for her.

"She was dry-eyed, not upset, never gave me a hug, it was all, Do whatever you've got to do," says Kathy. "We were only in the house thirty minutes or so." Lynn's obvious lack of grief bewildered Linda. "She wasn't crying—it was disturbing to me," she says.

Kathy knew her son and his wife had occupied separate bedrooms for a while, but it puzzled her that Glenn hadn't died in his own bed. "He wasn't [found] in the bedroom he lived in, he was in the spare bedroom. His was the first bedroom on the left," she says. "When the cops called to talk to us they said they went to the back bedroom."

Before they left for the funeral home where they were to discuss arrangements for the service and interment, Lynn said she needed to choose some clothes to dress her husband in for his wake and burial. Linda recalls that Lynn wanted to control that too. "We were talking about what he would wear and she got up to get his uniform, his T-shirts. Mom said, 'I'm going with you.' Lynn didn't want her to, but Mom said, 'He's my son and I'm going.'

"Helen had to stick her nose in it too. She couldn't just let Mom go back there and get his stuff," Linda says. With Helen trailing her, Kathy followed Lynn down the hall to Glenn's bedroom and watched as she found his regulation police shirt and pants and picked out a white T-shirt for underneath. Seeing her son's clothes carefully put away in the dresser was too much for Kathy to bear. "Mom broke down crying and said, 'I can tell this is Glenn's room, he folded everything so neatly,' " says Linda.

They all went to the H.M. Patterson & Son funeral home on Old Canton Road in Marietta where Glenn's body had been taken after the medical examiner was finished with him. Lynn launched matter-of-factly into how the funeral should be conducted. "She scheduled it for two on Monday afternoon, which screwed up a lot of the people he worked with, because they couldn't come," says Linda. Next she haggled over the wording of the death notice that was to be put in the local papers. The funeral home director asked for details of Glenn's immediate family, checking the spelling of their names and their addresses.

When she'd finished, the new widow made a shocking announcement. On no account was she to be described as "Glenn's wife, Lynn Turner" in the obituary notice to be published in both the *Marietta Daily Journal* and *The Atlanta Journal-Constitution*. The others looked at her askance. "She was very adamant that she did not want her name in the papers as Lynn Turner. She said she didn't want the police and news media getting hold of it, she didn't want it on the radio or in the papers, didn't want to deal with the press. She said she wanted to be listed as Julia in the obituary. Yet no one knew her as Julia. I had never even heard the name before. It blew my mind," says Linda.

She tried frantically to sort out the questions that flooded her head: Why would anyone who'd just lost her husband so tragically care so vehemently what a newspaper called her? What was the problem anyway? Wasn't Lynn the name she went by? And Glenn had died at home of natural causes, hadn't he? "I was hurt, sick, I knew she was somehow involved, I didn't know how, I didn't have a clue. He'd been perfectly fine the night before. I couldn't figure it out how she had done what she had done, but I knew she had done it."

With the Turners stunned into silence, Helen took over. She too was all about business; she knew how many death certificates were needed to pay bills. According to Donald Cawthon, she said, " 'If that's not enough I can just make copies,' and the funeral director tells her, 'Ma'am, it's against the law to make copies of death certificates.' But the Momma was in charge. She had Glenn's birth date, Social Security number with her. She had everything."

Glenn's family had just two requests. One was that the notice ask that any contributions to be made in his memory to the Fraternal Order of Police in Marietta or to the Police Benevolent Association in Decatur. The other was that Glenn's closest friends, the men who had been in his wedding party, should be his pallbearers.

Next they were shown coffins with many different features and price ranges. Glenn's family could scarcely bring themselves to look at them. "She wanted us to pick out the casket," says Kathy. "I told her I wasn't going in there, I didn't care what it was like." Lynn shrugged and asked Linda to do it. "It was like she was picking out a dress or something. She acted like it was no big deal. It was weird," Linda remembers. "I told her I could not go back there to pick out what he was going to be buried in."

Next on Lynn's to-do list was to organize the proceedings at Cheatham Hill Memorial Park cemetery. The staff recall the young widow arriving at the cemetary office flanked by a posse of Cobb County's Finest.

"Usually it's the family who come in and make arrangements, but Lynn Turner was escorted by officers and officials from the county police department to give her guidance and support. There was about eight of them." A manager who requested anonymity says, "Although he wasn't killed in the line of duty, they wanted to help her. His family was not there. I believe they wanted him buried at another cemetery, but she overruled it. I don't know why she chose us. There was no family link, but there are other police officers buried here and we regularly have high-profile funerals."

Even allowing for the fact that people grieve differently, there was something about Lynn's attitude that didn't endear her to anyone in the room. Far from being tearful, Lynn was pretty combative. She wanted things done the way she wanted. The manager looked around at the faces of Glenn's fellow police officers, and knew something was wrong. "They were in disbelief when he died and you could see from their faces that they knew there was more to it. It was clear they didn't care for her one bit, but they stood by her because she was Glenn's widow."

It was obvious to the cemetery staff that they were there because Glenn would have wanted them to be. The Cobb County Police Department was a very strong brotherhood, a very tightly knit group of men, and they were determined to give him a proper police officer's send-off. Lynn wanted much less fanfare, but they persuaded her that Glenn would have wanted a hero's funeral and they were determined to give him one.

Lynn's choice of grave was also puzzling. The site she picked out was all by itself. It contained just one space, not two, so that she couldn't be buried there. "She chose one isolated by a pine tree on one side and an adjoining space already purchased by someone else. This means no one can be next to him. Yet she had countless options of which space to choose," said the manager.

Her decisions also seemed odd to David Dunkerton, who had called to offer his help with the harrowing business of arranging the burial. "I met her at the cemetery. She picked out the marker, but that was it. I said, 'How about putting his badge on the marker?' and she said, 'I'm leaving it to you, I'm in a hurry.' It was just another display of her callous behavior towards him.

She couldn't even pretend to care he was dead," he says.

Before Glenn was dressed for viewing, David made sure that his partner took the symbols of the job he loved so much to his grave. "When you complete the motorcycle course you're authorized to wear a gold-colored pin in the shape of a wheel with a set of wings coming from it. I took mine and got it gold-plated and I pinned it on the turtleneck he was buried in," he says. A similar one was attached to the chest pocket of his shirt along with a gold-tone nameplate engraved with "M. G. Turner: Field Training Officer," and the Cobb County Police Department badge he had been so proud of.

On Sunday, March 5, Glenn was laid out for his wake in his long-sleeved uniform shirt, with CCPD patches on the shoulder, the gray uniform pants with the black stripe down each leg and his white ceremonial gloves. The gold-rimmed glasses he was rarely seen without had been lovingly placed on his face. Lavish floral tributes and photographs of his beloved family surrounded him.

That day Glenn's bereaved family was sickened by Lynn's apparent lack of anguish or respect for the comforting rituals that accompany a death. When people would offer their condolences to her, she seemed exasperated by the whole affair. At her side throughout was Paul Rushing, her dead husband's one-time colleague in the Cobb County motorcycle unit.

During the hours her husband's body lay at the funeral home, no one saw Lynn near his casket. Two viewing times were scheduled, the first from 1:00 to 3:00 P.M., the second from 6:00 until 9:00 P.M. Lynn kept her distance from Glenn's family throughout. "She never went in the room where his body was at," says Kathy. "When I arrived I was waiting for Dillard and the rest of his clan to come so that I could show them where to go. I walked in and she's standing in the hallway. I hugged her and I said,

'Do you want to go in?' and she said, 'No.' I went in and I never saw her again."

Lynn also rebuffed her father-in-law's attempt to comfort her, says Kathy. "At the wake my ex-husband told her mother, 'She won't talk to me,' and she said, 'She won't talk to anyone but Mrs. Turner.' When Dillard told me that, I said, 'Talk to me? She doesn't talk to me. There's nothing she's saying to me.' When she was leaving he went to her car to speak to her and she rolled up the window. Helen always said that Lynn was strange to her."

To Kathy, it seemed like the apple didn't fall far from the tree. "Helen didn't associate with me at the funeral home either," she remembers. "I stayed right by Glenn's casket and I greeted people, and she was in the other room the whole time." At the evening session, Linda was infuriated by her sister-in-law's impatience. "The viewing wasn't even over—I couldn't tell exactly what time it was, but I know it was nowhere near nine o'clock—when she came up to me and said, 'I gotta get the hell out of here.' Then she took off." James overheard her irritation too. "Lynn was making all kind of comments at the wake like, she had to get the hell out, that she had been there long enough," he says. "She did not want to be there anyway."

Nobody was more outraged by Lynn's behavior that day than Donald, who says he couldn't bring himself to view his best friend in his coffin. "I was standing out in the hall, too shook up to go in there, and I heard this big old laugh coming and a voice say, 'Aw, damnit, who the fuck does the Cobb County Police Department think they are? I am in charge of this fucking funeral. I don't want no fucking flag on there. If they keep messing with me, I'll shut this whole fucking thing down.'

"By the time she hit the corner, there I was, and she just stopped. And that's when Paul Rushing came over and shook my hand and said, 'He didn't have an enemy in the world, did he?' I said, 'Well, he had one,' and he just walked away. I was just about to go and get her, but Eddie Campuzano grabbed me and said, 'Don't do anything, calm down. She's not worth it.' All she did was to turn and look at me, then she walked on. One of her friends glared at me, and I told her flat out, 'That bitch killed him. She murdered him.' "

On the day of the funeral, the casket was draped with the Stars and Stripes. Glenn's fellow police officers in full dress blues were his pallbearers. The bike unit turned out in force, headed up by David Dunkerton. "I led the funeral procession on my motorcycle ahead of the hearse. As a sign of respect I had taken the identifying numbers from Glenn's motorcycle and put them on mine with black tape over them."

The CCPD's custom was that, although Glenn would have a full honors funeral, they could not hand over the flag that draped his coffin to his kin because he didn't die in the line of duty. Determined that his buddy would be afforded every symbol of dignity, David bought one out of his own pocket. "I also took his helmet to be displayed at the funeral and was told, 'Make sure you bring it back,' but when I went up to the casket I placed it at his feet. I also put my white ceremonial gloves in there," he says.

At 11:00 A.M. on Monday, March 6, Glenn's widow took her rightful place in the front pew at the Marietta Seventh-day Adventist Church where, like his mother, her husband had been a member. Next to her sat Paul Rushing, and that raised many eyebrows in the packed church. Her behavior at the grim occasion appalled Glenn's brother.

"I sat behind them at the service in the church and she was laughing and poking him in the side. It was all I could do just to not reach up and slap both of them," says James. Linda was just as angry at this final humiliation for Glenn, and Lynn's lack of consideration for his heart-broken family. "At the funeral she was sitting up front with Paul Rushing like she's at some party, laughing and cutting up. It's not what you do when you are just about to bury your husband." Lynn's antics only bolstered Glenn's partner's already low opinion of her. "I know people grieve differently, but the way she behaved was entirely inappropriate," she says. Mike Archer was also disgusted. "She was hanging on to Rushing like he was her pacifier. He was her crutch—she used him to get her through the funeral, she never left his side."

Kathy's pastor, Dr. Wayne Owen, officiated. After the service was over, the dozen Cobb County Harley-Davidson bikes led Glenn on the last sad journey to his final resting place at Cheatham Hill Memorial Park where he was to be laid to rest under the tall pines. A marble slab bearing his name and a police badge would mark his grave. The honor guard folded the flag David had bought and handed it to his widow. "That was a horrible moment," remembers Linda.

After the brief committal service, the mourners gathered to talk and share their memories of him, reluctant to go about their lives and leave Glenn to this desolate isolation. After a while, one of the cemetery employees discreetly explained that the burial could not be completed until they were gone. As they made their way back up the hill towards the reception area where tea, coffee and cookies were to be served, Linda noticed Lynn beside her. "She went off to my right to play with a little girl. Then she came back in front of me, and Paul Rushing came over. She looks over and she's like, 'I gotta get the hell out of here,' and she left with Paul, laughing." The cemetery manager also noticed her unfeeling conduct. "After the committal service she did not come across as grief-stricken," she says.

Lynn's repeat performance at the graveside upset

Donald to the extent that he had to exercise every ounce of self-restraint. "I couldn't stand her and I could see what she was doing, but I didn't want to make a scene. I had enough sense not to make a scene at Glenn's funeral."

With the passing of the man who had been her first love, Stacey Abbott's dreams of being reunited with him also died as she stood at his grave a few days later. "I was leaving for a snowboarding trip when my mother called. I was devastated," says Stacey. "That entire weekend is still a blur. I had times of refusal to believe that it was true. I went through times of crying, of anger. I don't think it really set in until I came home soon after his funeral and went to his grave. It was still brown from the dirt being placed there. The grass had not grown up yet. I lay there and cried for hours. My best friend in the world was gone, and I would never have him back again."

In the days and weeks after her son's death Kathy tried to reach out to Lynn, offering to be with her as she sorted through and disposed of his personal things. But far from welcoming a helping hand, Lynn made it obvious that she wanted nothing more to do with any of her in-laws. "She allowed me to come to the house for a couple of weeks after he died, to pick up some things, but she wouldn't let me go upstairs. She'd open the garage door and let me come in the basement and I would take mostly junky stuff, except for the quilt his grandma made for him and the gun that was his daddy's, things like that. Most of it was junk I took out just to be nice to her, and I would say to her, 'Lynn I love you and God loves you too,' and give her a hug."

As far as the Turners were concerned, Lynn was out of their lives, and by her own choice. They were left grappling for something that would help them understand and come to grips with their loss. They came up with more

questions than answers. How could a healthy young man
be dead in a week? From the flu? Everyone gets the flu at
some point and nearly everyone survives. Only the very
young and elderly are thought to be at serious risk. How
could he have been treated in the emergency room and
discharged the same day, and be dead the next?

It didn't make sense. Although they instinctively felt
that his widow must have had something to do with it,
there was not much they could do except try to find
another logical explanation. When they received Cobb
County Medical Examiner Dr. Brian Frist's autopsy report a month later, it was unequivocal: cause of death
was cardiac dysrhythmia due to cardiomegaly. In plain
English, Glenn had expired of natural causes due to an
enlarged heart.

Frist's report noted that Glenn had been ill for four to
five days before his death. When he was examined at the
Hospital, he had flu-like symptoms and was dehydrated.
Fluids were administered and he left with a fistful of
medications that Frist listed: phenobarbital/belladonna
elixir for stomach cramps, a Phenergan suppository for
vomiting and Zantac for ulcers. He noted that during the
last night of his life, Glenn had reportedly been disoriented and extremely thirsty. Frist also made mention of
the fact that the police at the scene saw no clues of anything untoward; there were no bruises or marks on the
body that would suggest foul play.

There was nothing more to be done. The forensic people had come up with nothing. Glenn's friends had little
choice but to accept the situation. "It was over," says
Donald. "We just thought it was just a fluke, a flu thing,
and then the heart thing—it's not uncommon in athletes,
he was a good-sized man and he was active, he did things
and unfortunately that was his demise. We left it alone.
We all had doubts and stuff in our minds. It was an unfortunate death at a young age."

Mike Archer got the results from one of the men charged with investigating Glenn's death. "Major Turner called me personally because I had been inquiring personally at Precinct Four. He told me that Glenn died of some virus that hit his heart. 'Are you sure?' I asked. 'Yeah, that's what it was—a virus hit his heart and killed him. It wasn't anything else.' I literally couldn't believe it."

Natural causes may have been the official finding, but the Turner family, especially Kathy, couldn't understand the county's lack of interest in conducting a more thorough investigation. "Glenn never was out of work. I knew he'd been sick and thought it was the flu, but I wasn't sure about that either," she says. And if there was something wrong with his heart, why had it not been picked up during his annual physicals?

She wanted to see the autopsy report. She had no idea what she was looking for, but she was sure it must contain something that would explain the tragedy to her. "I thought, Lynn must have gotten the autopsy report and I kept phoning her, but she didn't return my calls. I called the medical examiner's office about a couple of months after Glenn died and asked if they had released it, and they said yes. I asked the man there, 'Am I going to get one?' and he said 'No.' I said, 'Did Lynn get one?' And he said, 'Yes.' I asked if I could get a copy and he said yes, I could, and then when I got it, I thought— I don't know what I thought. Lynn wasn't talking to me and that was very, very hurtful."

After reading over the report, Kathy called the medical examiner's office and made an appointment to meet with Dr. Frist. When she and Linda got there, they were told he was unavailable and were instead handed off to an assistant. Although Glenn's mother and sister tried to convey their disbelief that a young man who had been brimming with life the week before, a workhorse who rarely had so much as a sniffle, who never complained about being tired despite juggling two and three jobs, had been cut down by a simple virus. The underling made it clear that they were wasting their time.

"I made an appointment for the afternoon. We spoke to a deputy who later on denied we were ever there," remembers Kathy. "I told him, 'I have some questions about the autopsy report. There are some questions in here that I would like to have answered.' And he said, 'I'll do my best to help you.'

" 'There was green substance in his stomach. What was that?' I asked.

"He said, 'Everyone has green substance in their stomach.'

"I said, 'Really?' And he said, 'Yes.' I felt I had to believe him because of the way he treated me. He was very abrupt. He wasn't giving in to us on anything.

"I had markings on the report where I was going to ask questions. I asked about the enlarged heart. I said, 'Glenn never, ever, anytime that I had known, had an enlarged heart.' That blew me off. He got yearly physicals from the police. They [cops] had to be in good physical condition. And when he had that motorcycle wreck, if he had an enlarged heart, I would have known about it then. There was nothing said about him having an enlarged heart."

"Couldn't the coroner look into it?" she pleaded. Weren't there more tests he could do?

The assistant shook his head. There was no reason to justify more tests; the doctor who'd signed the death certificate said Glenn's heart had conked out. It was tragic, but it happens, he explained. There was no reason to think there had been any crime committed. If they insisted on having his body dug up and sent back to the lab, given the absence of suspicious circumstances, the county wouldn't pick up the bill. She would have to pay for it herself. "How much would that cost?" she asked. The man across the desk shrugged and replied, "Maybe ten thousand dollars."

Faced with a brick wall, she fretted over her daughter-in-law's coldness to her. Why was Lynn acting so strangely? Kathy took her doubts to the police department. "I made an appointment at the detective's office and he blew me off too," she says. "I asked him, 'Why is Lynn treating me the way she is?' He said, 'Because she thinks you think she is guilty.' Kathy remembers being genuinely surprised. "I said, 'I've never said a thing like that. Why would I think she's guilty?' "

And with that, the cops dropped the ball. "I can see dropping it that day because you have two of your own sitting there, you have a dispatcher and you have a dead officer of ten years that everyone genuinely loved," says Donald. "You are emotionally caught up, so you drop the ball. But next week, pick the ball back up, there is no statute of limitations on murder, and you go back out there and investigate. The M.E. dropped it too. He did a terrible job. You make a note and you drop it in the drawer? Somebody should have done something. Kathy and Linda went to see him, but they saw an assistant. And he dropped it too; he didn't even relay to Frist that they all had been there. He should have said, 'Hmm, I better go back and take a look at that.'

"But they got wrapped up with their emotions. We're all human, just because of your profession don't mean you're invincible. We were standing on the tarmac outside the funeral home, they were all there, they weren't five feet away from me, and I heard them raising hell. They were saying, 'She's a goddamned 911 operator and she didn't call nobody? Why didn't she call us?' James had another explanation: "For an average person they would probably be suspicious, but Lynn was conniving and so articulate, she convinced them. They didn't know her as well as we did," he says.

While his family wrestled with their pain, Lynn went on with her life, seemingly unperturbed about losing her husband in such tragic circumstances. In fact, to the Turners, it was almost as if she got a kick out of making them even more miserable than they already were. Less than two weeks after Glenn died, she showed up at the McDonald's where Margie worked, pulling up to the drive-through window in his car. Margie was sick to her stomach.

If the sight of her sister-in-law made Margie ill, her brother contemplated taking justice into his own hands. "I was so upset about all this back then, I had just gone through a separation with my fiancée, we were supposed to be married and we broke up, and that all happened like boom, boom, boom, and I thought, I don't care, I'll take care of her, forget the police department, I'll do it myself.

"I had planned it out in my mind like a sniper, I'd take her out. That's a terrible thing to say, but I really did. I mean, I had already made up my mind how I was going to do it, where and how it was going to be done. I had a place up in the woods where I could sit and take her out with one rifle shot. When I look back at that now, I think how horrible it was to think that, but that's how I thought at the time, because she took someone we truly cared about from us, and she had no regard for us—nothing. She could care less. That's how much I felt like she did it.

"I was really torn. The only thing that kept me from doing it was, I knew in my heart that it was not what Glenn would want. He would not want me to do that. But to me, that was the only way I could see—and this is long before we knew anything about the Thompson family. I knew that Randy was someone she'd been seeing, but I didn't know him personally and I didn't know to what extent she was seeing him or anything else. And then when the police department came back and said, 'You're wrong,' then I really felt guilty, because here I was contemplating doing something against somebody who had nothing to do with it."

CHAPTER EIGHT:
Playing House

In the days after the funeral, Glenn's family and friends all went back to work and tried to carry on without him. Lynn, on the other hand, had no intention of returning to her job as an emergency dispatcher. "She never went back. They kept calling her and she wouldn't return their phone calls, they couldn't get ahold of her," says Mike Archer. "The way I heard it, the major over there called her and left a message. Then one of the other dispatchers came up in the back [of the building] one day and Lynn had dropped off her police supplies, her badge, clothes—everything. She just threw them in a pile and left them at the back door of headquarters.

"She didn't want to face anybody. She had started a different life, she had that new life in Forsyth." With Glenn's death, her life had also become less complicated; she was no longer juggling parallel lives in two different counties with two men who had no inkling of each other's existence. She also knew she was about to come into some serious money. "She didn't officially resign until the check finally came from the county for forty-seven thousand dollars, and that took several weeks," says Donald.

In February 1995, Randy Thompson told his folks that he was quitting his job at the Butler dealership and moving back to the town where he was raised. "The car selling was not working out for him, for one thing, and he was just not the salesman type. He wanted to get back to Cumming and get into the sheriff's department," his father later explained in court. For a couple of weeks he moved in with his sister Angie to be nearer the job, and Lynn.

Four days after burying her husband, Lynn signed a lease on an apartment in Cumming and described Randy as the "occupant." He was the secret that many of Glenn's fellow cops had kept quiet about, at least to the Turner family. They weren't the only ones in the dark—she'd kept silent about the new man in her life to her own family, and when she moved in with him, she didn't even tell her mother.

Now she cut off any remaining ties with Glenn's family. For a few weeks after the funeral, Lynn had given a grudging welcome when her mother-in-law tried to reach out to her, but showed little sympathy and less understanding for Kathy's bereavement. "Even when I went over to the house, she was not giving me anything, but at least she was letting me be there," says Kathy. "I didn't know what was going on in her life and I tried to be very nice to her. Here she was, a widow woman, and she was young and I was feeling sorry for her. But she didn't care about me being nice to her at all. I don't know how she could look me in the eye and give me a hug.

"After she got the autopsy [report] she just quit answering my calls, and I never went back because there was nothing I could do, she just wouldn't open the door," Kathy says. "I called her mother and she didn't want to talk to me either, and so I thought, I guess the connection is severed here."

Lynn had already found herself into a job in the Forysth County Sheriff's Office's 911 center. To help her move from Marietta to Cumming, Lynn enlisted the assistance of one-time date Bryan Bennett. She had kept in touch with him even though he stopped seeing her as soon as he found out she was married. She had called him the day after Glenn died, blaming the tragedy on an irregular heartbeat.

The Turners made one last attempt at salvaging some of Glenn's belongings from Old Farm Walk once Lynn had moved away. When they arrived at the door they found the house locked up and they could only peer in the windows. "We could see one of Glenn's uniforms hanging up in the garage. She was supposed to have taken them back to the police department. We would love to have gone through the place, but it was technically still hers—it was up for sale at the time," says James. Tempted though they were, they knew such a course of action would play directly into Lynn's hands. "We knew that she would love to get something on us, so we thought, We're not going to do that," he says.

"The man who bought the house said he begged her to come over and clear out the basement, but he didn't know the story—he didn't know they were Glenn's things. He said he wished he had known, because he would have gotten them to us. We never knew what happened to the stuff, I guess it was probably just thrown away."

James, who was then working as a bail bondsman, was having an especially tough time coping with the loss of his brother. He was haunted by his own prescient words as Glenn's best man. "I'm the youngest, but everything kind of fell on me for several reasons. One was the infamous toast I made at his wedding. I didn't mean it literally— that's what I felt, and I never dreamed that it would ever come true. It bothered me, but what bothered me more was, I knew in my heart that his death wasn't right. I felt like she did it, but I didn't know how she did it, and nobody seemed to help.

"I talked to a couple of officers that I knew who worked there with Glenn at the time also, and everybody is telling me, 'Look, James, he's one of ours, if there's something wrong here we are going to find out about it.' They said they would leave no stone unturned," he remembers. "You are brought up to trust police officers and they know their job, you don't, so you trust them and that's what we did. I guess the most heartbreaking thing of all was when they came back to us and said, "You know what, you're wrong, there wasn't nothing that happened," and then it made me question myself that I had accused someone wrongly. Even though I had never confronted her, never accused her, I knew in my heart and in my head that she had done it."

He began looking for answers on his own. "I ran all sorts of searches that I had access to, looking for information about Lynn, who was always very secretive about her background. It was, 'This is my mom, this is my adopted dad,' and that was it. We didn't know a lot about her. But I didn't do much. The Cobb County Police Department was already checking into her and I didn't want to do anything that would mess up what they were doing. I had to step back," he says.

Despite the leeriness of Lynn that he'd shared with his dad, Randy Thompson couldn't keep away from her. On the apartment lease Lynn had listed other sources of income apart from her day job as a 911 operator. She claimed that she also did some work for a Cobb County attorney, mostly running errands for him, like traveling to Tennessee, where she had pretended to be an undercover drug narc. Nita Thompson remembers being skeptical: "She would make these trips to Chattanooga where she told us she was undercover for someone. I wasn't really sure if it was true. I didn't really listen to a whole lot Lynn said. I let it go in one ear and go out the other. With her, I didn't know what to believe and what not to believe." Lynn had also said Lynn had a wealthy cousin who was always good for money if she was in a bind.

Randy didn't know as he started playing house with Lynn that she was already plotting out her financial future. Growing up in Cumming, on Wallace Tatum Road, he had lived across the street from a small holding owned by a family named Cable. By the time he was 14, he was earning pocket money baby-sitting the Cable children and helping out with chores around the farm. Rebecca Cable met Randy again years later when he walked into her insurance agency looking for auto coverage. He told her he was with the sheriff's department and she advised him to also consider taking out life insurance. He bought a $25,000 policy and named his parents as his beneficiaries.

When he and Dara were married he'd made her the beneficiary of the policy. After their divorce, and soon after he'd hooked up with Lynn, he went back to the Cable Insurance Agency and asked Rebecca to make another change, this time to Lynn Turner. It wasn't his idea, it was Lynn who had urged him to do it, he admitted. Rebecca advised him that a better plan would be to split the beneficiary of his life insurance between his parents and his little son.

While Randy was trying to provide for Lynn should anything happen to him, he had no idea that back in Marietta, Glenn Turner was working himself to the point of a breakdown to pay his wife's bills. She didn't tell him that she had big plans for the rest of her life and they didn't include what she viewed as the major stumbling blocks to her happiness—Glenn Turner and not enough cash.

One of the first people Randy bumped into when he returned to Cumming was Terry Pruitt. After his marriage to Dara broke up he had lived for a while in the basement of a house owned by Terry's uncle. They talked and laughed about the blowout bash the guys had thrown for him when he'd left his deputy sheriff's job two years before. Terry had attended the affair with his then girl-friend, Samantha Butler and by all accounts, it had been an unforgettable party that had kept going over two nights.

He told Terry that he'd taken an apartment at Oakland Oaks and he was living with a woman named Lynn. Why didn't Terry and Samantha drop by? Soon the two couples became a regular foursome. "We saw them just about every weekend. We'd go out on Lake Lanier in the boat that Lynn bought, a brand-new, eighteen-foot Sea Ray." It never occurred to him that Lynn was married to someone else. "I never saw her wear a wedding ring, ever," Terry later testified.

It seemed to him that Randy's live-in lover was either very well off or had won the lottery. "She bought him boots, leather jackets, just all kinds of stuff. And she bought cars—it seemed like he had a new car every six months, and I knew he couldn't afford new cars." The autos even had expensive-sounding names. "For a while he drove a black Monte Carlo," he said.

Lynn pulled all the stops out for Randy's 27th birthday on June 12. She mulled over how she could top the gifts she'd already given him, like the $1,000 boots and $20,000 cars, and came up with a doozy: tickets for an all-expenses-paid cruise. He raved about the upcoming trip the next time he saw Terry and Samantha. "It will be fantastic, we are going to the Caribbean and we will be stopping off at the Bahamas, St. Thomas and Puerto Rico." He'd stopped and looked over at Lynn, who smiled back at him, flushed with satisfaction and clearly enjoy-ing being a sugar mommy. "It will be so cool. That's why we want you guys to come with us."

"It sounds great, man," Terry had said, "how much is it?"

"About two and a half thousand," Randy replied.

"I can't afford that," Terry protested. He worked for Fix, the family electrical and plumbing business, and although he did all right, he didn't have that kind of cash to squander on a luxury cruise.

"You don't have to, we're paying for it. In fact, it's already paid. Look, here are your tickets! All you would need is some spending money, you know, for drinks and stuff," Randy told him.

It was first class all the way. The morning they were leaving, Randy and Lynn picked up Terry and Samantha in the limousine she'd booked to take them to the Atlanta airport to catch a plane for Miami, where they were to board the ship. "It was all Lynn's idea," Randy burbled excitedly. During the flight to Miami, he called his mother. "It was the first time he had flown and he was having a good time calling me from the plane," she says. For the next week, Lynn threw herself into the honeymoon she'd felt cheated out of when she found herself on the family cruise with Glenn Turner nearly two years before. The two couples spent lazy days sunning, swimming and sightseeing, and tropical evenings dining and dancing to the steel drum combo. When they'd had enough of the good life, she and Randy would retire to their palatial cabin near the top deck. Terry and Samantha were a few floors below in less grand, but still comfortable, quarters.

Six months after setting up home in the apartment she'd leased the week after Glenn died, Lynn plunked down a wad of cash on a house for the two of them at 5210 Tallantworth Crossing, and on September 1, they moved in.

Randy couldn't wait to show the place to his folks, and to his delight, Perry and Nita were suitably impressed. It was much more spacious than their modest family home, and decorated expensively. Looking around at his son's stylish new digs, Perry remembered thinking Lynn had good taste and seemingly, a bottomless wallet. That must be some powerful, well-paying job she had with Forsyth County. Hadn't she said she was a 911 dispatcher? Surely they didn't get paid the kind of money a place like this must have cost. That grandma, the one she told Angela had left her all this dough? She must have been some rich old bird.

"It was a very expensive home. I think it was in the one hundred and seventy thousand price bracket, and the furnishings were first class—furnishings we were not used to having. There was a big TV screen, and all of the couches and chairs were leather, and there were nice things—very nice things," he testified. Helen Gregory was introduced to Randy for the first time when she was invited over to see the new house. Lynn had told her about him, but up to this point, they'd never met.

A few visits later Randy introduced his mother and father to Simon, the cockatoo that Lynn had bought him. It had cost over $1,000. "That bird was everything to Randy," says his mom. "He had two large cages for it, one he kept at his apartment and the other he kept at work. Simon would hop on his shoulder and get in his truck and go with him. Randy would lay down on the bed or the couch or whatever and if he had a blanket or anything over him, Simon would get under the blanket and lay down with him. Simon loved Randy too."

That August, Linda Hardy, who was still totally unaware of her sister-in-law's new life with Randy over in Cumming, received a call from Janet Hammond at the Deferred Compensation Service Center in Ohio. She told Linda that Glenn's widow was claiming she was the beneficiary of his Cobb County deferred compensation (PEBSCO) account. She said Glenn had originally named his sister as his beneficiary, but shortly before he married Lynn, he had sent in a form changing it to his wife. The thing was, he had forgotten to sign it, she added. They would be sending a document to her and all Linda had to do was to sign the waiver and return it so that they could hand over the cash to Lynn.

Linda had no intention of doing anything of the sort. Glenn was no idiot, if he hadn't signed that form, then he didn't want Lynn to get his money, she figured. He may have mailed off the form to shut his wife up, but the lack of his signature proved he'd wanted Linda to remain as his beneficiary. On August 22, she wrote to the claims adjuster:

Dear Ms. Hammond,

> *Per your request, I am stating in writing that I will not be signing the release form naming Lynn Womack as the beneficiary for my deceased brother. I have been advised that as long as his signature was not on the change form, the paperwork is not valid for her to be the beneficiary. Please let me know what steps I need to take next in order to clear up this matter as promptly as possible.*

> *Thank you,*
> *Linda Hardy*

Janet Hammond forwarded Linda's letter to her superior. In the accompanying note she said that she had contacted Alisa Moody, Lynn's friend and former lodger, who claimed to have witnessed Glenn fill out the form. On September 5, Hammond again wrote to Linda to inform her that if she and Lynn couldn't resolve the matter amicably by November 1, then the claim would have to be settled in court and that any attorney fees would be charged to Glenn's account. On the same day, Hammond sent a note to Lynn confirming that she had received an affidavit from Alisa Moody, but advising that without

Linda's signature, a court would have to decide how the funds would be disbursed.

Linda wrote back:

> I don't understand why this issue is to be resolved between Lynn and myself when she was not even named as beneficiary on this policy. You state that Alisa Moody witnessed Glenn filling out the paper work to change his beneficiary. But Glenn failed to sign anything. If she had truly read and witnessed anything, why didn't she see that he did not sign it? I understand that anyone could have filled out the paperwork for him, but unless he signed it, it would not be valid. She was Lynn's roommate and best friend, so that also raises the question of whether she really witnessed anything or not. I truly don't believe that Glenn ever intended to make the change legal, or he would have followed through properly. He was a Cobb County Police Officer for 10 years and also a notary, and knew that even a document as small as a traffic violation must be signed to be valid, much less something of this importance.

Over the winter, Lynn and Randy settled into something close to domestic bliss. On weekends, she got an advance course in parenting when little Nicholas came to stay. By June she had some news for Randy: she was pregnant and he was going to be a father again. Helen took the prospect of being a grandmother in stride and offered the couple congratulations. Randy's family weren't sure how to react. Besides, Lynn was strangely secretive about her pregnancy. "Not many people knew about it, she was weird about it," says Nita. Despite the 259-mile round-trip between their home and Cumming, she and Perry had dropped by several times since he had moved in, mostly to see their grandson when he was spending time with his father. They were still getting used to their son's new living arrangements and they could see that the relationship had some hiccups. During the last few months they'd overheard frequent angry outbursts and arguments, and they were concerned how a new baby was going to fit in.

Nita, who had never warmed to Lynn, recalled a strange conversation she'd had with her on one of these visits: "We were standing in front of her garage and she volunteered the information that her ex-husband had passed away, and I said, 'What happened to him?' She said, 'It was the flu or something. He had been in the hospital,' and then I asked her if he had insurance money to pay for his funeral and she said, 'Yes.' She said he had not changed the beneficiary since they had been divorced and that the money came to her. I asked her if she gave the money from the policy to Glenn's family and she said that she had."

The row about Glenn's PEBSCO account dragged on over the winter. On March 19, Lynn had a lawyer, D. Richard Jones, write to Janet Hammond demanding she hand over the disputed funds to his client. At the beginning of April, Linda wrote asking to be put in touch with the company's legal department, which was handling the dispute. She also wanted to know if an interpleader action was ever filed.

By now Lynn had gotten herself a new job in the Forsyth County District Attorney's Office. Chris Childers, who now runs his own security business in Jasper, Georgia, had just begun working right down the street as a plainclothes officer with the criminal investigations section of the Forsyth County Sheriff's Office. He told reporter Janet Midwinter that Lynn caught his eye because in the somber atmosphere of the office, she "stood out like a sore thumb." "Everyone else wore suits or fairly plain dresses, but she had the big pouffy hair and wore reveal-

ing dresses, and her make-up was done. It was the whole
package and she was dressed to the nines for a reason.
They dress pretty conservatively in the D.A.'s office, but
Lynn stood out. What it looked like to me was that she was
trawling for a boyfriend."

He had taken a case file up to her office for review,
and Lynn started to chat. "It was nothing major, no big
deal, just friendly conversation. I think the second time I
went there she asked me if I was single, and I told her I
was, but I didn't have a lot of time to date. She said, 'We
have to go out sometime.' I thought that was a little forward, but I decided, Well, that's okay, that's fine.

"I was attracted to her, she was good-looking, well put
together and well spoken. I thought this was someone
I could go out with, and so, like all good investigators, I
went to find out a little information on her. I spoke to
a couple of people and nobody really knew that much
about her, except her husband had passed away."

At that time Chris was also working at a high-end
restaurant and nightclub, called the Marina Beach Club,
in Cumming, where all the Atlanta Braves, the Falcons
and different football teams used to hang out when they
came into town. "It was a very nice place. People who
came there dressed very nicely, no blue jeans or anything
like that," he says.

"It was a restaurant, but on weekends they had deejays
and dancing and stuff. And I was working security at the
door, one of my many part-time jobs. She came in with
some people from the D.A.'s office after work, and she
said, 'How come you never called me?' I said, 'Well, I
don't have your number,' and so she took one of the
club's business cards off the desk and wrote her name
and number on the back. I still have it.

"The next week I was in her office again and I was
talking to one of the secretaries and I asked what the deal
was with Lynn. The woman said, 'Oh, she's living with

Randy Thompson.' I said, 'What?' I was like, Well, that cuts her out. It's an unwritten rule in law enforcement that you don't date cops' wives or girlfriends. At some point they may end up becoming your backup and that could get really uncomfortable.

"So I said, That's that. But she kept calling down to my office and I would just blow her off and say I had to work or whatever. The next time I was up at the D.A.'s office, I walked in and she said, 'I know about you.' I said, 'Okay, what do you know? Fill me in.' And she said, 'I know that if we ever went out I would never have to worry about money.'

"I thought that was the strangest conversation to have with someone you hadn't even been out on a date with. I asked, 'What are you talking about?' And she said, 'I've found out about you and that I wouldn't have to worry about money.' I told her, 'I don't know what you've heard or what you think you know, but I am a broke police officer. I work two, sometimes three jobs to try to make ends meet. I am not wealthy by any means. Any money my parents have, they worked for, and I am not entitled to any of it.' I remember this because she was at a filing cabinet putting a file away and she slammed the cabinet and said, 'Well, that's not what I know.'

"I was thinking, You're a nutcase. I saw right then that I was not going to have anything to do with her at all. I said, 'Well, since we're airing out everything, I know that you're seeing someone.' She said, 'Who?' and I replied, 'Randy Thompson.' She said, 'Huh,' and just kind of blew air out, like she was disgusted. 'Well, he's going to be out of the picture before too long.' I told her I didn't date other cops' girlfriends and she got really mad, she was red-faced, and said, 'I don't understand what the problem is.' I could only say, 'You're living with a police officer,' or a former police officer or whatever he was at the time. I kept saying, 'I just don't do that, sorry.'

The next time Chris was back down in the office, one of the secretaries starts laughing and tells him it was good that he didn't go out with Lynn. When he asked why she said, 'She called into work this morning and said she was in the hospital.' 'What's wrong with her?' he asked. The woman replied, 'She's having a baby.' Lynn hadn't told anyone at work that she was having Randy's baby, she had hid it for nine months. The D.A.'s office couldn't believe it, because they were having to scramble to find somebody to cover for her while she was on maternity leave. At the end she wore baggy shirts and sweaters so nobody noticed. She had to have been pregnant while she was trying to seduce me," says Chris.

On January 30 Lynn gave birth to a daughter named Amber. For a while, as she threw herself wholehcartedly into motherhood, the tension between her and Randy abated. But not for long—soon they were back to arguing constantly. His parents began to stop by less and less as the couple's incessant bickering spoiled their visits. It was upsetting for Nita and Perry, who cursed the day their son had become involved with this woman.

"She wanted her and Randy to get married," says Nita. "He finally—I think she was pregnant with Amber at the time—he bought her a ring and she wore it for hardly any time. And then she wouldn't marry him. Randy wanted to do right, but she knew she had him because of the baby, and then she wouldn't get married." Their bills began to pile up, and to earn more he joined the Forsyth County Fire Department, moving Simon's second cage to the firehouse. A month before his daughter was born, he had started looking into having his "fiancée" named as his beneficiary on a State Farm Insurance policy.

Nothing Randy could do seemed to satisfy Lynn. The attractive girl who had once declared how much she loved him had turned into a shrew, and Randy, clearly unhappy, was biting back. But she wore the pants in the relationship and she held the purse strings. She handled all their money and even balanced Randy's checkbook for him.

The relationship looked like it had totally imploded by the late fall of 1996. At the Forsyth County Sheriff's Office, Officer Jessica Marshall took the November 21 call. Lynn told the cop her boyfriend had been drinking, they'd gotten into a spat and he had smacked her on the mouth. When Jessica got to the house, there was no sign of Randy, but Lynn showed off her bruised lip. Shortly afterwards, Randy had arrived home, having been driven back by a firefighter pal nicknamed "Possum."

At the sight of the two women, Randy began cursing and yelling that Lynn was "crazy." "Possum" calmed him down and Officer Marshall called for backup. Sheriff's Deputy Norman Woodward pulled up and arrested Randy on the spot. As Randy was led outside in cuffs, he slammed his hands on a truck parked in the driveway. After he'd been taken away, Lynn called Major Ron Casper, her boss at the sheriff's department, to fill him in before he heard it on the grapevine.

When his parents found out, they were shocked. Playing the martyr, Lynn then told the police that she was sure that Randy hadn't hit her on purpose. They'd argued, he'd lashed out to get away from her and his hand had accidentally connected with her face. Despite her explanation, he was charged with simple battery, sentenced to 10 months probation and fined $400. In court Lynn changed her tune, claiming that it wasn't the first time he had hit her, he was a mean drunk and cited a previous altercation in which he had dislocated her shoulder and bruised her ribs. Although she'd wanted to press charges then too, the cops, apparently harboring doubts about her version of events, had refused to charge him.

The whole incident was hogwash, according to Randy's mom. "I remember that because she finally admitted to me that he didn't hit her, at least not on purpose," she says. "They were fighting and he was trying to leave, but she didn't want him to leave so she jumped on his back and as he was trying get her off him he hit her in the mouth with his elbow, is what she told me. She told the cops that he deliberately hit her, but then after the fact, she told me that he didn't, it was an accident."

Although the hostility between them eased somewhat over Christmas and New Year, the joy of the season did not trickle down to Randy. By early 1997, it was clear that his home situation was getting to him. A few weeks before, he succeeded in getting Lynn named on his State Farm policy. On the night of February 1, Lynn again called the sheriff's office and this time reported that her boyfriend had swallowed a bunch of sleeping pills. She said she was afraid he was suicidal and asked them to send an ambulance. Responding officers Bo Norris and paramedic Jeff Lisle answered the call. A doctor arrived and checked out Randy and what he'd thrown down his throat before deciding that he hadn't taken enough of the pills to do him any serious harm. The doctor and the EMTs left him to sleep it off.

It was little wonder that Randy drank or tried to opiate himself. Living with Lynn was becoming impossible. They fought like cats and dogs. Any issues they had between them had been exaggerated by the mood swings caused by Lynn's pregnancy, and she could scarcely stand to have him in, or out of, her sight. Although she told him she no longer had any use for him, she was jealous when he wasn't around. When he took off to play golf with his buddies, she'd get on the cell phone to bust his chops. If she couldn't find him, she would vent her fury on his parents.

"She would call and complain about Randy, ranting and raving that he'd done this or that. I eventually told her to stop calling me. Randy was my son and I wasn't going to listen to her anymore. I'd take his word over hers every time," says Nita. When she couldn't get Randy, who'd turned off his phone to stop her reaching him, and knowing his mother would hang up on her, Lynn would call Perry and harangue him instead. "He would talk to her and try and calm her down." Nita despaired. What had her boy gotten himself into?

Over spring and summer the relationship became so fractured and was punctuated by so many violent rows that by November, Randy ended up at New Day Counseling and Assessments for anger evaluation. He knew he should get away from her, but Lynn was like a drug, no matter how bad he knew she was for him, he was unable to resist, and kept going back for more. Besides, she was the mother of his little girl.

What added to his desperation were his pressing money troubles. Teresa Green, who had worked with Lynn at the Forsyth County Sheriff's Office 911 Communications Center, said that Lynn would transfer money from her bank into Randy's account to help him make his child support payments to his ex-wife. And if Randy couldn't stand living with Lynn, it was becoming mutual. Teresa recalled that an exasperated Lynn had said on several occasions that she hated him.

CHAPTER NINE:
Another Death

It was shortly after this string of ugly incidents that Lynn became pregnant with their second child. Policewoman Jessica Marshall, who had been dispatched to the house to break up the fight that had ended with Randy's arrest, became Lynn's new best friend. Together the two women would go on shopping sprees or just hang out at Lynn's home, where Jessica was privy to the couple's frequent falling-outs and reconciliations. She described them as having "a love/hate relationship."

Not even the son who was born on June 18, 1998 could heal the chasm that deepened when Lynn developed postpartum gynecological problems. The little boy was named Blake, and Lynn was told he would be her last child. She underwent a hysterectomy and was then put on hormone replacement therapy to combat the uncomfortable effects of early menopause.

After Blake's arrival, Lynn insisted that Randy take out additional life insurance, and he doubled his coverage to $200,000. Later that year, he inked yet another policy with Cotton States for $36,000 and again he made Lynn his beneficiary. Even that didn't stave off her demands, yet although he wanted to bail out, he was reluctant to give up on his life with Lynn. He already had a

broken marriage behind him and felt guilty about his oldest child being shuttled between him and his ex-wife.
The last thing he wanted to do was to walk out on his
younger kids. "He was raised right," his mother explained. "He knew the right thing to do and he wanted to
do the right thing, and that's what he was trying to do.
She was having no part of it."

But although he tried to keep it together, there were
many nights that he bunked down with friends, unwilling
to face Lynn's wrath and wearied by the constant conflict.
Lynn knew just how to push his buttons. If he wanted to
see his kids, he had to come home. Once he went back,
she'd make life so impossible that he'd leave again.

"There always seemed to be a little tension floating
around the room. She was always picking fights with him
about anything, and that upset me," says Angie, who remembers Randy being much happier when he was away
from Lynn than when he was with her. "He and his son
came by my house a few days after the birth of my second son, and I took a picture of Randy, his son and both
my boys [she now has three]. Randy looked like a rac-
coon because he had been standing out in the sun earlier
that day collecting money for the fire department drive
for burned firemen, and had his sunglasses on, and ended
up with the circles around his eyes." That he'd spent
hours in the heat for his fellow firefighters didn't surprise
her. "He had a heart of gold, and would have done anything for anyone."

For the next couple of years he tried to make the best
of it. When things became too hot to handle at home, he'd
move out for a few weeks, begging a bed from coworkers
or from Terry Pruitt. But when the separation from his ba-
bies became unbearable, he'd crawl back, his tail between
his legs like a whipped dog. His family had no idea just
how intolerable the situation had become for Randy until

January 23,1999, when they were made painfully aware of how hopeless and miserable he felt about his life.

Earlier that evening, Jessica had dropped by the house. Deputy Chris Shelton was also there. It was one of Randy's "away" spells, and Lynn told her that he had called the previous Saturday and said he was sick. When she had phoned him back on Sunday to ask how he was, he had been abrupt with her. As if to demonstrate her power over him, she then fished out a voice message he had left six or seven months before and played it to them. In it Randy said he was calling to apologize for a recent fight. "I'm sorry," he had said, "I guess I've just got a split personality."

Nita and Perry were asleep when the phone rang. Perry shook himself awake and grabbed the receiver to stop it ringing again and disturbing Nita. She woke anyway. The alarm clock by his bed showed him it was the early hours, but he was too groggy to take in whether it was two or three o'clock in the morning. Propping himself up on one elbow, he answered, "Yeah, who is it?"

"Daddy, I have done something stupid." Perry sat bolt upright. Randy's speech was slurred and he didn't sound good. "What have you done?" he asked.

"I have taken some pills."

"What have you taken?" Perry quizzed him. Randy didn't answer.

He tried again. "How many did you take?"

"I don't know," said Randy.

"Are you by yourself?" his father wanted to know.

"No, Terry is with me."

"Wake Terry up and put him on the phone," Perry told him.

"I can't, Dad, he's got to go to work tomorrow, I don't want to wake him up," Randy replied.

"Okay, I'll tell you what I'll do," began Perry, who had gathered his wits and delivered an ultimatum in a tone that invited no argument. "I'm going to hang up the phone and give you three minutes to have Terry call me back, and if he doesn't call me back, I'm going to call 911."

Although it was less than three, it seemed like an eternity to Randy's troubled parents. When the phone rang again, Terry was on the line.

"Randy is acting sleepy," he said.

"Can you get him to the hospital?" Perry asked.

"Okay," Terry said, "I'll take him to County."

"Then we're on our way. We'll meet you there."

Grabbing their clothes and pulling them on as fast as they could, Nita and Perry were out of the door and in the car in a few minutes. The journey from Warner Robins to Cumming takes two hours—if you don't encounter traffic or go through Atlanta. Their minds rushed back to that winter night nearly two years before when Randy had emptied a bottle of pills into his mouth and Lynn had called for the emergency services. Despite the seriousness of her son's actions, Nita knew instinctively that as distressing as they were, they were not suicide attempts, but cries for help.

"We got up and flew as fast as we could," says Nita. "I wasn't scared, because I knew Randy, and I knew, though he might do something like that, he wasn't stupid enough to kill himself. If Randy had wanted to die, he had a gun. All he had to do was put it to his head and he would have been gone." But if they were just false alarms, cries for attention from Lynn, as Nita believed, he was crying out to the wrong person. "She was driving him crazy. She wouldn't let him see the kids. It was bad. She is just a mean person all the way around."

By the time they arrived, Randy was in the emergency room and acting as if nothing much had happened. "They had pumped his stomach and he was laughing and cutting up about the whole thing," said Perry. He and Nita were mad at him, but at the same time they were thankful beyond words that he was going to be all right. A couple of doctors came in to talk to Randy and, concluding he was no longer a danger to himself, they released him to his parents' custody. "The doctor told us that he hadn't taken anything to kill him. Randy didn't like pain—anytime he had a headache, he called me. We brought him home with us for a week," says Nita.

His sister Kimberly agreed: "I think it was just him trying to say, 'Something is not right here.' Maybe this would wake her up and get her to change the way she was to him," she later told *Dateline*. One thing she was sure of, this destructive dance with Lynn, the going back to her and then moving out again was taking too much of a toll on her brother. "I know you love your kids, but the best thing to do is to move on," she advised him.

Everybody urged him to make a clean break with Lynn. He needed to find a permanent home of his own and start over. Until he found a place, he stayed with a firefighter pal, Glen Everett. On April 1, 1999, with Perry's help, Randy moved into unit G-5 at the white-painted Overlook Club Apartment complex at 815 Tolbert Street. But most of his clothes and, for a time, his beloved bird remained at Tallantworth Crossing, where he continued to cut the grass and do chores around the house after arriving with toys for the kids. Lynn told Jessica that since the split she and Randy were getting along much better.

Their attraction for each other baffled many of their friends. One of them was Cumming Police Department Officer Casey Tatum, who had known Randy since the fifth grade, worked with him at the Forsyth sheriff's department and was renting an apartment at Oakland Oaks at the time Randy and Lynn lived there, before she bought the house. He believed they just couldn't let each other go.

Even after Randy had left for good, Lynn peppered him with random calls, and often a blistering argument would ensue. They bickered constantly over the children. According to Tatum, Lynn used the children as bait to lure Randy back under her control. If he wouldn't come home, then she would only let him see his youngsters at the firehouse. She would not allow them to stay overnight at his apartment. He knew he was being played, even though he was at a loss how to cope with it. "She will not let me see my kids and I can't handle it. She has to be in control of everything," he told another friend, Melanie Harper.

His parents also saw less and less of their grandchildren. "Finally Randy said, 'I just can't take this anymore,' and he moved out, but she still had control over him because of them. He wanted to see his children and she would jerk him around with these kids. He'd get mad about something and she'd call him and say he couldn't see them, and all sorts of bad stuff. She was a controlling freak. She wanted to control everybody," says his mother. "When Randy lived with her we'd go up pretty often to see him and the kids, but she wouldn't let him bring them to see us. After he moved out we hardly ever saw them."

One of the bones of contention between the couple was Randy's refusal to hand over child support payments. "I'll pay, but I'll pay it to the [family] court. I'm not giving anything directly to you," he told her. He no longer trusted her with his cash or his kids. In fact, now that he knew she had cheated on Glenn Turner with him, he had begun to have doubts that his baby son was even his child. He told Tatum that he was going to demand a paternity test to find out if he was the real father.

He had also confided his suspicions about little Blake to his former wife. Dara remembered him saying that Lynn was trying to pressure him to cough up money for the children, but when he had countered that he was going to

The Seventh-day Adventist Church where Glenn's funeral was held. His mother prays for him there every Saturday. *Courtesy Onnie McIntyre*

Cheatham Hill Memorial Park. Riders from the Cobb County Police Department Motorcycle Unit escorted Glenn to his final resting place. *Courtesy Onnie McIntyre*

The home Glenn shared with Lynn at Old Farm Walk in Marietta. She claimed he tried to fly off the second-floor deck. *Courtesy Onnie McIntyre*

Never forgotten: Every year on the anniversary of his death, Glenn's family and friends gather at his grave to share their memories.
Courtesy Onnie McIntyre

Glenn in uniform.
Courtesy Kathy Turner

Glenn and his big sister, Linda Hardy. Like her mom and her brother James, she refused to accept that Glenn died of natural causes. *Courtesy Kathy Turner*

The house at Tallantworth Crossing in Cumming where Randy Thompson and Lynn lived with their two children. *Courtesy Onnie McIntyre*

The unit at the Overlook Apartment complex on Tolbert Road where Randy's firefighter buddies found his body when they broke down the door. *Courtesy Onnie McIntyre*

Twelve years on. Left to right: Donald and Silvia Cawthon; Linda Hardy; James Turner; Glenn's mom, Kathy; and James's wife, Tracie. *Courtesy Onnie McIntyre*

The radiant bride-to-be displayed no sign of pre-wedding jitters at the bridal shower Glenn's mom threw for her at the church school hall in August 1993. *Courtesy Kathy Turner*

ask the court to order a paternity test, she had backed down and dropped the subject. He also complained how Lynn, who had showered Nicholas with love and bought him toys that made him the envy of every kid in the neighborhood when she was trying to seduce Randy, had started "getting ugly" with the child for no reason. He also told Dara that Lynn had warned him when he left that if she couldn't have him, nobody else would.

Months went by before he saw Lynn again. While they were on the outs, Lynn had set her sights on a new potential boyfriend who also worked for the sheriff's department. At one point she was so smitten with him that she threw Randy's and Nicholas' clothes into bags and told Randy to remove them.

During the time they were estranged, Randy called Teresa Green while she was at work and asked her out. She told Lynn, who persuaded Teresa to call him back so she could eavesdrop on the conversation. Although Lynn was no longer in love with Randy, she had no intention of letting him out of her clutches. She started sending him flowers, signing the cards that accompanied them "From a secret admirer," just to see if Randy would take the bait and call to ask if they'd come from her. Teresa remembered that Lynn would also send flowers to herself in a twisted attempt to hook the man she'd selected to replace him.

To Teresa, Lynn had enough money to play expensive games. When the two women would be together on a lunch break, Teresa saw her deposit large sums of cash, $2,000 to $3,000 at a time, into her bank account. She always had a plausible explanation for her affluence—one she gave was that her stepfather had given her the money after selling a tractor or some other piece of farm equipment. And Teresa couldn't help but notice that her friend often splurged on enviable personal luxuries, like the designer sunglasses that cost $150 a pop. When she hosted cookouts at her home, she fed her guests prime steak and copious amounts of liquor.

Despite the fact that both were going on with their separate lives, Randy still couldn't make a clean break from Lynn. He hated being an absentee dad. Entries in the diary he kept in the late summer of 1999 reveal how she continued to use the children as a weapon:

> *Monday August 23: Lynn called about 5.45 p.m. She was mad because I haven't called her today. She was being an asshole and she told me when I had time for her and the kids to let her know. She's just playing her game. She called me later and accused me of having a girlfriend.*
>
> *Tuesday, August 24: Tried to call to check on Blake, he was sick at his stomach last night. She won't answer the phone or return a page. Paged again and I left a message on her cell phone. She called at 7:30 and wanted to fight on phone, I told her I had to get ready for work. She told me that we were going to finish it now or not at all. I said we would talk later. That wasn't good enough. I hung up. She called back I didn't answer. She left a message not to call or page her and to leave her and the kids alone.*
>
> *Wednesday, August 25: She called and begged me to come over, I told her no. She got mad and I had to hang up on her to get off the phone. She rang again told me not to bother her or the kids.*

After he had told her was he meeting up with a friend who Lynn clearly loathed, the next day's entry shows how unhealthy their relationship had become:

> *Thursday, August 26: Lynn called about 7:00. She was talking shit for about an hour. She called back around 10:30. During the conversation I said something about F. Brown. She told me if I went anywhere with him not to ever call her other than [about] kids again. I plainly told her to get*

lost—if she thought she was going to tell me what to do
we had to talk about that for an hour. I tried to get off the
phone for 45 minutes. She told me since we were going
her separate ways I could come over. She asked me if I
would bring a condom and bring extra for her to keep. I
used a condom and left her one. Neither of us enjoyed it.

Yet according to Perry Thompson, Randy began talking about getting back with her for the sake of his kids.
Nita was glad for her grandchildren since she had questions about the way they were being raised. The control
freak Lynn wasn't her idea of a warm, loving mom.

"To me she was too hard, she was too strict with them.
I just felt she expected them to know more than they
could have at the age they were. She expected them to be
more mature than they were. She never let them be children," she says. Nor was Nita any fonder of Lynn's own
family. "We had nothing to do with them. They didn't
like Randy, who knows why? I don't know. But because
they didn't like my son, I didn't like them. I was a very
protective mom, because I was adopted when I was six
years old—my mother gave me away—and I think that
made me be more protective of my children. They didn't
like him and that hurt Randy and therefore it hurt me and
made me not like them."

The idea that they might try being a couple again
didn't make anyone else happy, least of all Casey
Tatum. A few weeks before, Randy had said something
that took his friend's breath away. He confided that he
had grave suspicions about the death of Glenn Turner.
The confession made his cop buddy think back to the
fall of 1999, when he had gotten a call from Lynn, ostensibly worried about Randy. "Have you seen him?"
she asked. "Can you check on him for me, I've been trying to call him and he's not answering," she'd asked. It
chilled him to the bone.

In the weeks that followed, Nita and Perry Thompson called several times a week to make sure their son was all right. Despite his fragile psyche, they knew that Lynn would give him no peace. "She held his children over his head; she wanted to control him," says his mother. She was also concerned about his health; he was plagued with a chronic respiratory condition, a potentially career-ending condition for a firefighter. She told him he needed to get to a doctor.

In May 2000 Randy underwent sinus surgery, but it was not as successful as he had hoped and he continued to have respiratory problems for most of the summer. In October he was diagnosed with a staph infection and attached to an IV line that fed antibiotics into his body. Within a few days he was fine, but on his doctor's advice he also had a procedure to install a catheter in his chest so he could be hooked up without having to continually re-puncture his veins if the infection kept occurring.

Despite his nagging health problems, Randy was feeling good about himself. He loved being a firefighter. He had enrolled in EMT school, reconnected with God and had begun attending church regularly. He'd also resolved to tackle the problem of his continually clogged tubes. He made an appointment for December 15 with infectious disease specialist Dr. Michael Dailey at his Roswell office.

He told Dr. Dailey that he'd had surgery twice, in 1996 and again earlier that year, but still suffered painful bouts of sinusitis. He said that he'd gotten shots at the Atlanta Allergy and Asthma Clinic and was taking Zyban to help him quit smoking, all in a bid to overcome the recurrent sinus condition. After a thorough checkup confirmed he had clear lungs and no heart irregularities, he was put on a course of vancomycin. To rule out possible damage to his immune system, Dr. Dailey ordered immunoglobulin and HIV tests. He told Randy to bring in the CAT scan he'd had taken in the summer.

At a follow-up visit the next week, Randy complained that he was still in chronic pain. Dr. Dailey inserted a PICC line through which antibiotics were fed. Just before Christmas, Randy told his mom that he was going to try to work things out with Lynn. If seeing his kids and being a proper father meant moving back in with her, then that's what he would do. He confided even more to his dad. "He loved his children and he told me because of that he wanted to make the marriage . . . work with Lynn, make a relationship work with Lynn. They had been talking and they had not been fussing or fighting because they were fussing and fighting a lot and things were beginning to work out," said Perry.

Randy told the same thing to fellow firefighter Paul Adams, who had been his friend for over ten years, and proudly showed him a brand new $700 watch Lynn had given him. At the same time, he also voiced concern that she went through money like water. "She's inherited some cash, but she is spending too much of it, and somebody in this family needs to put a rein on her spending so much," he said.

The day after Christmas he was back at Dr. Dailey's, suffering from such a severe bout of phlebitis in his left arm that the catheter had to be removed. As soon as the flare-up was under control, it was replaced. On January 1, he arrived at his parents' house with Nicholas in tow. "Perry and I both had had the flu that Christmas and been sick about a month. Randy and Nicholas were going to come Christmas and they couldn't because Perry and I were both sick and in bed," says Nita. Randy seemed to be feeling good, except for an aggravating headache.

When the pain persisted and grew more intense, he went back to see Dr. Dailey on January 5 complaining of severe headaches and persistent bloody noses, for which he was given Lortab 7.5. Although the catheter in his chest appeared to work efficiently, the sinusitis had now lasted for a worrying twenty-eight days. The doctor upped the dose of vancomycin, recommended he cut back on the Lortab and asked him to make another appointment the following week. The doctor noted that his patient still looked "chronically ill."

On January 19, Randy was back in the doctor's office. Although the diagnosis hadn't changed, Randy said he felt better. Dailey told him he wanted to monitor the situation and asked him to come back again the next week. Later that day Randy had driven to Zacks with Paul to sell a pair of stereo speakers. They had arranged to have dinner together that night, but when his buddy arrived at his apartment, Randy was full of apologies. He explained that Lynn had called and asked him to meet her at the North Point Mall in Alpharetta, to pick out a birthday present for Amber, whose birthday was the following week.

She'd suggested that afterwards they'd take the kids out for dinner. He admitted that he hoped this conciliatory move on her part signaled a change of heart, and that she would let him back into her bed. He even joked to Paul that he was banking on "getting me some" that night. But later, when he spoke to his mother, his mood had swung drastically and he sounded depressed. He told her that they had taken the kids to the LongHorn Steakhouse using the gift certificate she and his dad had given him at Christmas, and Lynn had done or said something that had obviously upset him. But he didn't tell her what it was.

At 7:45 the next morning, Paul got a 911 page from Randy. "I don't feel so good, I'm breathing funny, can you come over?" he said. When Paul got to Tolbert Road, he found the place in a shambles; his friend had been sick in the kitchen sink, in the living room and on the bathroom floor. He was also hallucinating—at one point he mistook Paul for his pet cockatoo. Feeling distinctly uneasy, Paul looked around. What the hell was happening here? The recliner and an end table in the living room were kicked over, the door to the laundry room was pulled off its hinges. "I don't know what's wrong with me," Randy said. "What do you think made you sick?" Paul asked him. "I don't know. I went to LongHorn's with Lynn and ate there," Randy had replied.

While he was surveying the mess, the phone rang. It was Dara. "I'm calling because he was supposed to give me a check for child support today," she said. Paul spoke to Randy, then told her, "He's real sick, he's vomited everywhere and can't come to the phone. But he says he left the check in your mailbox at two o'clock this morning." Next, Lynn rang. When Paul told her that Randy was too sick to take her call, she asked, "What's wrong with him? I need to talk to him." Despite Paul's pleading, Randy refused to let him call for an ambulance. About half an hour later, Lynn called back wanting to know, "Is there anything I can do?"

Just after midday, she arrived at the apartment with lunch in a Burger King bag—a cheeseburger, fries, three cheese sticks and sweet tea. She gave one tea to Paul and the other to Randy, who took one sip and threw up again. Lynn produced a Phenergan anti-nausea suppository and administered it to Randy. She stayed about an hour, but returned later that afternoon between three and four. "What the hell is wrong with you? Do you think it is food poisoning?" she asked him. She left and reappeared around six in the evening, staying for a while before saying she was going home to put the children to bed. Between her visits, she had called Randy's folks. "He's sick and vomiting, and talking out of his head," she told them.

Randy's friends Melanie and Clint Harper arrived around seven. They had been on a trip to Chattanooga, found out Randy was sick when they got home and dropped by to check on him. Melanie later told the TV show *Dateline* that when she and Clint had arrived at the apartment, Randy was lying on the couch, and when she spoke to him, he seemed unable to recognize her.

She crouched beside him, took his face in her hands and was alarmed to see that his eyes lolled from side to side. He was also hyperventilating.

Melanie, who was the daughter of Nita's best friend and had been close to Randy all of their lives, looked at Paul. They knew he needed help, but were reluctant to raise the alarm. What if this was another suicide attempt? If it was, the hospital would have no choice but to inform the fire department, and that would almost certainly mean curtains for Randy's career. She told *Dateline* what happened next.

Lynn came back. "He needs to go to the hospital. I'll call, but I can't go with him because I have no one to look after the kids. But call me and let me know what's going on," she said to them as she left. By 10:30 P.M. his condition had worsened. He was rushed to Joan Glancy Memorial Hospital in Duluth in neighboring Gwinnett County. After he was gone, his three friends cleared out his medicine cabinet and flushed his pills down the toilet. Paul went home to catch some sleep and the Harpers followed their sick friend to the emergency room.

In one of his more lucid moments, Randy was able to tell Dr. Claud Morgan that he had been vomiting all day and had not been able to eat or drink anything. He was hyperventilating, confused, dizzy and disoriented. Then he slipped back into delirium. Melanie told *Dateline*, "At one point he looked at me and said, 'Simon, get in your cage.' I told the nurse, 'Simon is his bird, he's hallucinating.' She asked me, 'Isn't he on pain medication? Well, it could be from that.' "

Dr. Morgan suspected a stomach virus and put him on an IV with fluids. He said Randy should have nothing but clear liquids for the next twelve to twenty-four hours. When he seemed to improve, Dr. Morgan wrote out a prescription, and after Paul and Melanie said they would stay the night with him, he was discharged. A follow-up appointment was scheduled for Monday, January 22, before Melanie drove him home.

He made it up the stairs to the apartment under his own steam and lay down on the couch while Melanie poured him a glass of Gatorade. He said he wanted to sleep, and she left. When she called later to check on him, he was angry that his painkillers were gone. "He said, 'My head is busting. I don't know what y'all's problem is, I don't know why y'all think I've been taking too many, but I'm not.'" His bitching was reassuring to Melanie. He'll be fine, she told herself.

Paul called at eight the following morning and was relieved when Randy told him he was feeling much better. He checked in on his friend several times throughout the day, and each time Randy seemed to be okay. When Nita phoned that morning he also reassured her he was feeling better, although his head still hurt. When Paul called back at 8:30 that evening he was troubled to hear his friend gasping for air as he said that he was feeling sick. Lynn had dropped by at lunchtime to bring him the prescription she'd had filled for him, and a grilled cheese sandwich and tea that so far, he'd managed to keep down. "Do you think I'm going to die?" he asked Paul. "Of course not," Paul replied, but he made him promise that if he got any worse, he would go back to the hospital.

At 6:45 the next morning, Paul called his mother. He had worried about Randy all night, and asked her if she would take him back to Memorial. Around seven, he rang Randy. There was no reply. He called Lynn on her cell phone and told her he was concerned because Randy wasn't answering his phone. "He's probably still sleeping, keep trying him," she said. He called again just before 9:00 A.M. and this time, when there was no reply, he rang fellow firefighter Barry Hood. He confirmed that Randy hadn't shown up for work. "I'm on my way over, I'll meet you there," Barry told him.

Forty-five minutes later Barry pulled into the Overlook Club complex. He ran up the stairs and pounded on the door, calling Randy on his cell phone while keeping a finger pressed on the doorbell. He listened for a noise, a shuffling sound that would indicate that Randy was hauling himself out of bed, but the apartment was ominously silent. He looked down and saw that Randy's truck was parked below.

Busting the lock and pushing his way in, Barry found Randy in the living room, sprawled on the couch, his head propped up against the arm, his left fist clenched under his body and his left foot on the floor. He was wearing nothing but white Jockey shorts and a thick gold chain around his neck, and Barry could see the catheter taped to the right side of Randy's chest. Barry crouched down beside him and saw that Randy was past resuscitation. Sitting back on his heels he dialed Lynn's number. He told her that they had forced their way into Randy's room and found him on the couch. They couldn't get any response from him. When she hung up, she called Paul and told him: "Barry can't wake Randy up."

Paul called it in. The police and Forsyth County Coroner Lauren McDonald III arrived shortly afterwards and pronounced Randy dead at the scene at 10:26 A.M. on Monday, January 22. With no foul play detected, it was presumed that he had died of natural causes. He was 32 years old.

CHAPTER TEN:
Smelling a Rat

On the day her son died, Nita had gone out to lunch with some of her colleagues at work. She told them that he'd been sick, but had improved to the point where he was having the stent removed that morning. "We'd been talking about him the whole time, and I said, 'I am going to call him as soon as I get home to see he's okay.' When I got back, I went to where we clocked in and I saw my sister-in-law standing by the door talking to my friend Cherylene, and I could tell by the look on her face that something had happened. I fell to my knees and asked, 'What's wrong?' 'It's Randy,' she said, and before she could tell me he was gone, I knew it. And I just went all to pieces.

"They called for an ambulance. Cherylene and my sister-in-law brought me home, and we tried to get hold of Perry, who was out on the road. He was in Fort Walton Beach in Florida. Somebody at Frito-Lay patched Angie through and she told him about Randy. He called me and said Frito-Lay told him they'd fly him home, they'd send somebody down there to get him—whatever. But he said, 'I can get there quicker myself.' So the guys down there unloaded the truck for him real fast, and he headed home. He arrived at seven thirty that night."

Forsyth County Sheriff's Officer Miles Butler had phoned Judge Dickerson's office, where Lynn now worked, and asked to speak with her. He'd told her that Randy's truck was parked outside his apartment, but they couldn't get in and he wasn't answering the door or the phone. Helen Gregory was at her job in another part of the courthouse when Lynn buzzed her. "Mom, they have called me about Randy," she began. Her daughter's voice told her immediately something was not right. Helen said she'd be right down.

When she reached the judge's office she asked, "What's happened, what's wrong?" Lynn shrugged and replied, "They said they will get back in touch with me. They can't get in, he won't answer." Moments later the phone rang again and Lynn lunged for the receiver. Helen watched as her daughter listened in silence, then hung up without uttering a single word. Lynn turned to her. "He's dead," she said. And then, according to her mother, Lynn sunk to the floor and fell apart.

Shortly afterwards, Miles Butler arrived at the office in person, asking to speak to Lynn privately. He described how they'd found Randy home alone and dead in the living room. When he'd gone, her sympathetic boss and her shocked colleagues tried to persuade her to go home. Your mother can take you, they told her. Lynn was having none of it, she was staying put, she told them, and she worked for the rest of the day, leaving at her usual time.

As soon as Melanie Harper got the news, she called Lynn. "Are you okay?" she asked. "I'm as well as I can be. I just got out of the bathroom from puking my guts out, but I'm okay," Lynn replied. Melanie later recalled feeling terrible for her. "You could tell she had been crying, so my thing is, 'Bless this poor girl's heart.' Here the father of her two children is dead, and she has nobody," she told *Dateline*.

It was a blow Helen Gregory could scarcely withstand. She had been battling breast cancer for months and was working only sporadically following sessions of debilitating chemotherapy. She was really too ill to be back at the job so soon after the energy-sapping treatment, but it was better than sitting home worrying about her illness. "I was capable of working a bit and I was afraid that if I didn't, I would give up, and didn't know what would happen to me. And so I pushed myself and made myself work," she said.

Her daughter was apparently made of the same stern stuff. She recovered enough to make a call that afternoon to the Social Security Administration to find out what benefits she was due. At nine the next morning, her coworkers were astonished to see her back at her desk. Among the calls she made was one to Bryan Bennett, who had visited them at the Cumming house, to tell him about Randy's death, which she blamed on complications of the sinus surgery.

Randy's family, who were desperately trying to come to terms with their loss, thought it was the staph infection that had killed him. It must have gotten hold of him before he got the antibiotics, they reasoned. The next day, operating in a haze from the sedative the doctor had prescribed for her nerves, Nita started to go through the dismal ritual of laying her only son to rest. It helped, but only slightly, that she was familiar with the people to whom her son's body was now entrusted. "My youngest daughter's family owns the funeral home [in town], and we went over and picked out the casket. I decided I wanted Randy in his dress fireman's outfit, and we saw to that. Then we went to the cemetery. I didn't want to put him in the ground, so we've got him in the mausoleum here. It's kind of a blur," she says.

Nita also drew strength from having her 9-year-old grandson around. He had arrived later that day with her former daughter-in-law. "As soon as Dara found out, she brought Nicholas. Then she went back home and got their clothes and came back. She stayed with Brandie and she and Brandie went out and bought me clothes to wear to the funeral," she recalls.

Randy's parents were devastated, and his three sisters were beside themselves with grief. Angie, who was pregnant at the time, was inconsolable, and Brandie wrote a heartfelt note to her dead brother telling him how much she was going to miss him, and put it in the casket. Lynn never came near them, but she made a phone call that Nita will never forget: "It was the day Randy died or the day after, but she called me and wanted to know if we had heard anything about her causing Randy's death. I told her no, we hadn't heard anything. Then she asked if we did hear any rumors, would we believe them?" Nita says she was shocked and replied, "Certainly not."

A viewing was scheduled for Wednesday the 24th at the McCullough Funeral Home on South Houston Lake Road in Warner Robins. Lynn put in an appearance, but just as she had done at Glenn's funeral, she would not go in the room where Randy was laid out. "I spoke to her at the viewing, on the Wednesday night before we had Randy's funeral and that's the last time I talked to her. She and I never really got along. There was just something, I guess it's a mother's instinct, but I just could never like Lynn, there was something there kept me from liking her. We often had words," Nita admits.

The funeral was held at eleven in the morning on Thursday, January 25. Lynn was alone, her mother too weak from the chemotherapy to be at her side. Quiet and composed, she didn't shed a tear. As his heartbroken family and friends clustered around the casket before it was closed, she hung back. Perry took pity on the young mother of his grandchildren and gently took her by the arm. "I'll take you to see him," he started to say. She pulled away, shaking her head. "No, I don't want to look at him," she said.

The following morning, Nita prepared to say good-bye to her only son. Like Glenn before him, Randy was accorded a uniformed officer's farewell, with full cere-monial pomp, at Parkway Memorial Gardens in Warner Robins. The night before, an honor guard from the Forsyth County Fire Department had kept a round-the-clock vigil by the casket. His fellow firefighters were the pallbearers, and they turned out in force in their dress blues. Just past midday three helicopters flew over the mausoleum while the committal service was underway. His family asked that donations in Randy's name should be made to the Georgia Firefighters Burn Foundation in Atlanta.

"Randy wouldn't have believed the funeral that he had," says his mother. "Barry Head, who found Randy dead when he and another guy, they had to break into his apartment, did most of the planning. They put him on his fire truck and they had two ladder trucks at the cemetery with their ladders up so that everybody walked under them. They had bagpipes playing, the helicopters flew over and one of them went off on its own. There were so many people. The funeral home is new, and it is huge. We had the service at the chapel there and it was packed. There were people standing outside in the vestibule, there were firemen lining the wall, all the way from Randy's casket to the back of the church. Randy would have been awestruck. So many people came from Forsyth County, people who took off work to be there.

"At the cemetery, the honor guard folded the flag that was on the casket and gave it to me. They gave Randy's helmet to Perry and [when it was over] Lynn stood out there at the cemetery and pitched a fit, cussing and rant-ing and raving because she wanted that helmet. We didn't

see her, but we were told later that she had carried on because she wanted it," says Nita.

As the cortege was pulling out of the graveyard,
Melanie Harper's cell phone rang. It was Lynn: "Guess
what you are going to be hearing next?" she asked. "You
are going to hear that I killed Randy and that it seems
a lot like my ex-husband's death. You wouldn't believe
that, would you?" Stunned, Melanie spluttered, "No, I
don't believe that."

But plenty of other people did. For six years, Glenn
Turner's family and friends had kept their feelings in
check. They had believed the Cobb County Police Department when they said they had looked into all the
facts surrounding the tragedy. When someone dies in
suspicious circumstances, the first person police typically look at is a family member. And when other police
officers had called up saying, 'I suspect something,' they
had assumed that his wife would be interviewed. The department had been told about the things she had been
doing—running around on him, and seeing other people,
and that Glenn had told her he was going to leave her and
move in with his dad. There had to be an investigation.

But the coroner had pronounced Glenn's death to be
from cardiac dysrhythmia and the autopsy had confirmed
that conclusion. There was nothing more to be done. His
friends and colleagues on the force knew that, despite
their suspicions, it was final.

After Glenn died, Mike had quit the police force, and
was working as a car salesman at Tom Jumper Chevrolet
when he heard the news. Everyone he worked with knew
about his friend. "I had pictures of him and a poem about
him on my wall, and I talked to other police officers about
him because Lynn used to come in with Randy. I told the
other salesmen my story with Glenn and how I always
thought she had done something to him," he says. "One
morning I came into work and one of the guys saw me

and said, 'I need to tell you something. You need to sit down.' I kept standing and he said, 'No, you really need to sit down. I got a call from someone who said they found Randy Thompson dead in bed yesterday morning.' " Mike also learned that Lynn had dropped by the dealership to borrow a "loaner" car to drive to her boyfriend's funeral.

"When he told me that, I just slammed my hand on the desk and yelled, 'I told you! I knew it!' I picked up the phone and called over to Forsyth County and got Lieutenant Goss on the line. He was actually the one working the investigation. I told him the whole story. I told him everything, and when I got off the phone I thought, 'I've got the damn ball rolling on this.' He wouldn't tell me a lot about Randy's death. I told Randy Raines, another salesman who was an ex–police chief, and he called Robert Hightower, the ex–Cobb County director of public safety who is now with the GBI. He gets off the phone and says, 'Hightower says he will open the investigation.' "

Mike dialed Donald Cawthon's number. "Guess what? Lynn Turner's new husband was found dead."

"You've got to be kidding me," gasped Donald.

"He's dead and from the same symptoms as Glenn," Mike yelled, releasing years of pent-up rage and emotion. After a brief conversation, they were agreed: if this poor guy, who they'd never met, had died anywhere around Lynn Turner, then she had to have had something to do with it. There could no longer be any doubt; it confirmed what they'd believed all along, that their pal's death was no accident. "We've got to get through to someone," Donald said. Like Mike, he'd beaten a dead horse about Glenn for months after his death, only to be told the case was closed. Surely somebody would listen to them now.

He called Glenn's sister, Linda, whose marriage to Jimmy Hardy had ended in the years since her brother's death, and who was then living in Virginia. She was out at the night class she was taking in medical terminology. By the time she got home, listened to Donald's message and got hold of her mother, it was nearly ten o'clock. Kathy phoned Mike Archer and asked him, "Mike, what in the world can I do?"

"Get hold of Bob Hightower," he told her. But according to Kathy, the GBI man was in no mood to listen. "He [had been] Glenn's boss, and he blew me off, so I called Mike back and asked, 'Who else can I go to?' He said, 'Let me do some thinking.' And he talked to some people, but they just blew him off too." Mike confirms that he made no progress that night and recalls calling one of the CCPD detectives. "I got on the phone and said, 'I bet she poisoned both of them.' He told me I was watching too much TV."

Oblivious to the Thompsons' heartbreak and unaware of Kathy Turner's determination to make someone in a uniform take her seriously, Lynn started cleaning up. A few days after she'd buried the father of her children, she got a call from Rupert Sexton at Cotton States Insurance. His daughter had told him about her tragedy, and the name had rung a bell. He wanted her to know that Randy had a policy with his company that was worth $36,830. She said she would drop by his office on Samaritan Drive and pick up the check.

Back in Cobb County, Glenn Turner's friends were buzzing with the news about Randy, and convinced that the deaths of two healthy men being struck down with a mysterious sickness while involved with Lynn was more than just an unfortunate coincidence. "What were the odds of that happening? You had a better chance of hitting the Mega Millions jackpot twice in the same lifetime," they clucked amongst themselves. Surely now the truth would come out. They didn't know what exactly she had done to Glenn and Randy, they were just absolutely sure it was something lethal.

To Donald Cawthon, the idea that the deaths were

nothing more than a quirky twist of fate was ludicrous.
He was no longer going to shut up. "When I got that call
from Archer saying, 'You are not going to believe this,
her second husband's died'—we thought she was
married—from that moment on, it was balls to the wall. I
was, 'You are going to listen to me, I am going to shove
it down your throat. I am going to keep you in the media
and on the front page. He was murdered, Randy Thompson was murdered, and this proves that Glenn was murdered,' and it was to anybody and everybody that would
listen." One person who was paying attention was *Atlanta Journal-Constitution* reporter Jane O. Hansen, and
she started asking questions.

Mike Archer also bent the ear of his former colleagues
and began poring over the documents that had lain un-
touched since a few weeks after his friend's death. "Back
when Glenn died, I was told, 'Sit back, let us handle
it, we're going to dig into this.' When Randy died, I got
a copy of the police report, and I found out they didn't
question one person. They just did the basic autopsy and
that was sloppy." The papers in front of him raised more
questions than they answered. To him, the lack of an in-
quiry couldn't have smelled worse than a decomposing
pile of mackerel.

But Glenn's friends had one ally they didn't even
know about. Mike Edwards had never known either man.
His interest in the case stemmed from being married to
the mother of one of Glenn's friends. His stepson always
maintained that Lynn Turner had had something to do
with his death and Edwards hadn't bought her story
about finding Glenn wandering around the basement in a
trance. He was supposed to have been suffering from the
flu, for God's sake, not some condition that could support Lynn Turner's contention that he was out of his
brain.

As a seasoned police chief in Riverdale and a former

assistant superintendent of the Georgia Police Academy in Forsyth, where he'd overseen the development of law enforcement training courses and programs, he seriously doubted that a police dispatcher used to dealing with the effects of an illness like the one she described, and having spent a night chasing a hallucinating husband around the basement trying to stop him from doing damage to himself, would take off and leave him unattended. He wondered about the shopping trip. In his experience, when someone offers an alibi nobody asked for, that's when you should get suspicious.

Edwards told *Dateline* he had chewed over the case for a while without coming up with anything concrete that pointed to Lynn's involvement. Then Randy Thompson had died. Any shadow of doubt that she was not involved disappeared and he contacted colleagues over in Forsyth County. He had no authority to start an investigation in another jurisdiction, but he could chip away behind the scenes. You've got to look at her, he told them. This is not just a young woman dealt an incredibly cruel hand by fate, losing the two men in her life while they were both in their early thirties, because the similarity of the circumstances made it just that—incredible!

Although Randy had been autopsied the day after he died, the medical examiner's report was not released until May. In textbook terms it stated cause of death: cardiac dysrhythmia, acute coronary insufficiency atherosclerotic, coronary heart disease. When Nita received her copy, she shook her head in disbelief. Whatever illness had taken her son, there had been nothing wrong with his heart—of that she was certain.

In the intervening weeks the *Journal* fixated on the titillating prospect of a double murder mystery. At the beginning of the summer, Mike Archer got a call from Jane Hansen who told him that the GBI and the cops in Cumming said they didn't know about Glenn's death until

June. When Mike called over to Forsyth to find out what was going on, he was told, "We didn't drop the ball on this. You didn't give us anything to go on." He was flummoxed. "I am the guy who sells cars, I told you everything I knew," he said.

Although publicly they played their cards so very close to the chest that Glenn's frustrated friends and family began to despair of ever being heard, the wheels of justice were turning in Forsyth County.

The detectives started taking affidavits from everyone they could track down whose paths has crossed those of Lynn Turner. On June 25, the Forsyth County coroner told Lt. Goss that after Randy died, Lynn had called asking for a copy of the autopsy report, and he had sent it to her. Since Randy's death, Lynn had carried on pretty much as normal. Paul Adams told Goss and David King that two weeks after his funeral, she had invited a bunch of people over for a cookout.

Lynn also turned up for work at Judge Dickerson's office every day. At the end of June, the Cumming district attorney, Phil Smith, advised the judge that an investigation into the death of Randy Thompson was ongoing and that he was looking closely at Lynn. On June 26, she was suspended with pay. As she cleared her desk she shrugged unconcernedly and told her flabbergasted colleagues, "Whatever it is, I didn't do it."

On July 6, now promoted to captain, Frank Goss sat down with Nita and Perry Thompson at their home. They told him about their son's long battle with sinus problems and how he had been so much better in late December when he'd stayed with them. He had called after ten o'clock on January 19, after having had dinner with Lynn, and he had been upset over something she'd done. Whatever it was, he'd kept it to himself. Nita told about Paul Adams's call the next day. He'd said that Randy was very sick and he couldn't get him to go to the hospital.

Nita told Captain Goss about Lynn bringing food to Randy. After he died, she didn't come and see him until the day of the viewing, and even then, she wouldn't look at him. A few days later, she'd called to complain about someone from the funeral home asking for settlement of the bill. Nita said she'd ranted, "Who does he think he is?" Perry added that they'd been told that Lynn had gone to see Judge Joyce Hawkins in an unsuccessful attempt to get into Randy's apartment before his parents were given access.

Angie Bollinger made a last visit to Tolbert Street. Accompanied by Frank Goss and Barry Head, she retrieved envelopes containing bills, several insurance policies and the lease on her brother's 2000 Chevy truck. She also picked up some photographs of his children and his favorite picture, taken at the 1996 Olympic Games in Atlanta. After she left, the apartment was secured.

While Glenn's buddies and Mike Edwards prodded away at the authorities in Marietta, and the Forsyth police quietly continued their inquiries, it wasn't anyone with a badge who truly kicked the investigation into high gear—it was Glenn's angry mom. When Randy Thompson's death still didn't spur the Cobb County authorities to take another look at the events surrounding Glenn's death, she resolved that whatever she had to do, she would not rest until she'd found out what really happened to her son. Since the night Linda had called her to tell her about Randy, she had tossed and turned, trying to fathom how she could make people listen.

Who would care the most? she asked herself. Six years after she'd buried her son, there wasn't a day gone by that she didn't shed a tear for him. Why would Randy Thompson's mother feel any different? Since the police didn't want to know, she had to reach out to that poor boy's family herself. She could at least let them know that another man had died in copycat circumstances. But how could she contact them? A friend offered to go online to dig up some information. She called back with Randy's obituary notice from the Cumming paper.

Kathy wrote down the names of the family members listed in the piece, then looked them up in the telephone book. There were lots of Thompsons in the Cumming area, but only one Bollinger. It had said in the paper that amongst his survivors, there was a sister, Angela Bollinger. She dialed the number: "Hi, my name is Kathy Turner, my son was married to Lynn Turner. I was so sorry to read about your brother," she began. She went on to tell her how Glenn had died in mysterious circumstances and how his family all shared this feeling that his wife knew more about his death than she would admit.

Angie listened silently until Kathy came to the end of her story. When she did reply she told Kathy that the deaths were just a coincidence, a horrible one, granted, but she didn't really see where the two were connected. Her family had been given what seemed a perfectly logical explanation for Randy's death. He had died of natural causes due to an enlarged heart. Discouraged, Kathy apologized for calling and hung up.

Later Angie phoned her father and Nita, and recounted the strange conversation she'd had with Glenn's mother. Although she was convinced that Kathy's belief that Lynn was implicated was no more than a wild accusation from a woman clearly still bereft from the passing of her son and looking for a scapegoat, a seed of doubt had been sown in Nita's mind.

Despite Angie's lukewarm response, Kathy would not give up. She looked at the obituary notice again, checked the name of the funeral home and got the number from the phone book. She told the person at the other end of the line who she was and explained that she wanted to write a letter of condolence to Randy's mother. "If I send it care of you, would you make sure she gets it?" she asked. "Sure, we'll do that," the voice said. Kathy wrote how sorry she was for Randy's loss and said she would love to get together to compare notes. They had their sons in common and she could tell Nita more about the woman who was the mother of her grandchildren. She enclosed her phone number. For nearly four months, she heard nothing.

Then one evening, the phone rang. It was Nita Thompson on the line. "She had mailed it to the funeral home and they figured it was just a condolence card. Then one day at church, Michael, who is Brandie's brother-in-law and runs the funeral home, said to me, 'You've got some stuff at the funeral home. Come by and get it.' I went that Monday and the card from Kathy was there. I immediately called her." When Kathy picked up, Nita explained, "My daughter didn't take down your phone number when you spoke to her, so we couldn't get in touch with you."

Unlike the Turners, the Thompsons had never seriously questioned the medical examiner's ruling in Randy's death. Though Nita didn't really understand why her boy had died, he'd had this awful staph infection that had gone untreated for a while before he'd been put on antibiotics.

Kathy described how she had gone to the Cobb County medical examiner to beg him to take a second look at Glenn's death, how she thought there had been foul play and how she and her family had been swept aside. Nobody had wanted to listen to them; everyone decided that they were crazed with grief or just plain crazy. It was a tragedy and eventually, they would come to terms with it, they had been told. But the Turners couldn't and wouldn't let it rest, she said. How could they get over Glenn's death, when the woman they believed had caused it was walking around free as a bird? Now another man had died, and Lynn had probably already set her sights on some other guy. Who would be next?

They agreed that both families should sit down together and compare what they knew. A couple of days
later, they sat in Kathy's living room swapping stories
about their sons, compared what they did for a living and
were amazed at the similarities between them. They
shared tales of Lynn, who had come into their boys' lives
like a whirlwind, seducing them with her money and her
controlling personality, and how the relationships had
foundered just as quickly. Nita also found out that pretty
much everything Lynn Turner had told her about her deceased husband was a pack of lies.

As they talked late into the night, Nita's mind was in
overdrive: she instinctively knew Kathy Turner was right.
She was saying the same exact things she and Perry had
agonized over: Glenn was ill, okay, that she knew, but he
had been a big healthy guy who should have been able to
shake a bout of flu and recover. Hadn't they said the same
about Randy? And wasn't it weird that Kathy was as
shocked as she was to learn that their sons had previously
undetected heart conditions that had supposedly killed
them? Medical exams were routine in their line of work,
where fitness was so important, and neither man had ever
been diagnosed with a damaged heart.

Nita remembers staring blankly at the death certificate
signed by Forsyth County Coroner Lauren McDonald
III. She hadn't wanted to believe what she read: cardiac
dysrhythmia. She had thought that had to be a mistake—
the infection was one thing, but there had been nothing
wrong with Randy's heart.

"I knew there was something else. For goodness' sake,
he was a fireman, he had to be in good health, you have
to be in good shape to do that," she says. "I knew that
Randy saw Dr. Shannon Mize, the same doctor that we
had used all these years, and we even went by to see him
and he told me, 'There's nothing wrong with Randy's

heart.' I said, 'I know that, I just wanted you to verify that
there wasn't anything wrong with Randy's heart.' " Before they left Kathy's house, they had resolved to work
together to do everything they could to put their sons'
killer behind bars.

Nita was as good as her word. She called the GBI
Crime Lab and told them she wanted Randy tested, and
made an appointment for her and Perry to meet with
someone. A few days later, they were ushered into Mark
Koponen's office at the State of Georgia Medical Examiner's Division of Forensic Sciences in Atlanta. They told
their story: their son had died unexpectedly, and now
they'd learned that a young police officer had died six
years before in almost identical circumstances. Both men
had been involved with the same woman. They told him
about the call from Kathy and their growing belief that
she was right.

While they talked, Dr. Koponen sat in silence. When
they finished, he picked up some papers and waved them
in front of them. "This is so ironic. I just got Glenn
Turner's death certificate today and this is another young
man that shouldn't be dead," he said bluntly. Then he
added that, because he was now having grave reservations
about the examination done on Glenn Turner, he was ordering an investigation into the death of Randy. The
Thompsons, who had feared they too would be dismissed
as crackpots, were floored. A feeling of relief swept over
them and they didn't know whether to laugh or cry.

What Dr. Koponen didn't tell them then was that when
he had performed the autopsy on Randy on the afternoon
of January 22, he had detected calcium oxalate crystals
on the kidneys, and had found that puzzling. He had ordered toxicology tests on the blood, and told the lab to
look for any trace of ethylene glycol. The lab had come
back saying that while there were traces of ethylene glycol present in the blood, it was such a negligible amount

that it couldn't have killed him. Only then had he attributed the death to natural causes.

Still, he hadn't issued his autopsy results right away, he had sat on them until May 2, when, with no other evidence having come forward, he had signed off on them. After the Thompsons left his office, he called Brian Frist, the medical examiner for Cobb County. He asked to see the autopsy report on Glenn Turner and to have any tissue samples taken in 1995 sent over to his office.

When they arrived, he found that they also contained calcium oxalate crystals, but no toxicology test had been done for ethylene glycol. He sent the samples to the state laboratories at the Georgia Bureau of Investigation. A few days later they came back positive. He then ordered retesting of Randy's blood and urine. The results were too similar to be a coincidence. By May 24, 2001, Dr. Koponen was sure that he was looking at two homicides. Both Glenn and Randy had died after ingesting ethylene glycol, a poisonous substance commonly known as antifreeze.

CHAPTER ELEVEN:
Follow the Money

While the medical examiner was coming to the same conclusion that Glenn Turner's friends had held from the minute Randy Thompson drew his last breath, the campaign for justice being waged by Donald Cawthon, Mike Archer and Mike Edwards now picked up some serious steam, thanks to the persistence of the two grieving mothers.

On March 24, Dr. Koponen called the Cumming Police Department and said he had received information that the ex-husband of Lynn Turner had died in conditions disturbingly similar to those of Randy Thompson and had suffered from the same vomiting and sickness in the days before his death. Koponen said he was going to test a tissue sample from the autopsy of Glenn Turner, and what he expected to find were the same kind of crystals he had found in Randy Thompson, the kind of crystals found in antifreeze, the stuff put into automobiles every winter. When he called back some days later with the results, Cobb County officials had no choice but to order an investigation into what was almost certainly Glenn Turner's murder.

The Cumming Police Department called the Georgia Bureau of Investigation. Since two counties were involved,

on June 20, Special Agent David King, a twenty-year veteran of the GBI, took over as lead investigator on the hunt
for Randy Thompson's killer or killers. The two families
had made it clear they thought the common denominator
was Lynn. She'd been the wife of one man and the lover
of the other. She had been living with Glenn when he became sick, and made frequent visits to Randy while he
was ill, ostensibly looking after both men in the hours before they died.

She had the opportunity—that at least was clear. But
if she was the killer, why had she done it? What was the
motive? Both the Turners and the Thompsons had told
the same tale: Lynn had targeted their sons. To reel them
in, she'd conducted campaigns of calculated and ruthless
seduction. She'd bought nice homes, fancy cars, luxury
cruises; you didn't do all that on a 911 operator's pay.
Since everyone involved worked for the county, it didn't
take an Einstein to figure out that no one here was earning major bucks. King wondered how she bankrolled her
extravagant lifestyle.

He knew that the Thompsons had sat down with the
Turners to swap notes. They had talked about the control
Lynn exerted over their sons emotionally and financially,
her preoccupation with money and the sickeningly similar illnesses and deaths of Randy and Glenn.

Armed with a sheaf of warrants the investigators began to look at the bank accounts of all three. But before
they did, they talked again to the families. What had also
come out during their difficult and heart-wrenching con-
fab was that both men were heavily insured—Lynn had
seen to that. Fueled by that information, the cops began
to follow the money. They discovered that, in both cases,
Lynn had insisted that she hold the purse strings from the
start. While they were engaged, Glenn had named his fiancée as beneficiary to his PEBSCO account in place of
his mother. The papers were signed at their home on May

23, 1993, with Lynn's houseguest as the only witness. Four months later, just after they returned from their honeymoon, he also made her the sole beneficiary to his police retirement pension. In September he put her name on a $100,000 policy with Metropolitan Life.

Having rented digs for herself and Randy four days after Glenn's death, she immediately began pressing her lover about insurance. He had taken out rental insurance with State Farm years before and added a $15,000 life insurance when his son with Dara was born. In December 1995, a month before Lynn gave birth to Amber, he tried to put her on the $100,000 State Farm Insurance he had bought two years before when he had listed his mother and his ex-wife as beneficiaries. In 1997 he made her trustee of their daughter and a year later Lynn replaced Nita and Dara as recipient of the policy.

In September that same year, four months after their son Blake arrived, Randy doubled the amount of his coverage to $200,000. Two months later, he took out a $36,000 policy with Cotton States stipulating that if anything happened to him, Lynn was to get every cent. On September 10, David King and Frank Goss talked to Lori Conrad at the Forsyth County Human Resources Department. She told them that through his job, Randy had a $25,000 insurance policy that would go to his mom in the event of his death. He also had a 401K containing between $2,000 and $3,000. Nicholas and Amber were the beneficiaries of this.

Next the investigators checked to see what had happened to those policies. They discovered that when Glenn died, Lynn had won the jackpot. The day after she buried him, she'd called Met Life's 800 number to check on the amount she was due, and submitted a claim on April 11. They looked into his police pension and discovered that Glenn, who had worked two, sometimes three jobs to defray their mounting debts, had racked up 78.7 hours of

vacation pay amounting to $1,000, which she collected
two months after he died. She got $47,587.50 in cold cash
from his employee benefits plan along with monthly pension checks of $788. They would be adjusted to reflect in-
flation and would keep coming for the rest of her life. But
she'd really hit pay dirt when Metropolitan Life ponied
up: on May 10, 1999, she opened her mailbox to find a
check for $2,100 and exactly two months later she walked
into Wachovia bank holding another one for $99,000. As
far as the investigators were concerned, in Glenn's case, a
motive had been established.

They found she hadn't been so lucky the second time
around. Within a week of Randy's death, Lynn had called
State Farm. She told the agent that her common-law husband had died. She asked how much was in the account
and what she should do about having it paid to her. On
May 3, 2001, quoting Randy's policy number, she wrote
on her personalized notepaper to the State Farm office in
Winter Haven, Florida:

To Whom it May Concern,

Mr. Thompson passed away on January 22, 2001. I
am the beneficiary of the above listed policy. Please for
ward me all documentation regarding the processing of
this policy. Also, enclosed is a copy of the death certificate of Randy Thompson for your file.

Thank you for your assistance in the matter, please
feel free to contact me at the above address and phone
number or contact me at work.

Sincerely,
Julia Lynn Turner.

On May 8, she received a reply.

Dear Ms. Turner,

Please accept our sincere sympathy for your loss.

Unfortunately, our records indicate this policy terminated when the premium due April 11, 2000 was not paid by the end of the grace period.

From the information received, it appears Randy Thompson's death occurred on January 22, 2001. Since the policy was not in force on the date of death, we are unable to provide any benefits under your claim.

Please write or call us if you have additional questions regarding this matter. I am returning your copy of the death certificate for your records.

Christie Vosika,
State Farm Life Claims.

From all accounts, Lynn had been incandescent with rage. This was not something she had bargained for. It had never occurred to her that Randy had let his payments lapse nine months before he died. But there was little use fighting it. With nearly a year's worth of missed payments, State Farm was not going to give her a payday of any kind.

A month after Randy died, Lynn had called Lori Conrad asking for the phone number of the Cotton States Insurance company. A few weeks later, Lori told the investigators that Nita Thompson had called her to ask if her son had county insurance. The funeral home in Warner Robins had also called inquiring about a beneficiary.

The investigators pulled Lynn's credit history and bank accounts. They found that the lapsed State Farm policy had sunk her deep into a financial hole. She had unpaid bills up to her armpits and must have been counting on that $200,000 windfall to save her neck. If not satisfied, her pressing debts would bring her world crashing down around her; she would lose her house and be in hock to the bank for years. If they were looking for motive, it was staring them in the face. If she knew that all she needed to wipe her credit slate clean was one whopping check, then in her warped mind, wouldn't that be good enough reason to kill the father of her kids?

On July 17, 2001, Captain Goss went looking for Dara Taylor, now Dara Laughlin. She told him that although she and Randy had divorced after only a year, they'd sorted out their issues for the sake of their son. She said the court had ordered Randy to pay $299 a month in child support, and that when he'd died, he was a year behind in his payments. They had spoken during the week prior to his death to discuss when he'd pick up Nicholas, and she'd last spoken to him on Saturday, January 20, about 11:30 A.M., when he'd called her to tell her he had put some cash in her mailbox. She'd thought he'd sounded drunk, but when she asked if he'd been hitting the bottle, he'd told her that he was sick.

Dara also told Captain Goss that after she'd returned from the viewing at the funeral home, Lynn had called her and suggested they meet at O'Charley's, a restaurant bar in Alpharetta, to talk about Randy. When Dara got there, Lynn told her that she and Randy had gone shopping at the North Point Mall on the Friday before his death, then eaten dinner at LongHorn Steakhouse before going their separate ways around 9:30 P.M. The next day she had taken him chicken soup and Gatorade. She then said they should decide how to split up Randy's belongings, and they did. But later she called back and said she'd changed her mind about some of his things. A few days after they'd met, Lynn phoned again, demanding to know what items Dara had removed from his apartment.

That there was no love lost between the two women was obvious. "She was often ugly to my son," Dara told

Goss, adding that Randy had confided that Lynn saw her as a threat. "She would accuse Randy of having an affair with me and said that she didn't trust him."

A week after Randy's funeral, Lynn had called wanting to know if she had any insurance policies. Dara said Lynn had been very upset because she had discovered that a policy on which she had been the beneficiary had lapsed. "Why would he let that happen?" she'd asked.

On July 12, Lynn was fired. When she appeared at the office the next day to collect the rest of her belongings, she heard what her boss already knew, that the GBI were now involved. While Lynn was busy packing up, Daisy Weeks was talking to Frank Goss and David King over at the 911 headquarters. She told them that on Monday, January 22, Lynn had mentioned that Randy had been sick over the weekend, and she'd dropped by his place to deliver Coca-Cola and soup.

Daisy was questioned about the trip that she and Lynn had taken in May after they'd asked for and been granted permission to tour the Georgia State Crime Lab. She told the investigators that Lynn had said that when she'd worked for the Cobb County Police Department, her job required her to visit the morgue. Daisy had called a friend who worked at the Georgia State Crime Lab and arranged the visit.

She recalled that while they were signing in at the front desk, Lynn had remarked that the autopsy on Randy was taking much longer than usual. Daisy told the cops that Lynn had called her just about every day after that trying to find out the reason for the delay. She complained that his parents were stirring up trouble for her with their questions and were accusing her of having something to do with his death. "I don't know why they are saying that. The autopsy was done and how are they going to disprove its findings?" she had grumbled. As relations between her

and the Thompsons deteriorated even further, she'd told
Daisy, "Now they are saying I killed him."

On the afternoon of August 1, Frank Goss got a call
from Paul Adams, who had talked earlier to David King
of the GBI, but said he had just remembered something.
Just before the memorial service, he had gone to Lynn's
house to pick out some photographs of Randy to display
beside the casket. While he was there, Lynn had shown
him a sheaf of papers she said she had downloaded from
Randy's computer, and made an outrageous claim: "He's
been having phone sex with this woman up north." A
couple of days later she'd shown up at a fire department
debriefing where she'd babbled on about Randy and his
gal pal. Adams said he'd been furious with her, horrified
that she was trashing the name and reputation of his
friend and a woman she didn't even know. He had said
nothing at the time because one of the other guys told
him he had once called Randy's apartment and heard a
woman talking in the background.

Captain Goss tracked down Randy's alleged phone
friend. Elizabeth Hayes told him that she had spoken
with Randy on the phone three times. They had arranged
to get together in Atlanta during a stopover on a trip she
was making to Florida, but the meeting had never taken
place because, at the last minute, Randy couldn't make it.

What was more interesting to Goss was that Lynn had
sent Elizabeth an e-mail exactly one month after Randy
died. In it, she had written that she was upset with his
parents, especially his mother, who Lynn claimed was
trying to make her sign over insurance benefits to her.
Lynn wrote that she had been at work when Randy's
body was discovered and was actually on the phone with
the fire department as they broke down the door to his
apartment. It didn't look like he'd suffered, he had a
staph infection and a heart condition, but she was waiting

for the autopsy report to learn the exact cause of his death.

Elizabeth forwarded the e-mails to Goss who quickly realized that if Lynn had killed Randy, then they offered a fascinating insight into her duplicitous psyche. In the first, she had written:

> *I know you do not know me but I know that you know who I am. I am Randy Thompson's ex-fiancé [sic]. I am not even sure if the two of you were still having contact. But I know that you two cared about each other, I wanted to let you know that Randy passed away on January 22, 2001. You may already know this. I hope you are not offended for the e-mail— I was going through some old documents/e-mails and saw your name. . . . if you didn't know that, someone should let you know.*

Elizabeth dialed the number Lynn had put on her message. She sent tapes of the ensuing conversation to Captain Goss.

"Lynn? I was informed. I'm sorry, but thank you for taking the initiative to tell me," she'd said.

"I was not sure if you knew or not, and I knew that some people meant a lot to him, so I felt you should know," Lynn said.

"Did they find the cause?"

"The autopsy has not come back yet," said Lynn. "I think it's going to be related to the staph infection. My kids are doing okay. Blake is too young to understand and Amber cried some, but she knew that he had been sick. She even told me that 'Now Daddy won't hurt anymore,' " said Lynn.

"Amber is a beautiful little girl," Elizabeth said. "Randy sent me a picture of her. I have to tell you, I lost a husband when my kids were two and four, so I know what you are going through."

"Nicholas is the one that really is having a hard time," said Lynn. "I don't mean to sound nosy, but had you talked to Randy recently?"

"The odd thing is that I e-mailed him that week, I was going to Atlanta," said Elizabeth. "The last time we actually spoke on the phone was back in October when I was in Atlanta going to Hawaii with my son. We haven't talked anymore. He was never online. I don't know what you know about our friendship, but if there is anything you want to know, ask. . . ."

"The reason I asked is the last three or four weeks he had really changed, he was a totally different person," Lynn told her.

"How are you doing?" Elizabeth asked. "Back when we talked more often, it seemed like he wanted to get back with you."

"He had started trying to spend more time with the kids. He actually seemed happier. Not the grizzly bear he could be at times. He and I were even getting along, he had started going to church and even stopped lying to me . . . a *big* change. I mean, I'm not hateful or bitter, but I know your friendship meant a lot to him," said Lynn. "He and I would go for periods of time without talking and then out of the blue would start talking again."

Elizabeth told her how she had encouraged him to take his EMT exam and had sent him tests to use as study guides.

"I received his test grades a couple of days after he died, he actually passed this time," said Lynn.

She told Elizabeth how he would call her at two in the morning to cuss her out or leave a string of abuse on her answering machine when she didn't pick up the receiver.

Elizabeth admitted she had experienced the dark side of Randy too.

"He really seemed to change," claimed Lynn. "I had a really hard time at the funeral. His family treated me like crap. The two fire department chaplains did not even mention my kids in the ceremony. But when his chaplain spoke, he told me that only a couple of weeks ago, Randy had told him that he wanted to be a father to Amber and Blake, and he wanted to work things out with me. That broke my heart and I'm still having a hard time with it. I had no idea and he had really changed his attitude."

They talked about the children, how Blake looked like Lynn, and Amber took after her dad. "But at the memorial service here in Cumming, they did a video from baby pictures and you could really see Blake in him," said Lynn.

"I don't know what to say, I really feel for all of you," Elizabeth commiserated.

"It is kind of weird—talking with some of the people that he really cared about has helped me. It's kind of funny. . . . I can remember when he told me you were coming down to stay at the apartment for a couple of days. I was so jealous—but even when I was mad or jealous, if that is what made him happy, I was okay with it," Lynn assured her.

"I was no threat to you," said Elizabeth. "I cared, but not that way."

"It wasn't a threat to me. I was jealous of things that were actually good for him. You were very good for him, I think you really made him feel good about himself. . . . Very few people did that for him," said Lynn.

"I wanted to do that. I didn't like him being so hard on himself," said Elizabeth.

"At least there at last he was not. He even took the kids out to dinner the week before he died. Even when we were fighting and I hated him, I loved him," said Lynn.

"I am really surprised you knew, and had my name," said Elizabeth. "I believe he loved you."

"When he still lived here and you two talked, he tried to

make me jealous. Even after he moved into the apartment, he would on occasion try to make me jealous," said Lynn.

The two women agreed to keep in touch and exchanged numbers and personal notes.

"Almost all my friends are EMS/fire or cops," said Elizabeth.

"Well, I work indirectly in public safety. I worked for the Cobb County police for five years and the sheriff's office here for three, the district attorney's office and now the judge's office," Lynn told her before hanging up.

The same day, Captain Goss talked to Teresa Green. She told him that Lynn had "recruited" her to be her friend; a month after being hired by the sheriff's department, Lynn and Ron Casper had picked her out for a position in the warrant division. She said she had known Lynn for over five years, yet it was a while before she mentioned Glenn. Lynn had told her they'd only been married six months when he died of a heart attack. When Teresa started to say, "I had no idea, I'm so sorry," Lynn had brushed her sympathy aside with, "Nah, no big loss," then said it had been a disaster since day one, since before day one; they were totally unsuited and she had known that as soon as they walked down the aisle. She'd wanted to cut the honeymoon short. They should never have gotten married.

When Glenn had died, his family didn't want her to get the insurance money. Teresa told Captain Goss that Lynn always seemed to be flush with cash, and about the large bank deposits she'd seen Lynn make. She said Lynn claimed to have inherited a trust fund when her grandmother died.

Teresa said she had met Randy through Lynn in 1997. "Was Randy sickly, did he ever have problems with his digestion?" Goss asked her. She shook her head. No, the only time she ever remembered him being sick was back in 1998 when she and Lynn had taken him to lunch at the fire station on Settingdown Road. Randy had complained of a stomachache.

Teresa also told Goss that Ron Casper would visit Lynn at her home, and he had worried that scuttlebutt about his visits would filter back to the department. One day she was at Lynn's, and noticed that while Lynn handed her a soft drink, she'd given Casper an iced tea. While he was in the process of divorcing his wife, Lynn had helped him look for somewhere to live.

They stayed close after he met someone else, Teresa said. In January 1998, she and Lynn had driven down to Florida, where Casper was getting remarried. Lynn picked up an auto from a car rental place on Highway 9 in Alpharetta, and no sooner had they gotten there than Lynn started making noises about leaving. She was in such a hurry that after the wedding was over, she refused to wait until they could change out of their outfits before taking off, and they'd ended up pulling on jeans in the car as it was barreling along the highway. At one point, stuck in a traffic jam, Lynn got on the phone to the Georgia State Patrol Headquarters to ask what was going on, telling the operator that she had to get home in a hurry to pick up her child. Teresa remembered that Amber wasn't supposed to be collected until the following day.

She told him that she had been struck by Lynn's obsession with pharmaceuticals: the woman was a walking encyclopedia about prescription drugs and what illnesses they were used for. When Teresa was over at Lynn's house she had noticed that there were always Phenergan suppositories in her refrigerator. "Lynn also knew all about poisons that killed insects around the house," she said, adding that it had been Lynn and not Randy who always bought them.

She said she had last talked to Randy after Lynn stopped

working for the sheriff's department. Lynn had called her three weeks after Randy died, complaining about his parents. Teresa recalled her being angry that they refused to let her have some of his personal belongings that she'd earmarked for the children.

Two days later Goss and GBI Agent Tim Attaway called again on Perry and Nita Thompson. Goss had gotten a call from Perry saying he had taken his son's mattress from the apartment and that there were vomit stains on it—Randy had been violently sick the night before he died. When they arrived at the house he took them to a shed in the yard where he had stowed the bedding. After processing and photographing the mattress, they removed a section of it and put it into a brown paper evidence bag. It was sent to the Georgia State Crime Lab for analysis, along with a clear plastic tea container and a stained blue cotton blanket that Perry had also retrieved from the room where Randy had died. On the evidence sheet required with each submission, on the line that read, "suspected drugs," Goss circled "poisons" and wrote in "ethylene glycol." He also noted that the items were "recovered from the scene."

Nita and Perry told Goss that whenever they'd been around Lynn, she seemed obsessed with money; she always talked about it and about people who had money. They told him that Lynn had received an insurance payout after Glenn died, but she claimed to have turned it over to his family.

At the end of the month, Goss took a call from Chris Childers. He told them that in 1995 he'd worked at the Forsyth County Sheriff's Department, where he'd met Lynn, who was then working for the district attorney, and she'd hit on him pretty blatantly. She had told him that she and her husband were getting a divorce and she had no relationship with him. After she moved in with Randy

Thompson and became pregnant, he remembered her hiding her pregnancy from everyone, including her boss.

The investigators also pored over a 2001 day planner that Randy had kept, looking for some sense of his life and his state of mind in the days before his death. In his own words it showed a man determined to regain his health and lose weight. He had been intent on putting his life in order:

> *January 1: Wgt. 132 lbs—lose to 210. Get well—have in Hick. cath. [Hickman catheter]. Get in church—Get straight. make $60,000—get married. Get Bills straight+Payed off.*
> *Saw Amber & Blake Nick at Mom's.*
> *January 2: Pick up Nick from Brandie. Saw Kids. Neck hurts bad.*
> *January 3: Worked.*
> *January 5: Pay check 1243.00. Saw Drs. Dailey & Vanta. 1 more week of Vancomycin.*
> *January 6: Worked 3 calls. Washed and Waxed my truck.*
> *January 7: Went to Freedom Tabernacle Church—went to Altar—turned life over to Jesus. Went to see kids. Had lunch at Mary Ann's. Amy gave me new NIV Bible.*
> *January 9: Work—late, wrote up*
> *January 10: <u>Church</u>*
> *January 11: Dr. Dailey 3:00. Call Vanta on culture*
> *January 16: Hair Cut 12:30 Comm meeting 4:00*
> *January 17: Church 7:00*
> *January 19: 2:00. Dr Dailey 3:00*
> *January 20: Work for David at st 12. night shift*
> *January 26: Dr. Dailey 2:00*
> *January 27: Amber B/Day party 12:00 Chucky Cheese*
> *January 30: Amber B/Day*

As they read the diary, it was clear to the cops that Randy had died on the cusp of a new life. His intentions were there in black and white: he and Lynn would hammer out their differences and work at putting their relationship back together. After two years of living apart except for the nights they rolled together in the dark, he no longer wanted to wake up each morning in a different house from his children. Lynn and he needed to make their relationship legal and their children legitimate. They would get married, he would work two jobs—more if necessary—to help pay off their debts, he would get well and he would do it all with the help of God. His faith was central: the Church was turning his life around; he would bring Lynn and the kids into its nurturing fold and everything would work out fine.

The more the investigators turned the pages, the more they were convinced that Lynn Turner had a very different idea about the future. Her long-term plans didn't include Randy any more than they had included Glenn. She too wanted out of debt—and she had plenty of it. The Thompsons told investigators that as far back as November 2000 Lynn was two payments behind with her mortgage and was afraid the bank would repossess her home, leaving her and the kids homeless. She had complained to him about forking out for doctors' visits for the children out of her own pocket. But they suspected that she wasn't thinking of scaling down her lifestyle to make ends meet—she had a quicker solution to her financial crunch in mind. Randy's life insurance was going to take care of her money mess and more.

Shortly after Randy died, Lynn had called Perry and fumed about the funeral home. They were leaning on her to pick up the bill, she'd griped. She had told Judge Dickerson and her coworkers that she was going to sue the hospital. The people there had diagnosed and treated Randy. It was their fault that he had been released—they should have seen that he was desperately ill and they were going to pay.

While the investigation was gathering steam, Donald Cawthon made a discovery that blew the case wide open. At the time, he ran a business called Money Talks Cellular on Roswell Road, where one of his customers was Leon Hendrix, owner of the Chevron station in Sandy Springs where Glenn had worked, and kin to Lynn. His employees kept losing or breaking mobile phones and he'd bring them to have them repaired and replaced. Hendrix seemed unaware of the link between him and Glenn, and Donald couldn't help wondering what he thought about the secretive Lynn. It was all he could do to bite back the questions that were at the tip of his tongue. "My gut would just go off every time he came in, and it was all I could do to put on a straight face," he says.

With access to phones that Lynn, and possibly Glenn, might have used while working for Hendrix, Donald figured the one thing he could do to help the investigation along was to pass on the numbers to David King. "In a couple of days Hendrix came back, and we're talking and he says, 'I don't know what's going on, the damned GBI is calling my cell phone. How the hell did they get my cell phone number and are calling my girls?' And I'm just sitting there thinking, 'I gave it to them.' Finally, I said, 'You don't know who I am, do you?' And he said, 'Well, no, who are you?' I said, 'I'm Donald Cawthon, Glenn Turner's best friend.'"

According to Donald, what happened next blew a hole the size of Texas through Lynn's account of what she had been doing on the day her husband took his last agonizing breaths. She had never been a suspect in Glenn's death all these years before, but with both his and Randy's deaths now reclassified as homicides, Hendrix was visibly troubled by something that hadn't seemed relevant, until now. "He grabbed the counter and started to cry. Then he said, 'Can you get in touch with that GBI agent?' I got on the phone, and next morning, King went to his house. Later that day he called me and said, 'She sat in my gas station for four hours that morning. I knew something was wrong. She told me Glenn was sick and had been in the hospital, and she sat there just as weird-acting as she could be. Finally, that afternoon about two, she pulled out. If anyone killed him, she did. That's the nail in her coffin, Cawthon.' "

CHAPTER TWELVE:
The Arrest

While the police continued their probe, forensic specialist Mark Koponen was compiling a list of questions for Brian Frist, the medical examiner who had autopsied Glenn. On his mind were the following:

* Was there anything unusual about his autopsy other than the crystals in his kidneys? What type of medications would cause the same crystals to form?
* Other than antifreeze, what would cause these crystals to form in the kidneys?
* Could antifreeze be injected into the intravenous catheter in the victim's chest?
* How much antifreeze would have to be consumed to cause death and over how long a period?
* Other than flulike symptoms, what other symptoms would appear?
* On the poison determination report, it was stated that the blood specimen was negative for a significant quantity of ethylene glycol. Is it your opinion that there were enough crystals to cause death?

When Frist saw the report on Randy's death and learned that Lynn had lived with both men, then heard Koponen's questions, he knew at once what had to be done: he ordered that Glenn's body be reexamined. For the Turners, the news was both exhilarating and devastating. On the one hand, they were elated that after six long years, their protestations that his death was no simple medical tragedy had at last been heeded. But to retest his organs, his body would have to be exhumed; the sanctity of his grave, his final resting place, would be violated. They knew an exhumation was not a pretty sight. "It was very heart-hurting, very overwhelming," says Kathy. "But I wanted it done. It was horrible to think about what they were doing, but I wanted to know what really happened to Glenn. I was like, 'Do it, and get it done and over with.'"

Kathy had been told about the exhumation, not through official channels, but in a phone call from Jane Hansen, the *Atlanta Journal-Constitution* reporter who was rattling cages trying to shake the story loose. Kathy made plans to leave town. Although she wanted to be there when they lifted her boy from the ground, she knew that the cemetery would be swarming with media, and the thought of having a microphone stuck in her face at such a harrowing moment was more than she could bear.

Word of the medical examiner's order, coupled with news that the GBI had ordered new tests on tissues from Randy Thompson, spread like wildfire around the two communities. Cobb County District Attorney Patrick Head let it be publicly known that the forensic team would be looking for evidence of antifreeze. "The investigation has been reopened to try and identify whether it's murder or not," he said. CCPD Homicide Detective Scott Broehl affirmed that there were "striking similarities between the two men's deaths and their cases."

Lynn was saying nothing when reporters flocked to her door. Her lawyer, Rafe Banks, told the *Atlanta Journal-Constitution*, "There are all sorts of allegations flying around. Suffice to say, the families have the pot boiling."

On Monday afternoon, July 30, 2001, a backhoe rolled into the Cheatham Hill Memorial Park cemetery on Dallas Highway, Marietta. Standing by the open grave were two of Glenn's buddies, Donald Cawthon and Jeff Martin. Donald told a reporter what he'd been shouting from the rafters since his pal had died: "She told him she didn't love him the day she walked up the aisle with him." The grisly proceedings were filmed for the evening news by a local TV crew.

Two thousand miles away, Kathy tried not to dwell on what was happening to the remains of her son. She was on a car trip on the other side of the country. "I left with my mother on the Friday before to visit with my brother and his wife in California. They met us at the airport and the next morning all of us spent a week traveling up the coast to keep me busy. It was great to have something to keep my mind off it, but I had nightmares on that trip. It was tough being out there and wanting to be home with the kids at the same time."

But Glenn was not going through this ordeal without his family. James, who had vowed to be present at the disinterment, but dreaded being at the graveside with TV cameras trained on him, watched from the relative privacy of his car, parked on top of a nearby incline. His mobile phone was at his ear with Linda on the other end. His fervent hope was that it wouldn't be too late to find any incriminating evidence in his brother's remains.

The earth-mover rumbled into place and began to dig. When its shovel made contact with the concrete top of the vault, the rest of the dirt was painstakingly removed from the casket by cemetery workers wielding picks. Next, they attached metal straps to the backhoe which hoisted it up. For James, the sight of the coffin suspended in midair, swinging gently from its fragile-looking tethers, was almost unbearable. It was lowered onto a flatbed truck and removed a hundred or so yards away from the prying lenses to a screened area where it was loaded into a police department van for the journey to the medical examiner's office. There Brian Frist pronounced the casket and its contents to be in "very good shape." He said he was hopeful of uncovering new clues to Glenn's death. "If the evidence was there when he died, it will still be there today."

James kept up a running commentary of what he was seeing to Linda. "He was on the phone to me for two hours, for the whole time, telling me what's happening," she recalls. Their sister Margie took comfort in her everyday routine and went to work.

Under fire, Frist was emphatic that he'd done all he could at the time. He maintained that there was no record of the Turner family showing up at his office to see him, therefore there had been no reason for him to doubt his initial finding. Without new evidence, there had been no reason to suspect foul play. "With a three-day history of being sick, and a heart weighing five hundred grams, it would be easy to dismiss the crystals as being some part of an acute illness with dehydration," explained his former boss, Dr. Joseph Burton.

The second autopsy was performed the next day. This time, the greenish fluid that had been found in Glenn's stomach and had troubled his family, was tested explicitly for evidence of oxalate crystals. Present at the procedure were Mark Koponen, Chief Forensic Technician Mike Gerhard and Forensic Technician Judy Benson.

When the lid of the casket was opened, there was no doubt in any of their minds that Glenn had been loved by family and colleagues alike: he had been sent into the next life with plenty to remind him of the people he had left behind—the personal mementos beside him were testament to that. The family photographs, the withered flowers, his police badge and motorcycle cop insignia pins and the glasses that had been so tenderly placed over his eyes—they spoke volumes to everyone in the antiseptic and spine-chilling ambiance of the morgue. This was a man who was deeply mourned.

As he made his incision, Frist knew what he was looking for: the black plastic bag containing the body organs were underneath the chest plate. Each previously dissected piece of tissue—liver, pancreas, brain, heart, lungs, gastrointestinal tract, thyroid gland, spleen and kidneys—were reexamined and the findings meticulously noted. He earmarked a portion of each kidney and the liver to be dispatched to the State Crime Lab for further testing, and recorded the following data:

1. The kidneys show refractive crystalline structures within the renal tubules consistent with calcium oxalate.
2. The liver is positive for ethylene glycol, 1.6 mg/g
3. Cardiomegaly (enlarged heart)
4. Hemorrhagic congestion and edema of the lungs, bilateral.

Then he made his revised ruling:

Cause of Death, Sequel of acute toxicity—ethylene glycol. Manner of Death: Homicide.

So how did that square with what Dr. Koponen had found in Randy Turner's body? Although he had noticed crystals and had made the link between them and antifreeze poisoning during the firefighter's autopsy, the tests he had run had revealed only a minute amount of ethylene glycol. With the results of Glenn's exhumation in, he ordered new tests on Randy's blood, and this time, his long-held suspicions were vindicated. A mistake had been made by a lab worker—ethylene glycol showed up clearly in the blood and also in the urine.

The police in both counties had the ammunition they needed: both men had been murdered and by the same poison. Central to their case was the involvement of Lynn Turner. She had acute money troubles—she was a big spender with expensive tastes and an income that couldn't support her preferred lifestyle when Glenn died. She was a heartbeat away from watching the repo men seize her beloved autos, her home and everything in it at the time Randy had expired. Both men were worth substantially more to her dead than alive; she had everything to gain from their demise. With the second autopsy of Glenn done and dusted, she moved from being the prime suspect in one murder case to being the only one in two.

His family was relieved that the exhumation of Glenn had been a success; his body had given up the secret it had taken to the grave. Now it was time to lay him to rest, this time to be undisturbed for eternity. Once again, Kathy, her children, their friends and Glenn's buddies gathered at Cheatham Hill Memorial Park in Marietta. For the second time, he was accompanied to the cemetery by a color guard and buried with full honors as befitting a veteran officer. As the police chaplain, the Reverend Mike Cavin, tried to help them make sense of the nightmare, Glenn's fellow bike cops stood in silent tribute, their helmets under their arms. "I don't have answers," he told them. "What I do know is the good news—that love is not bounded by life and death. Your witness here today shows that. Even after all this time, you gathered out of your love for Glenn."

That summer was charged with anxiety for Lynn as her world began to close in. She confided to Jessica Marshall, "I almost puked when I saw Glenn's body being dug up."

Her friend stood solidly behind her. "I wouldn't believe you had anything to do with the deaths of Glenn
and Randy unless you confess to it," she said. "Well,
that's not going to happen, because I didn't do it," Lynn
had replied. She should never have married Glenn in the
first place, she told Jessica. "I didn't want to go on the
honeymoon. I didn't want to marry him." She should
have married Randy instead. "If I had married him,
things would have been different," she moaned. "I would
have been the beneficiary on everything. I could have
married him three weeks before he died."

Despite her declaration of her innocence, she knew
she was the only person the police were targeting. She
also knew there would be no move against her before the
lab boys released their final results. To be sure beyond
a shadow of a doubt that there was no mistake this time,
Dr. Frist had also sent specimens of Glenn's liver and
kidneys to independent experts at a laboratory in Willow
Grove, Pennsylvania.

To make matters scarier for her, Lynn heard in August
that the investigators were also taking a second look at
the death of the Forsyth County Sheriff's Office's Major
Ronald Casper, her former boss. He had died unexpectedly in 1998 while under investigation in the disappear-
ance of thousands of dollars from his office. Lynn had
been his administrative assistant at the time the money
disappeared, but was no longer working with him when
he fell under suspicion. Teresa Green told investigators
that Lynn and Ron were friendly and that she had been
surprised when Lynn did not turn up at Casper's funeral.
She also said that Lynn had quit her job at the sheriff's
office shortly afterwards. Teresa also said that she was at
Lynn's house one time when Ron dropped by and Lynn
had given him iced tea.

"Casper was an administrative captain in Forsyth
County, pretty much in charge of the money, and Lynn

worked for him," says Mike Archer. "This guy was a bean counter who dotted all the i's and crossed the t's, yet as much as forty or fifty grand ended up missing. They hired the GBI to look at it, but when they came in, there was so much money missing and the books were so badly messed up, they couldn't prove anything. But David King told me there [were] only two people who could have taken the money, Lynn or Casper. They said he died of some kind of spider bite.

"He wasn't that old, he was fifty or in his fifties," Archer remembers. "The rumor was, he was screwing her. I am sure he told her, 'You took that money,'—you know he didn't take it. She was screwing him and taking the money behind his back. He lost his job of twenty years and his career over it." To Mike, Lynn being somehow involved was no stretch. "I can see Lynn going to buy fricking poisonous spiders and putting them in bed with his ass," he says.

The soil was hardly settled on Glenn's grave when, armed with another exhumation order, the Cobb County medical examiner's team headed back to the cemetery. "James called and told me that they were going to exhume Ron Casper," recalls Kathy. "They didn't find antifreeze. She may have used something else, that's what they said. They said he died of a brown recluse spider bite."

"I got a call the day after Glenn was exhumed to tell me they'd dug him [Casper] up," says Donald Cawthon. "I asked when they would examine him, and was told they'd taken the samples. I asked when they were putting him back, and was told he was already down there. He was exhumed and reburied in twenty-four hours. A few days later I got a call and was told that nothing had showed up." Like Mike and Kathy, Donald was dubious about the spider. "How freak could that have been? Lynn was everywhere. Did a kid have it in a jar and she got hold of it?"

Next the police looked into the passing of the grand-mother who'd died in 1996 and whom Lynn had claimed left her a pile of money during that 1994 Christmas shopping trip with Angie Bollinger, but they took no further action.

As they waited for the results of the independent lab tests, the cops kept a watchful eye on Lynn and subpoenaed her financial records. It was ugly reading: she was in dire financial shape, with a heap of mounting bills on her credit cards and overdrawn accounts. She was in debt up to her eyeballs. Now they had established that she was in desperate need of cash. She'd already pocketed a bundle from Glenn's death, and she had expected to do even better when Randy died. Oh, she had motive, all right—but they still had no tangible proof.

All the test results came back in October. Both labs reported they had found deadly traces of ethylene glycol. To the forensic guys, it was a common enough substance. Each year there are over 100 ethylene glycol poisoning cases reported to the Georgia Poison Center alone, most victims being children or animals who have swallowed the stuff by accident.

What they hadn't worked out was, presuming she did do them in, how had she gotten her husband and lover to swill down enough antifreeze to kill them? It wasn't as if these were naive kids—Glenn had been a cop for ten years, and Randy had worked for the sheriff's office before becoming a firefighter. They weren't fools, they were not going to lift a bottle of antifreeze and knock it back just because she said they should.

The investigators were stymied: they needed something more than what was, although compelling, circumstantial evidence. Through the fall they plodded on doggedly, interviewing and reinterviewing everyone connected to Lynn, Glenn and Randy. Teresa Green told Frank Goss that Lynn had called her cell phone at 10:00

A.M. on October 15 while she was at work and left a message. Lynn had called back at 1:00 P.M. and remarked, "You find out who your friends are when all hell breaks loose," adding, "You know, legally, they can't make you not talk to me or contact me." She also maintained, "I had nothing to do with those two men's deaths, their families just have it against me," and ended the call with, "I've talked to several people at the sheriff department. I still have contacts there."

The investigation dragged on for another year. To Glenn's mother, progress in bringing her son's killer to justice was excruciatingly slow. "I got discouraged when I was waiting for the case to be opened up." Her dealings with District Attorney Patrick Head were far from encouraging: "I'd been to the DA's office multiple times and I thought, I am not going to go back. It was very hard, because they were not telling me anything. They'd say, 'We are busy working,' and 'It's coming, hang in there,' but you don't know that, and I was very concerned that it had been dropped.

"It was very frustrating, and I had to keep it going. I hated going into his office. It's a hateful thing to be in a D.A.'s office. If it wasn't for Russ Parker, the assistant district attorney who's now retired, I couldn't have gone on."

James tried to assuage his mother's fears. "The police were communicating. I deal with the courts and understand how investigations work a little better, and I thought they were actually telling us more than usual. But Mom and Linda thought they weren't telling us anything. I tried to explain that they were frightened someone would inadvertently say something that would damage the case."

As another Christmas came and went with no news, the Turners tried to go kick the ball forward on their own. They arranged a meeting with an investigator and an attorney who used to work at the medical examiner's office in Cobb County, and he told them that screw-ups were a common occurrence. They also met with high-priced attorneys in Atlanta to ask if suing the county would help. They'd never get a judgment, they were told. "If we wanted to spend twenty or thirty thousand dollars, they'd give it a try, but it wasn't going to go anywhere," says James.

In March 2002 Kathy put her pent-up rage into a letter. "I wrote about my feelings about what was going on and everyone said, 'Kathy, give that to *The Atlanta Journal.*' I didn't think I should, I hadn't talked to anyone but the reporter who had been covering the case, and she said, 'Oh yes, send it to me, send the rough draft.' I said, 'No, I will make it look better,' and I did. The paper didn't publish my letter, but they sure did talk to all the officials. That's the only time I really got angry, I thought they were not doing anything about this case, they were letting it get by. But I had no idea what they were doing. They had thirty boxes of paperwork. I thought it was dead in the air again, and I was wanting to make sure it wasn't."

Six months later, a grand jury was impaneled and heard testimony from just five witnesses, the medical examiners from Cobb County and Forsyth County, GBI Agent King, and forensic scientist Koponen. On November 1, 2002, despite the lack of eyewitnesses or an incriminating statement from Lynn herself, a warrant was issued for her arrest. That afternoon, she turned herself in to Cobb County authorities. After being arraigned for the murder of Maurice Glenn Turner, she was ordered to be held at the Cobb County Jail until a bond hearing could be scheduled. In court, the prosecutors said she was also being eyed in the death of Randy Thompson.

She stood red-eyed, handcuffed but expressionless, facing Cobb County Senior Superior Court Judge Conley

Ingram as the indictment was read aloud. After it was over, a statement for Glenn's family was made by Jeff Martin. "We are deeply saddened by the loss of our son, brother and uncle. We ask that everyone keep our family, the Thompson family and Lynn's family, in your prayers." Kathy stayed home. "It shouldn't have taken this long," she said simply when asked by a reporter what she thought now that her daughter-in-law had been arrested. Outside the court Nita Thompson said the day was "bittersweet. It's like living it over, but we don't want anyone else hurt like the Turners and we have."

Two weeks later, Lynn was back in court for a bond hearing. She had hired top criminal defense lawyer Jimmy Berry and his partner Victor Reynolds, a former chief magistrate judge, assistant district attorney and police officer, to defend her. Repeatedly, they tried to persuade Cobb County Chief Magistrate Frank Cox that while she was also the prime suspect in the death of Randy Thompson, that had nothing to do with the case on hand. D.A. Head opposed bail on the grounds that she might flee or commit other crimes to pay off her debts. GBI Agent King backed him up: "If she had an opportunity to get money, she would," he said.

The judge deferred his ruling, ordering psychiatric reports on Lynn.

After three weeks of captivity Lynn met with a court-appointed psychologist, Dr. Osama Sa'ad Hindash of the Cobb County Adult Detention Center Mental Health Services, who had to determine if Lynn would pose a risk to others if she was freed on bail. Looking over his notes he saw that she had no previous history of suicide, no reported abuse in her childhood and appeared to have no problem with drugs or alcohol.

During the session she fixed him squarely in the eye. When she spoke about Glenn and Randy, she became "somewhat agitated and restless. She is an intelligent and strong-willed woman who is not in touch with her feelings," he wrote in his report.

She repeatedly asked if she was talking too loud, telling Dr. Hindash that her ears popped because she had an upper respiratory tract infection. During the interview her eyes teared up and her skin was blotchy. "Maybe I'm allergic to you," she had joked lamely. Dr. Hindash concluded that she had difficulty expressing her feelings and seemed more irritated than anything else by having to talk to him at all. He recommended that Lynn not be released on the basis that she might harm herself or others and was a definite flight risk.

Jimmy Berry found his client another shrink, Dr. Alfred Messer from Atlanta. He found Lynn to be "alert, oriented and cooperative." She talked to the point, and she was neither delusional nor given to hallucinations, he observed. He also noted she'd had no prior problems with drugs or booze and had been a good employee. Her coworkers had offered to swear to her good character and truthfulness, he added. She had cried when he asked her about the two children she had not seen in nearly a month.

During their meeting she told him about the two episodes when she'd claimed that Randy Thompson had attacked her in drunken rages. Dr. Messer's conclusion was that she was harmless: "I cordially recommended Mrs. Turner for release on bond while she is awaiting trial. In my opinion she does not represent a danger to herself or others. Nor would she flee to South America. Her entire family lives in the area including her two young children."

In the first week of December, she was back in court to hear the ruling on her bond application. Noticing Judge Cox's expression of dismay as he scanned the list of over two dozen people he had lined up to give Lynn ringing endorsements, Jimmy Berry offered to pare it to just five. The rest of her supporters filed into seats to show the court that she had plenty of friends who didn't believe a word of the charges against her.

First to testify on her daughter's behalf was Helen. She told the court that she had worked in law offices for over twenty-five years. She said she would ensure that Lynn turned up for every court date.

"Do you have any reason to believe that she would flee the jurisdiction or not come back?" asked Jimmy Berry.

"No, none whatsoever," she answered resolutely.

"Is there any reason that you would believe that she would commit any crime while she's out on bond?" he asked.

"No, none whatever," she repeated.

"You are willing to post your home as bond?"

"Yes, my husband and I."

"And where will Lynn be if she is released?" he asked her.

"She can stay with us."

"She has two children? Are they with you now?" he asked.

"They're with us now," she told him.

Helen described taking Glenn to the hospital on the day Lynn had called her saying she'd hurt her head. She hadn't seen or heard much about Randy in the two years since he'd split from Lynn. All she'd heard was that he was sick.

Prosecutor Russ Parker also wanted to know if she was aware that her daughter was the chief suspect in the murder of Randy Thompson.

"That's what I read in the papers," she replied.

"Do you know that it's been reported that Randy died because of ethylene poisoning?" Parker asked.

"I've seen . . ." she began. "I've read it and I've heard it, but I don't believe it."

Then he asked if she knew that ethylene glycol had killed Glenn.

"I do not believe that," she said firmly.

Parker turned his attention to Lynn's finances.

"The residence your daughter lived in here in Cobb County, I believe that belonged to her?"

"That's correct, she bought it herself long before they were married," replied Helen.

"And the residence she lived in with Randy Thompson?"

"She bought it before he moved in," she said.

She told the court Lynn still lived in the Forsyth County home she'd shared with Randy.

"Are you aware of her financial obligations at this time?" Parker asked.

"Yes, I am," said Helen.

"And she is strapped for money?"

"My husband and I will see that everything is taken care of," she told him.

"And you've been doing that for a number of years, haven't you?"

"Well, we've helped her, yes. She's our only child."

She said she was not afraid for her grandchildren if Lynn was released. "She's a very good mother, a very loving mother. The children love her. They're very disciplined children."

She claimed to know little about the benefits Lynn had received after Glenn and Randy died, but acknowledged she did get something.

"Yet you and your husband on a pretty regular basis give money to Lynn?" Parker probed.

Helen shook her head. "Not really on a regular basis—we just help out with the children at different times—basically that's it."

Helen said despite the fact Lynn couldn't now work, she had been able to keep up her house payments by doing transcriptions and working for her stepfather.

"Mrs. Gregory, you don't plan to have any men moving into your house with Lynn, do you?" Parker wanted to know.

"Definitely not," Helen shot back.

Lynn's aunt, Sybil Graham, who'd worked for thirty-seven years in the legal system, said she was willing to help Lynn cofinance her bond. "I'll never believe she did it. I don't think my niece could do it," she said.

Next up was Tammy Sheriff. She told the court she had known Lynn since their daughters joined a cheerleading squad five years before. Her husband ran a small grading company and had written to the judge saying he would give Lynn a job if she made bail. They had talked to her a few days before, when Lynn called her collect from jail.

She was followed by Jessica Marshall, who described herself as Lynn's "best friend." They had met when she was working at the sheriff's office and they were both pregnant. She told the court that Lynn had given her a home when Jessica was going through a divorce. She had looked after Jessica's kids at night while she worked, and their children had become friends.

Prosecutor Jack Mallard wanted to know about Lynn's finances. "Did you know that with all the banks she was banking with over the last few years, that she was running overcharges, late fees every month?"

"No, I didn't know."

"Are you aware, being her best friend, that she's under obligation to about one hundred and seventy four thousand dollars at this time?"

"I do not know her financial situation," Detective Marshall replied.

Mallard pressed her on Lynn being the main suspect in Randy's death.

"I know it's being investigated, correct."

"And don't you think that's important in deciding

whether or not somebody will return to court if released on bond . . . ?" he asked.

"I know she would return."

"And do you have a magic potion that you can share with us? You only know that because she is your friend?" asked Mallard.

"I know it because if she had wanted to, she could have left before all this happened, and she hasn't," Marshall replied.

The last character witness for Lynn was medical supplies salesman Joe Moody. He had known her for twenty years. She'd grown up with his daughter, and when she'd started dating Glenn, she would bring him by Moody's house. He told the court he had been at their wedding and visited them when they moved to Cumming. Alisa had even moved in with the couple for a while. He had attended Glenn's funeral.

"If it were shown to you that Lynn Turner was actually seeing Randy Thompson prior to Glenn Turner's death, would that change your opinion of Lynn?" asked Mallard.

"No."

A disgusted Kathy Turner just shook her head.

The prosecution called Special Agent King. He listed his reasons why Lynn was a bad risk and also voiced concern that she would try to intimidate witnesses. "I've been contacted by some that have been interviewed in this case and they have informed me that she has tried to contact them, asking the status of the case, after they have been interviewed by the GBI."

"Would she commit other crimes?" asked Mallard.

"I think she is in a very bad financial situation and that she needs money badly. If she had an opportunity to do something to gain that money, I think she probably would," said King.

Lynn's attorney got to his feet. "How many conversa-

tions did you have with Lynn Turner between nineteen
ninety-nine and two thousand and one?" Jimmy Berry
asked King.

"Four, five, six, maybe more."

"Under what circumstances were those?"

"She was a suspect in a theft investigation I was conducting with the Forsyth County sheriff department,"
said King.

"And she talked with you at all times requested of her,
isn't that correct?"

"Yes, sir."

"And not having had a conversation with her since two
thousand and one, you indicated that you knew her very
well, and you have an opinion about her mental state today?" Berry asked.

"I base my opinion on the people that I have interviewed in the last year and a half . . ."

"Well, let me ask you something. I want you to look at
all these letters that have been submitted. Did you talk to
these people?" Berry pressed.

When King answered that he had not, Berry said,
"These were people who had known her for years and yet
the agent hadn't talked to any of them, none of their
names were even familiar to him?"

He also wanted to know how Lynn would run. Hadn't
King amply demonstrated that she had no money?

In December, on the basis of Dr. Hindash's report that
Lynn was a threat to the community, and despite his
inability to give any examples of Lynn's failure to show
emotion when cross-examined by her attorney, Judge
Cox nixed bail for the time being.

That Christmas, Lynn sat in jail wondering if she
would ever again be able to do the normal things a mother
does with her children. Their grandmother tried to make

the day as happy as possible, but what she was feeling was far from seasonal joy. Helen assured Amber and Blake that their mother would be home soon—it was all a misunderstanding.

CHAPTER THIRTEEN:
Awaiting Trial

L ynn was back in court to hear the judge's decision about her bail on January 10. Judge Cox was plainly not happy at the thought of releasing an accused (possibly double) murderer back into the community, but Dr. Hindash's unsupported conclusion that she was a cold fish who was a menace to herself and society weighed uneasily on his mind, especially as Hindash had admitted under oath that she did not need any behavior-modifying medicine or to be kept away from fellow prisoners.

"I have no legal right to keep Ms. Turner in prison when I can find no evidence that she is a flight risk or poses a danger to others," he said. Turning to Lynn he set bail at $200,000 and said, "It is my order that you will be required to live with your mother and to wear an electronic ankle monitor at all times." She would not be allowed to look for a job, he added.

As Helen Gregory broke into smiles of relief, several members of the Turner and Thompson families gasped. James Turner put his arms around his weeping mother. On the courthouse steps Perry Thompson lashed out: "We just didn't think anybody who was suspected of doing something like this would be turned loose." Glenn's former supervisor Mike Archer shrugged and declared that he still had faith that the justice system would eventually dish out the fate he richly believed Lynn deserved. "She's been running free for seven years. She always comes up smelling like a rose, so I am not shocked at all," he told the *Marietta Daily Journal*. Lynn and her lawyer savored the victory. She hugged him and told him she couldn't wait to get back to her kids.

While Lynn enjoyed her freedom, her attorneys got busy. By the first week in February, Jimmy Berry had filed fifty motions to be heard by the superior court judge who had been assigned the case, James Bodiford. He was particularly concerned about the huge media interest, fretting that the trial would degenerate into a circus. He wanted all hearings on his challenges to evidence to be held in camera and demanded that all print and TV journalists be locked out of the court until a jury was impaneled.

Furthermore, those jurors should be sequestered for the duration of the trial, he declared. With all the attention the press was paying to the case, he also feared the potential jury pool would be tainted. There would be no way to prevent those ultimately selected from reading potentially damning articles and learning about "evidence" that would never be allowed at trial. Unless the judge granted the motion, Berry would request that the trial be moved out of Cobb County.

"If the hearing is not closed we will push for a venue change," he said. "In my thirty-two years of practicing law, I have never had this many people who'd formed an opinion." His threat rattled neither the prosecutors, who professed to be open-minded about a move, nor Glenn's friends. "It doesn't matter if the case was tried in Alaska. You'll find twelve jurors who will look at the facts and find her guilty. If it looks like a duck, walks like a duck and quacks like a duck, it's probably a duck, no matter where the case is heard," Mike told the *Marietta* paper.

Even more crucial than a venue change was Berry's motion to bar any mention of Randy's death. The prosecutors immediately gave notice that they intended to ask for it to be admissible, citing "similar transaction," a legal term for allowing the court to hear about prior similar behavior to show an established pattern of criminality—in other words, she'd done it more than once.

"The state claims the defendant caused both Glenn Turner and Randy Thompson to ingest ethylene glycol. However, the state admits they don't know the exact method nor the time of ingestion concerning either case. They further make broad, sweeping statements that the defendant 'had access to the deceased shortly before he died,'" Berry complained. "The law is clear; before similar transaction can be allowed, there has to be enough similarities between the two incidents to demonstrate that one tends to prove the other. Yet this prosecution has no idea how or when my client is supposed to have killed the two men." If the ruling went against her, she would be put in the untenable position of having to defend herself in a case in which she had never been charged with any wrongdoing.

Berry also asked the judge to restrain the Turners from sitting too near the jury or expressing their feelings. "For the victim's family to sit in the courtroom and cry or show other types of emotions during the course of the trial will cause the jury to be sympathetic towards the alleged victim's family," he said.

He also wanted Lynn to wear her own clothes. "Forcing Mrs. Turner to appear in court in jail garb and/or chains is not only beneath the dignity of this Honorable Court, it is manifestly prejudicial to the right of Mrs. Turner to have a fair trial. She should be allowed to dress in appropriate civilian clothing and not be shackled and/or chained while in this or any other courtroom."

He then asked the judge to ban Glenn's police buddies from showing up in strength and in full uniform. "The defendant respectfully requests that this court enter an order directing that members of the police department, and any other law enforcement agencies, remain out of the courtroom and hallways adjacent to this courtroom during this trial. If they come to the courthouse, they should do so in civilian dress." While Judge Bodiford reserved his ruling on the other petitions before him, he did hand Berry one victory. Police officers would not be allowed to wear their uniforms in court. It would have a "chilling effect on the defendant's right to a fair trial," he agreed.

The pre-trial hearings dragged on through the spring of 2003. The most contentious motion at issue was Berry's demand that the court be closed. "The trial will be sensational enough by itself," he argued. "If the public is allowed to become voyeurs to the sensational and morbid aspects of the case, our client could never receive a fair trial." While Bodiford didn't give an immediate decision, he made it clear that he was not leaning in that direction.

Despite the gravity of the charges, Lynn's plight seemed hardly to faze her. It was almost as if she was in total denial of what lay ahead of her if found guilty, and was relishing being the focus of everyone's attention. Throughout the lengthy pre-trial proceedings, she never spoke. Spruced up as if she were still holding down a job in a professional office, she appeared in pantsuits to hide her ankle bracelet, and throughout the arguments, wrote copiously on a legal notepad. Local TV crews ringed the courthouse for every hearing, and the shocking case which had quickly caught on fire as "the Antifreeze Murder," was picked up by the networks and reported on CNN, ABC's *20/20*, NBC's *Dateline* and CBS's *48 Hours*.

On May 12 Judge Bodiford gave a thumbs-down to the defense team. He refused to close the court, saying that such a drastic move not only flew in the face of the justice system, but threatened the freedom of the press, and therefore was a device only be to used as a last resort.

On July 7, the district attorney argued that details of Randy's death should be heard by the jury. Lynn's lawyers lit into him: his case was circumstantial. If Lynn Turner did poison her husband and her lover, the prosecution had no idea how she actually did it. Pat Head hit back: the coincidences were too many to ignore. Two men had died of ethylene glycol poisoning, both had turned up at hospitals displaying the same symptoms, they both had been intimately involved with Lynn Turner and she'd stood to gain financially from their deaths. She'd plied them with food and drink in the couple of days before they died. Both murders bore her signature, he declared.

For two days, the two sides went at it hammer and tongs. Berry scoffed at the state's contention that the men had died of the poisonous substance, pointing out that witnesses couldn't even agree how much it would take to kill a man. Then there were the two suicide attempts. Randy Thompson had been an unstable character who had tried to take his own life on two previous occasions. Wasn't his death in reality a third try that had finally succeeded? Striding over to a large board set up on an easel, he pointed to three short sentences on it and maintained that the prosecution could not answer even these most basic questions:

a: Did she kill Glenn?
b: Where did she kill him?
c: How did she kill him?

"The answer to all three is, 'Don't know,' " he said.

Georgia Bureau of Investigation agent David King was Head's star witness. It was all about money, he said. Lynn Turner was a chronic spender. By the time Glenn Turner had died, she was drowning in debt. She owed more than $2,500 in overdraft fees alone. After she'd collected her dead husband's life insurance, she took her lover and his pals on a weeklong luxury cruise. And ever since, she'd been pocketing his pension of nearly $800 a month.

She was a heartless, calculating, cold-blooded individual. When Randy died, she had refused to leave work despite the urging of her colleagues. "I learned from my investigation that she was unemotional. Her reaction to Randy's death was not the normal reaction from someone who has lost a loved one," he said.

The district attorney summed up: "There is no other explainable reason for it to be other than ethylene glycol poisoning, and it is a poison used so rarely, it leaves little doubt that it is the handiwork of the same person."

Throughout the process, the two families sat together. They were pleased at the way things were going. The Turners especially were impressed by Bodiford's even-handed approach. "He does everything by the book, but he is also very fair and lenient," says James. "At the same time, he's not so by-the-book that it goes against common logic, and he gave both sides quite a lot of leeway. I was thrilled he got the case. I didn't want a judge who was up there trying to make a name for himself."

Considering all the awful things being said about her, Lynn seemed just as happy. During breaks she smiled and chatted with her aunt. But on July 12, the judge dealt a major blow. The jury would get to hear about Randy. As far as he was concerned, there were such glaring similarities in the two cases, he would allow the jury to weigh all the evidence. "It was more likely than not that participation in the death of Randy Thompson was criminal and was, in fact, executed by Lynn Turner. She had ample time and opportunity to give both of these gentlemen lethal doses of ethylene glycol. In fact, Lynn Turner was the only person in close proximity to them before they died," he said.

Bodiford went on to call her "indifferent" to the fate of both men, and commented on her moving in with Randy four days after Glenn had died: "This type of behavior does not seem to be in keeping with the acts of a grieving widow," he said in a glorious understatement. Then he cautioned that his remarks were not a presumption of Lynn's guilt or innocence. "A much higher standard than the preponderance of evidence used in this hearing" would be required at trial.

"I didn't expect it, I'm sort of numb," said Kathy as she was asked to react to the decision. But she later recalled that a friend in the judiciary system in north Georgia had told her, " 'Kathy, if you get that "similar transaction" thing in, you're good for it. You've gotten the most wonderful judge.' " To Glenn's mother, who still worried that Lynn would get away with his murder, this was very reassuring.

The Thompsons were also elated. "We were really afraid that today was going to be the end of our story. This is a ray of sunshine on a dark, dark day. None of us want to be here. But it is good news—really, really good news," rejoiced Perry to reporters. He was even happier a couple of months later when the Supreme Court of Georgia refused to consider Lynn's appeal against Bodiford's decision. Now there was nothing to stop the case going to trial on the date he had set, February 2, 2004. And it would be played out in the full glare of the cameras: WSB-TV Atlanta's formal application to televise all the proceedings had been approved.

While the months of legal wrangling dragged on, Lynn remained out on bail, but only by the skin of her teeth. In October she had found herself in front of Judge Bodiford again, this time charged with violating the terms of her bond. Her attorneys were asking for her virtual house arrest situation to be eased, but an irate Pat Head strenuously objected and produced witnesses to prove she was carrying on with her life as if nothing had happened.

Forsyth County firefighter Mark Davis, who'd worked with Randy, had spotted Lynn shopping at a Kroger supermarket. "I was shocked," he told the judge. "I thought she was in jail, and I was floored to see her out in public." He had called the Thompsons as soon as he got home. Forsyth County Sheriff's Deputy Lisa Frady bumped into her at Amber's school, Vickery Creek Elementary in Cumming. Another woman claimed to have seen Lynn hanging out at one of her old haunts, the Sidelines Grille sports bar in Sandy Springs.

Head demanded that her $200,000 bail be revoked and Lynn tossed back into jail. The days when the witnesses had seen her around town weren't the only times she had slipped away from her mother's house, he claimed. The court had stipulated she could leave home only to visit her doctor and attend court hearings, yet she had visited her attorney on at least ten occasions, albeit with the permission of the court officer whose job it was to monitor her.

To the district attorney her disregard for the court order was more proof of Lynn Turner's deviousness. "It shows she has the ability to manipulate a poorly supervised system," he complained. Jimmy Berry dismissed the accusation, claiming, "In nine months, she has done everything she was asked by the court to do."

The judge was not pleased. "Everything has been loosey-goosey," he objected. "There is nothing in the written order that says she can visit her attorney. At the same time, I cannot punish her if pre-court services said it was okay. Despite finding a violation, I don't see any reason at this point to lock her up." But for the next ten days, he confined Lynn to her mother's home until new restrictions were worked out. After learning that the ankle bracelet

BLACK WIDOW

195

frequently didn't work, he agreed to look into Head's request that she be fitted with a global positioning device.

News that the woman she believed had killed her son was flouting the court-ordered constraints, and apparently getting away with it, filtered back to Kathy Turner, and it made her furious. "It was extremely hard when Lynn got out on bail. We said, 'Why in the world is she out there?' And they [the authorities] said the judge had ruled that it was okay to let her be out. But she wasn't obeying [the condition of her bail]. She was under house arrest, yet she wasn't staying home half the time. She was taking subpoenas from her lawyer Jimmy Berry to people, and they didn't do anything about it."

If her newly curtailed freedom threatened to spoil Christmas of 2003 for Lynn, she didn't get any more joy from Judge Bodiford at her next court appearance. At an unusual 7:00 A.M. hearing on December 20, Jimmy Berry protested the prosecution's intention to present ethylene glycol tests as scientific evidence. Such tests used a method known as gas chromatography, developed to detect illegal drugs. "There is no real standard in the scientific community for really determining what amount may cause death," he claimed.

The prosecution produced Dr. Mark Koponen to give an answer. "A third of a can of Coke," he replied. "But levels vary." The problem was that you could hardly ask people to drink a glass of antifreeze to find how much it would take to kill them. But since it was not a naturally occurring chemical in the body, if it is found in someone who has died, it suggests poisoning, he explained.

With three thousand people dying of the stuff every year, there ought to be some sort of standard, huffed Berry. Apart from anything else, some household cleansers also contained the chemical, he said. Maybe it was the early hour, but he was laboring a losing cause. Judge Bodiford didn't buy Berry's reasoning and rejected his motion outright.

The day after, Lynn learned the new rules for her continued release on bail: she was placed on the Global Positioning System Program, and liable for all costs; she was allowed to take the children to school each morning, but she had to leave the house by 7:15 A.M. and return no later than 8:15 A.M.; she was permitted to drive the children to doctor or dentist appointments, but only after telling her lawyers where she was going, and providing them with a bill or statement to corroborate the appointment, which they in turn had to pass on to the judge's office; she could visit her attorneys, but they had to advise the judge of her visits; she was to stay within a proscribed part of the Gregorys' property, and she had to obey all the previous restrictions on her freedom.

After the holidays, Lynn's lawyers were back in court asking that the state be constrained from using the phrase "antifreeze murder." The word "antifreeze" carried "a prejudicial connotation calculated to induce revulsion and horror in the minds of the jurors towards the defendant," they said.

With the trial just a few weeks away, Judge Bodiford considered the motions still pending, most crucially, Berry's request to have the trial moved out of Cobb County, where he contended, publicity had killed any chance of his client getting a fair shake. Bodiford said he would decide after questioning the jury pool.

He too was concerned. He had ordered that a larger than usual number of potential jurors be called so he could weed out those who'd already made up their minds on Lynn's guilt or innocence. Of the sixty-two people questioned on the first day, nearly a third said she was a killer. "I already have formed a strong opinion about Miss Turner," admitted one. "I'm retired, I read two newspapers a day. I have the TV on all the time. My inclination

would be to say Miss Turner did it." One woman told the
court that two men dying in the same manner was highly
suspect. Another man candidly confessed that he could
not be impartial. "Do you think she is guilty?" asked
Berry. "Yes, I do," the man fired back.

Both the judge and the district attorney professed to
be amazed at the response. By the end of three days of
jury selection, the judge knew he had no option. "Based
on what we've observed in the last three days, I believe
a change of venue is appropriate, and I hereby grant it,"
he said on February 4. His preference was to move the
trial to Rome in Floyd County. The defense at first agreed,
then balked. The alternatives they suggested were in
Floyd, Columbia, Houston and Whitfield Counties. The
next morning, Judge Bodiford drove 126 miles to Perry in
Houston County, where he met with County Chief Superior Court Judge George Nunn, Jr. They set a date for
Monday, April 26, with jurors to be seated the following
day. Bodiford then wrote to both sides to tell them that he
and his staff would be put up at the Country Inns & Suites
in Warner Robins for the duration of the trial.

Jimmy Berry and Vic Reynolds fired off a letter voic-
ing their client's concerns about the new location. Randy
was buried in Houston County, and several of his relatives
were there. Moreover, Randy's parents lived in neighboring Peach County, and their home was well known since it
had been on TV. "We recall some of the news segments
on this story being taped from the Thompsons' residence," they wrote.

On March 12, prosecutors got the green light to refer to
the case as the "antifreeze murder." Banning it would be
"too restrictive," the judge decided. But he did throw out
one puny bone to Lynn: on the occasions he felt the use of
"antifreeze" was unwarranted, he would have it struck
from court records.

Notices were sent out to 120 citizens of Houston County

ordering them to report Monday, April 16, for jury duty.
The prosecution announced that its witness list had
swollen to 200, although it acknowledged that not everyone on it would be called. Although the case was now
to be held away from the prejudicial gaze of the Cobb
County residents, the media hordes made arrangements
to descend on Perry, and the local paper talked of little
else. Jimmy Berry and his partner refused to say if they
would give everyone what they wanted to see: Lynn
Turner taking the stand in her own defense.

CHAPTER FOURTEEN:
The Big Show

The trial finally got underway on Friday, April 30, in Perry's new courthouse. All eyes swiveled to follow the defendant as she took her seat, flanked by her attorneys. Court TV would also air the gavel-to-gavel proceedings anchored by homegrown Georgia peach Nancy Grace, who had been raised in Macon and worked as a prosecutor in Atlanta before trading her lawyer's duds for more telegenic outfits.

But while the locals on the steps outside strained to catch a glimpse of the blonde broadcaster, inside the building it was Lynn Turner who was the undoubted star of the show. It might not have been the role she'd have chosen for herself, that of accused murderess, but it did have its upside. She was back in her favorite spot—namely, the center of the action—and every camera in the room was trained on her.

She played it perfectly. Gone were the professional-looking tailored pantsuits she'd worn during preliminary hearings. For her debut on national TV she had decided on a mid–calf-length dress with a matching short-sleeved jacket in a grandmotherly shade of periwinkle blue. With her face-framing brown curls tamed into a tidy bob and her face scrubbed of its usual layer of paint, she looked more like she was headed to prayer meeting than beginning the fight of her life. If her heart was pounding or her stomach in knots, there was no outward sign of it.

Her appearance stunned Chris Childers. The Lynn he had known loved to flaunt her eye-catching curves in figure-hugging short skirts and low-cut tops. The flirt who had hit on him six years before was nowhere to be seen. "She had no makeup on, she had her hair pulled back and she had an older woman's kind of flowery dress on, which made her look about sixty. It seemed she was trying to make people think, 'Oh, this angel? She couldn't do this,'" he says.

She took one cursory glance at the families and friends of her husband and lover who packed the benches, then studiously ignored them. One person absent that day was dying to see her up close and personal, but Stacey Messex, who as Stacey Abbott had been Glenn's first love, made the decision to stay away.

"I wanted to see her face and look her right in the eye. I wanted so bad for her to feel the pain that I felt by losing Glenn. I wanted her to feel the sadness. I didn't go to any of the trial. I wanted to, but the media coverage was so heavy and I didn't want to be put in the spotlight," she says. "I also didn't want anyone to say, 'Hey, there is Glenn's ex-girlfriend. I wonder what she is doing here?' I never wanted there to be any question as to Glenn's faithfulness to Lynn or to give Lynn any excuse, other than just utter greed, for his murder."

On the bench across the aisle from Lynn and her defense team was Cobb County's A-team, District Attorney Pat Head and his assistants, Russ Parker and T. Bryan Lumpkin. Parker had 300 cases under his belt, including the 1995 conviction of Fredric Tokars, a venal Atlanta lawyer who'd hired a hit man who'd killed his wife in front of their two young sons. In 2000 Bryan Lumpkin forged a name for himself when he successfully employed evidence of a similar transaction in a previous case involving child molestation.

They were bolstered by legal heavyweight Jack Mallard, who had been lured out of retirement and sworn in as a special prosecutor for the trial. Mallard had worked as an assistant district attorney for both Cobb and Fulton Counties and had many famous wins to his credit. Back in 1982 he faced down child killer Wayne Williams in one of the most notorious cases ever seen in the Atlanta area, where for nearly two years, parents were near catatonic with fear as twenty-nine young boys went missing, then turned up murdered.

The way that he won the conviction of Williams should have struck fear into Lynn: although Williams had been accused of killing just two of the boys, Mallard persuaded the judge to let him introduce evidence from the cases of ten other victims. By the time he had finished, the jurors were ready to pull the switch themselves. Then, without Williams being charged in the single death of any of the other teens, the authorities in Atlanta had pronounced the cases solved, and closed them.

Head learned from the master of similar transaction and, just as Mallard had done in the Williams trial, he was not about to let this jury give Lynn Turner the benefit of any doubt. Flashing a confident grin as he walked over to the jury box, he told them, "We anticipate that this is going to be a little complicated, so we're going to encourage you to take notes, not only during the trial, but during the opening statement as well."

The warm smile disappeared as he launched into his opening remarks. "This case is about lust, greed and murder. It's about one woman and two men. Some of you asked about ethylene glycol. Some of you knew what it was. The evidence will show you that it is a clear, colorless, odorless liquid with a slightly sweet taste, that it is a poison to the human body.

"If a human ingests ethylene glycol, it can cause death. When it is consumed, the effects on the body are generally divided into three well-defined stages. Stage one can start from as early as thirty minutes or up to six hours after ingestion and it will continue for twelve hours. The liver begins to metabolize the ethylene glycol and you can expect to see symptoms such as depression, hallucinations, nausea, vomiting, flu-like symptoms. Death can occur during stage one.

"Stage two is ethylene glycol intoxication. It occurs between twelve and twenty-four hours after ingestion and the compounds that are produced by this metabolic process have an effect on the heart." He paused and laid his hand on his own chest. "At this point, mild hypertension or an abnormally fast heart rate can occur, also abnormally fast breathing or hyperventilation. Heart failure, death, can also occur during stage two," he continued.

"Stage three begins between twenty-four and seventy-two hours. Kidney failure can occur, even death. It is during this phase that calcium oxalate crystals are formed in the kidneys."

Then Head brought up the word that Lynn's lawyers had tried to keep from the jury's ears. "Antifreeze, the same stuff that's used in cars, contains between ninety-five and ninety-nine percent ethylene glycol. This is not a substance that ever occurs naturally in the human body," he told them. He went back to his table and picked up a photograph of a policeman. He showed it to the jury, then stuck it to a large display board facing them. "This case is about the homicide of Maurice Glenn Turner, a homicide that the medical examiner will tell you was caused by ethylene glycol poisoning."

He picked up another picture, this time of a guy in firefighter's gear, and positioned it beside Glenn's. "While this case is about the homicide of Glenn Turner, you're also going to hear about the homicide of Randy Thompson.

Randy also died from ethylene glycol poison." Head strode over to the table where Lynn was seated. Jabbing a finger at her, he told the jury, "There is one thread, there is one common denominator, and it's this woman."

He began to tell them about Glenn and the marriage that had brought him more heartbreak than happiness. He told them that despite the lack of normal wedded intimacy, the young officer had made sure that if anything happened to him, the wife he loved would be financially taken care of.

He told them about Lynn and Randy, and about the adulterous affair that began in the summer 1994 and was carried on that winter under the roof of his unsuspecting parents. In the winter of 1995, a couple of weeks after Glenn's wife and her lover had snuck off to a motel in Florida, Glenn had come down with a stomach bug so debilitating that his friends urged him to get medical help.

The day after her husband had been treated at the E.R., Lynn was a widow. "The defendant left the house on the morning of March third, and she later told the police she was going out to run some errands," said Head. "She returns home around two or two thirty in the afternoon and she finds Glenn in bed, dead. The medical examiner performed an autopsy and although he found calcium oxalate crystals in the kidneys, he failed to recognize the significance of those crystals at the time. He determined that the cause of death was natural."

Barely pausing for breath, the district attorney ripped into Lynn's callous disregard for Glenn and his devastated family. "Evidence will show that at both the viewing at the funeral home and at the funeral, the conduct of the defendant was not that of a grieving widow," he said.

He told the jury how four days after she'd buried her husband, she'd moved in with Randy Thompson and almost immediately begun collecting benefits from Glenn's death. Ticking them off on his fingers, he listed the checks that flowed into Lynn's mailbox, and described how she celebrated her good fortune by treating her lover and a couple of friends to a luxury cruise. On her return she was looking for still more money. Claiming that Glenn had made her the beneficiary in 1993 while they were engaged, she filed an affidavit with the county to have all the money in his deferred compensation account paid to her.

On August 30, she and Randy had moved into a new home she bought in Cumming, and five months later their daughter was born. When their son was born in June 1998, just as Glenn had done, Randy did the right thing by Lynn, making her the beneficiary of a life insurance policy. By the following spring their relationship had imploded and Randy moved into an apartment, where he lived alone.

"Prior to Randy's death, the defendant is in bad financial shape. On January the third, she is in a bank in Cumming about her overdrawn account and she indicates she will be able to take care of it . . . soon," said Head ominously. "On Friday, January the nineteenth, Randy cancels plans to have dinner with a friend so that he can have dinner with Lynn Turner. The next day, he's vomiting, hallucinating, nauseous, has flu-like symptoms.

"Randy calls his friend, another fireman, around seven thirty in the morning. He comes over and cares for him all day. The defendant also comes over that day. Late Saturday evening Randy is taken to the Joan Glancy Memorial Hospital where, like Glenn, he is treated and released. On Sunday, he is visited by the defendant. On Monday, sometime around mid-morning, Randy is discovered dead."

Glaring at Lynn, then turning to face the jury box, he added, "That same Monday, the defendant calls the Social Security Administration to find out about payment of benefits to her for Randy's children."

After pausing dramatically to let the point sink in, Head carried on. It was money and not mourning on her

mind. Within a week of Randy's death she called State
Farm to demand her $200,000. But this time, there was to
be no bonanza—the policy had lapsed. Yet she still prof-
ited from the tragedy: by March 1, the first of her
monthly $1,432 Social Security checks had arrived.

"An autopsy is performed by Dr Koponen, the medical examiner for the state of Georgia," continued Head.
"He finds calcium oxalate crystals in the kidneys, so he
suspects ethylene glycol poisoning. He asks that toxicology perform tests in the blood for the presence of ethylene glycol. The lab reported an insignificant quantity. So
he reported the death as cardiac dysrhythmia, heart
failure—the same as Glenn Turner."

He told how Randy Thompson's parents had raised
questions about his death and how the medical examiner
subsequently learned that a Cobb County police officer
had died in 1995 in parallel conditions. "That young policeman was married to Lynn Turner at the time of his
death. The discovery prompted Dr. Koponen to contact
the Cobb County medical examiner. As a result of his
call, the blood, urine and tissue samples of both men
were tested and retested. The toxicologist revisited his
data and discovered that he had miscalculated.

"Because of the similarities between the two deaths in
two separate jurisdictions, the Georgia Bureau of Investigation was also requested to handle both inquiries," he
said. He then told the jury about Glenn's body being exhumed. After his tissues had been tested by another laboratory and again by the GBI, the two medical examiners
now agreed: the manner of death for Randy Thompson
and Glenn Turner were both victims of a homicide.

Head began calling witnesses. First to take the stand
was Donald Cawthon. He told the jury that he and Glenn
had been hard-working, hard-playing young guys who,
along with another couple of buddies, were known as
"the Rat Pack." There were no secrets between him and

Glenn—they shared everything. "We didn't skip any issues," he testified.

Glenn had been a happy-go-lucky sort of guy, an easy-
going softy who fell hard for Lynn Womack and ignored
his buddies when they tried to talk him out of marrying
her. "He loved her," Donald said. Even after the marriage
had hit the skids, he'd hung in there trying to make it
work. It had been no secret that Lynn spent money as if it
grew on trees; the couple was plagued by bills, and to pay
them off, his friend worked around the clock.

Donald told the court that his buddies had suspected
that Lynn was playing Glenn for a fool. Glenn had admitted to him that the marriage was sexless, and eighteen
months after the wedding, exhausted from juggling two
jobs, he had made up his mind to leave. "He told me he
was going to file for divorce."

Under cross-examination Donald was quizzed about
his often-vented suspicions that Lynn had killed Glenn.
"Whom did you take your complaint to?" he was asked.
"I took it to the professionals, that's who I took my complaint to," he replied. "I expected them to do their job."

Cynthia McGhee, who'd worked with Lynn as a 911
dispatcher in Marietta, told the jury about being in the
Crystal Chandelier after Glenn and Lynn were married
and seeing Lynn hitting on another cop. "She tried to talk
him into leaving with her." On the day Glenn was buried,
she and some others had heard Lynn ask another police
officer, " 'Are you coming over tonight?' " Our jaws
dropped," Cynthia said.

"I didn't see any emotion in her whatsoever when
Glenn died. She wasn't crying or upset." Cynthia also told
the court that one day at work, she'd been intrigued to see
Lynn poring over a fat red copy of the *Physicians' Desk
Reference.* "When I asked her about it, she said she was
interested in medicine and how it worked in the body."

On Monday morning, after the weekend break, Mike

Archer took the stand. "Glenn said he was kaput with her. He had worked three hundred and sixty-five days and he didn't have a penny to show for it." Mike also told the court that Glenn had complained that his sex life was nonexistent after the disastrous honeymoon. He said that Glenn had told him that during one of their many rows, Lynn had spat out that she'd never loved him. "He said he was going to move out and live with his father."

Jimmy Berry tried some damage control. "The police department is a kind of rumor mill, isn't it? You guys are always together, you do things together and rumors spread. Were there a lot of rumors about Lynn?" he asked. "There were rumors about Lynn floating around at the time," Mike confirmed.

The parade of Glenn's coworkers and friends giving evidence carried on through Tuesday. David Dunkerton testified that a couple of months before Glenn died, he'd said, "If anything happens to me, look at Lynn." David hadn't been unduly worried about the prophetic remark at the time. "He was twice her size, I knew she wasn't going to beat him up."

Bobby Fisher recalled the conversation he'd had with Glenn just ten days before he died. "He told me that Lynn and him had gotten into a verbal altercation and that she made a threat to harm him. He said she had threatened to shoot him with his own service weapon."

The defense had had enough. The first two days had been powerful. The jury had sat spellbound as cops, so tough and unflappable on the job, had been overcome with emotion on the stand. Some had tears openly streaming down their faces as they remembered Glenn. Others bit their lips. All of them shared an obvious affection for the man they called, "a big teddy bear," "my best friend" and someone who "always looked on the bright side of things."

It was pretty obvious to Jimmy Berry what the prosecution was trying to accomplish. Since they had no hard

facts with which to prove their case, no confession or
eye-witnesses to Glenn's murder, they were painting his
client as the wife from hell, a raptor who sunk her talons
into a beloved officer who'd had the personality of a
saint, and emasculated him until he was powerless to resist her. And now here was a cop claiming that she had
even put her husband on notice that she would kill him.

"This incident, where Lynn threatened to shoot Glenn,
did you file a report about it?" Berry asked him.

"No."

"Why not?"

"I felt it was Glenn's personal business," Fisher answered.

The effect of Berry's effort faded as witness after witness painted a picture of a woman devoid of human
emotion.

Stacy Hendrix Roaderick, who'd been maid of honor at
the wedding, said Lynn had told her that when Glenn was
sick the only foods he could hold down were Popsicles and
Jell-O, so she was feeding him plates of the stuff. Pat Head
then asked her, "How did Lynn act at the funeral?"

"She was very calm, she didn't cry." Lynn had been
decked out in a hot-pink suit, Roaderick claimed.

When she'd finished, Berry was on his feet. What
color was the suit again? After a few pointed questions,
her conviction wavered as Stacy admitted she wasn't sure
about the suit after all. But Berry was. "It was pale gray,"
he told the jury.

On Wednesday, Samantha Garman Butler and Terry
Pruitt described the cruise that had been Lynn's 27th
birthday gift to Randy. When they'd said they couldn't
afford the trip, she'd paid. Pruitt testified that Lynn had
forked out $2,400 for the fares alone. Samantha Butler
said that over the next couple of years, they had drifted
apart, but after she'd heard about Randy's death she had

called Lynn to offer her condolences. Lynn had told her that the night before he died she had given him Jell-O. When they talked Lynn was still smarting from what she perceived as a snub from Randy's family. "She said she was treated like an outcast at the funeral and that Randy's ex-wife sat up front with them."

Glenn's sister, Linda Hardy, was called next. Her loathing for her sister-in-law was palpable. She told the jury that Lynn had pursued her brother relentlessly. When they married in August 1993, the whole Turner family had turned out in force at the wedding to wish the couple luck.

Pat Head asked her to tell the jury about a conversation she'd had with Glenn about two weeks before he died.

"He was sitting on my couch and he made a statement that Lynn was moving to Cumming and that he was staying in Cobb County. He said he was in the process of deciding where he was going to live because he had no interest in the home, so he was making plans to move either to my father's or to [his friend] Jeff Mack's mother's home."

"Would you have offered him a place in your home?" asked Head.

"That was a given," she replied. "But he hadn't made up his mind at that point in time. That's a big thing for anybody to go through."

Head asked her to cast her mind back to the phone call she'd received from Lynn on the night Glenn died. He produced a piece of paper in a clear plastic envelope. Head asked her if she recognized it. "Yes, sir, this is the piece of paper I was writing notes on when she made the phone call to me on the Friday night," said Linda.

"And to the best of your knowledge, did you try to write down everything she told you?" the D.A. wanted to know.

"I tried to write it fast because I was in a panic and wrote it down the best I could."

"Referring to your notes there, so you see 'three o'clock' followed by the words, 'Flipped out'?" he asked.

"Yes, sir. That meant three A.M. She told me Glenn flipped out. Right below is where he broke the lamp and right below that, he thought he could fly off the porch, and it keeps going," she said, deciphering her scribbles for him.

"Okay, do you see another series of words there starting with 'nosebleed'?"

"Yes, sir. She had told me he had a nosebleed and was throwing up; that he had two fluids, IV fluids, shots and he drank something—this was all at the hospital—and that his blood pressure was real high," answered Linda. She added that her sister-in-law had reeled off a list of the medications he had taken, then started to give her a rundown of Glenn's condition in the days prior to his death. Linda had been so shell-shocked that she couldn't write down what Lynn was telling her fast enough.

"Are there some notations that indicate nine o'clock?" Head asked.

"The Friday morning, she said that Glenn had gotten up and was feeling better, he ate some Jell-O. She had errands to run and she left the home between nine and nine thirty, and when she returned, she found him dead in his bed," Linda told him.

In an effort to pinpoint Linda's antipathy to her sister-in-law as stemming from the disputed PEBSCO account, which had eventually been settled when she and Lynn agreed to share it equally, Vic Reynolds asked, "You and his wife split the proceeds of that account. Correct?"

They did, Linda confirmed.

"And since your brother passed away, I presume that your contact with Lynn Turner has been extremely limited, if any. Correct?"

"I have had contact with her," Linda replied. "May I explain?"

If Reynolds was looking for a brief "yes" or "no," he was out of luck. Judge Bodiford was not about to cut her off.

"After his death, we tried to get some of his belongings. We got a few little bags full of clothes, I sent her letters asking repeatedly, very kindly, for some of his personal things, even the book where people who went to the funeral signed in. We did not have any idea who went to the funeral."

Linda testified that Glenn's family never did receive any of Glenn's treasured mementos. "I even got a thank-you note for going to my own brother's funeral, but she wouldn't send me any of that. She did send me some of the wedding photos and a teddy bear and a flag [from the burial service] but not any of his other belongings. We did not get anything to remember him with."

When Linda's testimony finished on Thursday morning, Randy Thompson's stepfather took the stand and Jack Mallard took over for the prosecution. He asked Perry to tell the jury about Christmas 1994, when his son's supposedly divorced girlfriend showed up Christmas Eve with a carload of parcels for Randy and everyone in his family. The gifts were so lavish—he instanced the $1,100 cowboy boots his son had happily strutted around in—that Perry had felt embarrassed accepting them.

Perry Thompson admitted that Randy had taken an overdose of sleeping pills back in March 1999. Then two years later, when his relationship with Lynn was at its most poisonous, Randy had called him in the middle of the night. "I've taken some pills," he'd said. His friend had rushed him to the hospital, but after Randy's stomach was pumped, Perry and Nita had been allowed to take him home.

"Do you have an opinion as to whether Randy, your son, was of the frame of mind to have committed suicide?" asked Mallard.

"He wanted to get things worked out [with Lynn] because of the children. And, well, he had gotten back into church. Randy was raised in the Church and we are not devout—I don't know what the word is, we are not that strict with religion. But we believe in the right things. Randy was raised that way. He had gone back to that and the Christian way of life, and he had become saved. And he was in the process of going through EMT school at the time. He had failed the course once and he was so determined to get that diploma and finish that course, so he had gone back to do it again. He completed it prior to his death. We received his diploma a couple of weeks after he died," said Perry.

"So he was an EMT at the time [he died]? He had been certified?" asked Mallard.

"Yes, sir."

"Let me ask about the family and children. He has how many children?"

"He has three," said Perry.

"What about the first one?"

"Nicholas is twelve now, by his first wife—his only wife."

"And did he have anything to do with Nicholas?" asked Mallard.

"They were extremely close, extremely close. He saw Nicholas on a very regular basis and brought him down to see us on a regular basis," replied Perry.

"Did he love his two children with Lynn Turner?"

"Yes, sir, he did."

"I'll ask you, in your opinion, what is your opinion regarding his state of mind as to whether or not he would take his own life?" asked Mallard.

"I think Randy had every desire in the world to live. We

are an extremely close family, all of us. My children and my wife and I, and Randy, had bad times just like anybody, but Randy was not that type of person to be suicidal."

"Is there any way, in your opinion, that he would drink antifreeze and kill himself?" Mallard prodded.

"No," said Perry flatly.

During her testimony, Randy's sister Angie described going shopping with Lynn. Money seemed to be no object. She testified that Lynn had told her she'd inherited a stack of cash from her grandmother. "What did she tell you about Glenn Turner?" she was asked. "She said he died in the line of duty. I didn't question it and she didn't offer anything additional."

After the emotional testimony of Linda Hardy and Randy's family, the prosecution called Samantha Gilleland, the manager of the Orr Animal Hospital, a Forsyth County animal shelter. She told the court that in the spring of 1999, after her relationship with Randy had become unglued, Lynn had shown up at the shelter and asked her what happens when an animal swallows antifreeze.

Jimmy Berry objected vehemently. After the judge ordered the courtroom cleared to hear his protest, Berry told him, "I think [her testimony] is calculated to bring in emotion even more than it's already been brought into the case. To put something like that in is devastating and it has no correlation to anything in reality."

But his plea fell on deaf ears; the judge overruled him and had the jury brought back in. Gilleland said that Lynn had appeared at the shelter after a horrible animal cruelty case had been in the news that had seemingly touched her heart. She wanted to play with the rescued creatures. On her first visit to the shelter, and according to Samantha Gilleland she made several, they had talked about antifreeze. "We discussed the stray cat problem she was having at the time, and she asked if the antifreeze had the same effect on cats as it did on dogs. I couldn't tell her, no one had ever asked me that before."

Samantha added that she had advised Lynn to trap the strays and bring them to the shelter to be put to sleep. "She wanted to know how the euthanasia process went and I explained that it was an injection. She asked me what we used, but I didn't know the name of it, I just called it 'the purple stuff.' She asked me if anyone could get it, and I told her, 'No, it is a controlled substance.'"

"Did she ever ask the name of 'the purple stuff'?" Berry wanted to know.

"No."

Berry asked how Lynn had reacted to Gilleland's advice about catching the strays.

"She thought it was kind of cruel to trap them only to put them down."

Samantha had forgotten about the visits until the investigation into Glenn's death hit her local news and she recognized Lynn on TV. "I told my sister, 'I know her, that's the woman who asked about antifreeze and cats.'" Then she'd called the police.

As he listened to her testimony, Donald Cawthon's mind went into overdrive. "I always wondered what happened to her dogs," he recalls thinking. "They were huge dogs—one of them weighed about one hundred and eight pounds. I never knew what happened to them. I can see her feeding them antifreeze to see how much it took to kill them."

To him, it wasn't much of a leap to imagine that she would then gauge the poison's effect on a human test subject. With Samantha Gilleland's description of Lynn's turning up at the sanctuary for no obvious concrete reason, like adopting a pet or to have an injured animal treated, her pointed questions on how to get hold of the euthanasia drug and how it was administered took on a sinsister meaning. Then her honing in specifically on antifreeze, wanting to know if the veterinary workers had any experience with treating animals that had swallowed the poison—suddenly it all clicked into place for him. Lynn had been doing her homework!

"I could see Lynn going into a bar and feeding someone antifreeze too, just to see whether it kills them or not, then reading the newspaper or checking the Internet to read the article on his death. And if the ME's office don't find it, she thinks, 'I got my tool,' " Donald says. "I think she was poisoning Glenn for a long period of time. He really didn't use any sick leave until that year, and he used up a lot of sick leave. She was poisoning him little by little, but he wasn't dying and she thought, 'Damn! I'll load him up on this.'

"I had a cat that died and the vet said it could have been antifreeze or a disease cats get. I asked if he could find out, and he said, 'If it's antifreeze it's hard to detect.' I think she did her research. Somewhere while working for the county Lynn found out that if you give someone antifreeze, they'll never find it unless they are looking for it."

Donald was convinced she was going down, but Lynn was acting like a woman with nothing to fear. "At the trial she'd stand in the hallway and gave me 'Eat shit' looks," he says. During breaks in the proceedings she would laugh and joke with her family and friends, and stare down Linda or Kathy when she brushed into them in the bathroom. Her attitude had seasoned court officers scratching their heads.

"The deputies and court personnel told me, 'This lady is walking around as if she's at some weekend picnic or something. She acts like she doesn't have a care in the world. She's walking around with this big old smile as if all this is bullshit.' She was like, 'How dare you waste my time having to come down here?' I really believe she thought she was going to get away with it," he says.

Her confident mind-set came across on camera. It forcibly struck J. L. McMichael, who was glued to Court TV coverage in his living room in Florida, where he'd moved in November 2002. "When the trial began, I thought of going up there, but they would have ended up throwing me out of the courtroom. I watched it on television. I just wanted to choke or squeeze her fricking neck off. She was sitting there like she was 'it.' I thought, If I could get ahold of you, I'd break your neck, girl. Nancy Grace called her a Black Widow, and that's exactly what she is."

The jury had Thursday night to mull over Samantha Gilleland's stunning testimony. On Friday morning, May 7, they heard from Randy's ex-wife, now Dara Laughlin. She described the phone call she'd received after his death, after Lynn had found out that he had not been making his insurance payments. "How could be so irresponsible?" Lynn had burst out angrily.

Dara was followed by Forsyth County firefighter Sergeant Casey Tatum. On cross, Berry's partner, Vic Reynolds, wanted to know about Randy's state of mind shortly before he'd died. Tatum emphatically denied the suggestion that Randy had committed suicide. Reynolds then began to challenge how much he really knew about his friend's mounting troubles. "Did you know that Randy was taking between twenty and thirty pills a day for his staph infection?" He then proceeded to list painkillers and drugs for depression. He asked Tatum if he knew that Dara Laughlin had been suing Randy for arrears in child support payments for their two children, or that he had fallen behind with both rent and car payments.

In the middle of the trial, James Turner received a shocking e-mail. "It was from someone who said she was a relative of Lynn's. She wouldn't tell me who she was. She said she lived in the Marietta area, lived very close to Lynn. She had known Glenn. She said that she was not surprised [when Lynn was arrested] because she had thought for a long time that [Lynn] had done something to him." The mystery e-mailer wrote that there were strange goings-on at Lynn's house and at a relative's who lived close by, she would see new stereo equipment going in and out. "She said, and she used these terms, they were even doing drugs," says James.

"I e-mailed her back: 'I would like to talk to you and the D.A. would like to talk to you. Give me a number where I can reach you.' It took her a day and a half to get back and she said, 'I am sorry, and I am sorry for what she did to Glenn, but I can't be involved.' I never heard from her again."

CHAPTER FIFTEEN:
The Verdict

Refreshed by spending the spring weekend with their families, the jury filed in on May 10, bracing themselves for a day of detailed and sometimes baffling testimony from forensic scientists and medical experts.

Cobb County Medical Examiner Dr. Brian Frist admitted that he had been perplexed by Glenn Turner's enlarged heart—at 500 grams it was 150 grams heavier than normal. Dr. Frist had noticed some calcium oxalate crystals in his tissues, but, he said, "I didn't pay much attention to them."

He testified that he had been sure of his diagnosis of heart failure until he heard about Randy Thompson. The circumstances of Randy's death and his connection with the defendant had prompted the exhumation of Glenn Turner. When ethylene glycol was discovered in his retested tissue, he became convinced that Glenn had died from poisoning. But to be sure of that, he had to satisfy himself that somone could unknowingly swallow enough of the deadly chemical to kill him.

He bought a container of Firestone Antifreeze, a brand available in any local auto supply store, and poured it into the same things several witnesses testified Lynn Turner had fed her husband in the days before he died.

As he spoke and over the objections of the defense, a slide show of Lemon-Lime Gatorade, green Jell-O, iced tea and chicken soup was played for the jury. The jurors were shown two seemingly identical glasses of Gatorade and were told one contained antifreeze, the other did not. While the antifreeze didn't prevent the Jell-O from setting or discolor the other liquids—information that had Berry and Reynolds squirming with annoyance—there was only one way to test how it tasted, and that was to sample it himself. He described how he'd dipped his finger in iced tea laced with antifreeze and licked it. "It tasted like sweet tea. Then I rinsed out my mouth."

Dr. Mark Koponen told the jury that he had seen cases of ethylene glycol poisoning prior to performing the autopsy on Randy Thompson, so when he'd discovered calcium oxalate crystals in Randy's kidneys, warning bells went off. And when he'd received the initial results from the lab confirming the presence of a minute amount of crystals, but certainly not enough to have killed a man, he'd been stumped. "I was incredulous," he said. After learning that Dr. Frist over in Cobb County had also found crystals in Glenn's liver six years before, Koponen ordered the tests to be run again. This time, like Frist, he no longer had any doubt. Both men had been poisoned, and the likeliest culprit was an over-the-counter commercial auto antifreeze.

The defense fired back: surely any of the six prescription medicines Randy was taking could have caused his death? In the weeks before his death, hadn't he downed a potentially dangerous cocktail of antibiotics for his staph infection that included assorted pain medications, an anti-anxiety pill and Xanax? "If he took too much pain medication, it might make him appear to be intoxicated, but it wouldn't have caused his death," countered Dr. Koponen. Xanax was "difficult to overdose on," he added.

Next to testify was the state's chief medical examiner,

Dr. Kris Sperry. He assessed as nil the likelihood of Glenn's and Randy's deaths being a coincidental stroke of sheer bad luck. "There are really no coincidences in life," he said. These were the only homicides by antifreeze poisoning in the state of Georgia.

"If there are similarities between the two situations, there is a reason why these exist," he maintained. Thompson probably drank the deadly antifreeze mix twice, once before he was hospitalized and the other shortly before he died. "It was the second dose that ultimately killed him," he said.

"Could you die from cumulative doses?" Pat Head asked.

"Yes. Over a relatively short period of time, the damage accumulates to the point where it could cause death. For most adults, a hundred milliliters, or three ounces, is enough to kill you. But there are adult deaths from as little as an ounce," he said. "If someone gets medical care quickly, there's a better chance of survival."

Vic Reynolds went on the attack. The GBI labs were not above making mistakes. It was one of their pathologists, Chris Tilson, who'd admitted on the stand that he had misplaced a decimal point the first time around. When he ran subsequent tests, his new findings showed 380 milligrams of the toxic substance per liter in Randy's urine, ten times larger than the 38 milligrams per liter he had previously noted. "It was a mathematical error and I took full responsibility for the mistake," Tilson testified. He had realized his blunder in September 2002 and retested the urine samples. When his results showed elevated amounts from his original findings, he also retested the blood.

Reynolds then waved a document at Tilson. It was a report on chemicals in embalming fluids and some contained ethylene glycol, he said. One brand he had in mind contained as much as 55 percent of the stuff!

The prosecution shot down the likelihood of antifreeze seeping into the men's livers on the mortician's slab with witnesses from the Dodge chemical company and Pierce Chemicals, both of which had supplied embalming fluids to the Patterson Funeral Home where Glenn's body was taken in 1995. Under oath, spokesmen for both firms denied that their products contained ethylene glycol. "I have looked back in our records to 1988, and we have never purchased it," said Mark DeBenedetto, the senior chemist at Dodge.

They were followed on the stand by a forensic scientist at National Medical Services, William Dunn. "Would you expect ethylene glycol to be found in a normal human liver?" asked Assistant District Attorney Bryan Lumpkin.

"No I would not," he replied.

"The fact that Mr. Turner had been embalmed, does that cause you any concern?"

"No, it does not," Dunn shook his head emphatically.

The defense then brought out toxicologist Dr. Robert Palmer, who had a private practice in Colorado. According to him, the three stages of poisoning that Pat Head had outlined for the jury in his opening remarks were no more than a useful but superficial version of what actually happens.

"Unfortunately we all know that everybody is an individual, and patients don't read the textbooks and they don't follow the rules to the stages of a poisoning," he said.

"The first stage, what would that normally be called?" asked Jimmy Berry, dazzling in a white suit.

"The first stage is often referred to either as the inebriation stage or the central nervous system stage." Anyone who's taken it would look drunk, he explained. "They get a little stumbly, a little wobbly."

"And during that first stage, would that be when one would be throwing up?" asked Berry.

"It's an automotive product and if you took a big enough drink of it, probably that would cause you to throw up, yes," said Dr. Palmer.

Berry wanted to know if calcium oxalate could have come from the embalming fluids or flowers or anything else decomposing in a coffin. "A number of plants have oxalate in them. The plants supply the oxalate, you supply the calcium and you have calcium oxalate crystals," the toxicologist testified. "But since the crystals were found in Glenn Turner's kidneys, they should have been in his other organs too. Since they aren't, I can't say for certain that he ingested ethylene glycol before he died. I don't believe the evidence supports the cause of death."

Later, in a crucial about-face, when he was being cross-examined, Dr. Palmer was asked to review Randy's blood and urine tests. He had never seen them before, he admitted. After poring over them for several minutes, he agreed that Randy Thompson must have died from drinking antifreeze.

On Wednesday, May 12, Detective Charlie Mazariegos told the jury that when he arrived at the house on the morning of Glenn's death, Lynn had spun the tale of waking in the middle of the night to find Glenn threatening to fly off the top of the second-floor deck. She'd followed him down to the basement and grabbed a container of gasoline that he wanted to drink, out of his hand. As he spoke, the jurors were looking at a photograph, taken in the Turners' basement, of a red gas can and a bottle of blue antifreeze.

Jim Berry went to work. Under cross-examination, he forced Mazariegos, a Vietnam vet, who had been the lead detective on the case, to admit he hadn't taken the antifreeze into evidence. After listening to Lynn's tale, he had smelled Glenn's breath and was satisfied he had not drunk any gasoline.

"Did you at least check to see if the container had been opened?" he asked.

"No."

He didn't fare any better when asked where things were located in the house. His memory and his answers were fuzzy.

"Aren't you trained to look for everything?" Berry goaded him.

But Charlie Mazariegos was not vague about the scene he had walked into that early Friday afternoon back in March 1995. As he described what he had found, the jurors were shown pictures of Glenn on his bed. The images were distressing: rigor mortis had already set in, his face was discolored and there was froth around his mouth, a common occurrence in people who die of poisoning. His family looked away, unable to bear the agony of seeing him as "evidence." Mazariegos testified that since no signs of foul play had been discovered, no further investigation was deemed necessary.

As a procession of cops trotted to the stand and backed that conclusion, Glenn's family gritted their teeth. "I lost a lot of respect for the Cobb County Police Department," says James. "I always had the utmost respect for law enforcement in general, and especially them. That's where he [Glenn] worked at, and they didn't do their job."

The prosecution then honed in on the money. They paraded a line of witnesses from banks and insurance companies to testify to the deep financial hole Lynn had dug for herself, and to demonstrate her deep interest in her husband's and her lover's life insurance policies. They produced documents and phone records to confirm her numerous calls.

Former cop turned insurance agent Vince Turley testified that Glenn, whom he'd known as a fellow officer, had called him in September 1993 saying he wanted to alter the beneficiary on his life insurance from his mom to his wife. As they'd chatted, Glenn admitted that it was his wife who had prompted the call. "I didn't do it right away and he called again. He said Lynn was all over his back to get it changed."

The day after he was buried, Lynn had called via the 800 number to find out how to collect. On April 12 she had turned up at the Metropolitan Life offices and submitted a signed claim form. Turley said MetLife had handed over checks for a total of $110,000.

In an attempt to portray his client as something far removed from a greedy predator, Vic Reynolds called Helen Gregory to the stand.

She told the court that since Lynn's arrest, she'd been looking after her grandchildren. How were they dealing with the trauma of having their mother tried for murder? Reynolds wanted to know.

"Lynn sat the children down and explained what was going on, and they understand. They're okay with what's happening," she replied. "I am trying to let them lead a normal life, getting them off to school and taking care of them."

"Would you describe your daughter as an emotional person?" asked Reynolds.

"No, she is not," Helen shook her head.

"What do you mean by that?"

"She just does not show openly her feelings or her emotions. I mean, it's all done privately," she said.

"Is that similar to anyone else in the family?" he asked.

"We're all that way," she told him.

"Obviously you knew Glenn Turner?"

"Glenn? Oh yes, he was my son-in-law," she said.

"Did he and your family get along pretty well?" Reynolds wanted to know.

"Yes, sir," Helen nodded.

"Did you have occasion to spend very much time with Glenn and Lynn?"

"I spent a great deal of time with them. They would come and have lunch with me at the office and I would visit them at home," she assured him.

"How did you learn that Glenn had passed away?" asked Reynolds.

"Someone called my home identifying himself as a deputy, I don't recall his name, and he asked me to come . . ." she said, her words trailing off.

"Don't tell us what he told you," Reynolds cautioned. "But based on what the conversation was, what did you do?"

"I got a telephone call to come to her house. I immediately left the office and went to Lynn's home. It was full of police officers and people," said Helen. "When I went in the front door, I could see her, she was sitting at her dining room table."

"Did you go to her?" he asked.

"I went to her immediately," replied Helen. "She was crying hysterically and I asked her what was wrong and she didn't respond. And I grabbed— She had her arms up and I grabbed her arms and I shook her and said, 'Lynn, what is wrong, honey? Tell me what is wrong.' And she just said, 'He's dead.' That's all she ever got out."

"She was crying?" Reynolds asked.

"She was hysterical," repeated her mother.

"Did you stay there with her for a while?" he pressed on.

"I stayed there until I took her home with me that night."

"Were you with her at the funeral home?" he asked.

"All the time," she replied.

"What was her behavior at the funeral home, Mrs. Gregory, do you remember that?"

"Lynn reacts when she's upset. Her voice rises and

she speaks in a loud tone, and that's the way I know when she's under a lot of pressure. She did speak in a higher tone than normal and I knew it was her way of, you know, her emotions. But she just does not cry openly," Helen told the court.

"Now on that occasion at the funeral home, Glenn's body was lying in state?" asked Reynolds. "Did Lynn go into where Glenn's body was?"

"No," replied Helen. "She will not go in where a body is. My mother passed away, who Lynn loved better than life. I believe she loved my mother more than she does me. And when she passed away, she fell to the floor in the hospital and cried, and I asked the nurse if they could give her something, she was so emotional. But from that period on, she never shed another tear or showed any emotion other than I could hear her crying at night."

"Did it strike you as unusual that Lynn didn't go to where Glenn's body was?" he wanted to know.

"No, not at all, because I have four brothers who passed away, my mother, my mother-in-law passed away, and she had never gone into a room with a body," she said.

"Did you go to the grave site and funeral the following day? Were you with Lynn?" asked Reynolds.

"Yes."

"Do you recall anything, to your memory, out of the ordinary or disrespectful by anybody there?"

"I did not see anything disrespectful," said Helen firmly.

Reynolds then moved on to Randy Thompson.

"Is he the father of your grandchildren?"

"Yes," she replied.

"Was the relationship on and off between him and Lynn?" he asked.

"He would get this feeling of wanting to leave for a period of time and then come back. But I never did get involved in their affairs at home. Mostly, when I was around, they were happy and I didn't see anything wrong," she maintained.

Helen described the morning when Lynn had called her to tell her that Randy's firefighter pals were going to batter down the door to his apartment. She told of rushing out of her office and racing down to Lynn's.

Vic Reynolds asked what she'd seen when she got there.

"Lynn was just bouncing on the floor and crying hysterically," she told him. "I stayed with her for several hours that morning while different people who worked in the courthouse came by."

"Were there any services held for him in your county?"

"No. Well, there was a memorial service after his burial," she replied.

"Did you attend that?" asked Reynolds.

"Yes, I went with Lynn," she said.

"And what was her state, emotionally, during that service, ma'am?" he said, trying to coax out an affirmation that Lynn was not devoid of feelings.

"She cried throughout the entire service," she said.

"Thank you, ma'am." Reynolds sat down, pleased with Helen's testimony.

At the bench, and out of earshot of the jury, A.D.A. Russ Parker told the judge he wanted to press Helen about her statement that none of the family normally displayed emotion in public, specifically, "We're all that way." That implied that Lynn was a biological child instead of being adopted, therefore her lack of feeling could not have been inherited, he argued.

"Judge, it has nothing to do with whether she was adopted or not," Reynolds protested.

"Let me think about it and I will give you the answer in thirty seconds," said Judge Bodiford, waving them back to their benches.

"Okay, the answer is no. I will not allow that," he decided.

Parker knew attacking Helen would only engender sympathy for Lynn Turner, but he seized the opportunity to drive one nail home. Questioning her about driving Glenn and her daughter to the emergency room, he said pointedly, "So, he wouldn't have gone to the hospital at all if you hadn't taken him?"

He also asked about the presence of Paul Rushing by Lynn's side at Glenn's funeral. "We stayed as a crowd," explained Helen.

"Did you hear your daughter ask several people to go out and have a few beers afterwards?" he asked.

"No, she did not," Helen said firmly.

The officer whose closeness to Lynn brought him under scrutiny from the prosecution and his colleagues on the force, came to her defense. Under oath, Paul Rushing recounted how they had become friendly when they both worked the same shift. The thirteen-year veteran cop told the jury he had been at both viewing days and Glenn's funeral. "Helen asked me to sit with them. I explained the request to one of my superiors and I accompanied [Lynn and her family] through the funeral and graveside services."

"Did you leave with her?" asked Vic Reynolds.

"No, sir, I left with my wife. She was there through the funeral and the graveside services. I rode to the funeral with my wife."

"Officer Rushing, have you been involved in any intimate way with Lynn Turner?"

"Other than friendship? No, sir."

"Have you been involved in any type of physical or sexual way with Lynn Turner?" pressed Reynolds.

"No, sir," he said again.

He said he had been interviewed three times by Cobb

County homicide detectives in connection with Glenn's death. Russ Parker rose to his feet; his mission was to rebut Reynolds' portrayal of Rushing as Lynn's "pal."

"I believe you are sort of a motorcycle enthusiast?"

"Yes, sir, almost to a fault," agreed Rushing.

"Would it be fair to say that you and Lynn Turner rode motorcycles together?" Parker wanted to know.

"Yes, sir, we had ridden motorcycles on a number of occasions together."

"Have you ridden up to Cumming, Georgia, together?" asked Parker.

"I don't know that we ever went to Cumming. We may have gone that one time when she bought a motorcycle— No, I'm sorry, that was Sandy Springs," Rushing corrected himself.

"Have you ridden together in other areas around the metro area of Atlanta?" asked Parker.

"Yes, sir, we have."

"And did Glenn at one point ask you not to spend so much time with his wife?"

"No, sir."

"He never asked you that?" said Parker incredulously.

"No, sir, he actually encouraged it," claimed Rushing.

"He liked you to ride with his wife?"

"Yes, sir. He didn't have time and didn't like her riding by herself," Rushing replied.

Parker moved on. "Did you go to Lynn Turner's house the day Glenn Turner was found deceased?"

"Yes, I did."

"Were you off duty?"

"No, sir, I was not. I had worked a morning shift."

"Who called to notify you that Glenn had died?" asked Parker.

"Lynn made the phone call and after about two words, she had to pass the phone off to somebody else."

"Did your wife Melinda go with you?" asked Parker.

"No, she was at work."

"You didn't go by and get her?"

"No, sir, I was on a motorcycle and it was raining," answered Rushing.

"Did you help Lynn put a message on her answering machine?"

"I don't remember. I may have. I did just about anything she asked me to do that day," said Rushing.

"At the funeral home, do you remember Lynn getting upset about an American flag on the casket?" asked Parker.

"No, sir, not specifically."

"Was she upset about anything?"

"Her husband had died, yes, sir, she was upset," said Rushing.

They bantered back and forth over what Lynn was angry about, but Rushing wouldn't bite. Parker tried a different tack.

"After the viewing, did she ask you out for a couple of beers?"

"No, sir," replied Rushing.

Next the prosecutor tried to make something of the fact that Rushing hadn't sat with Melinda at the funeral. Rushing said she was standing with the other policemen's families, as was customary at a funeral where the deceased was buried with full honors. In any case, she was only a few feet away.

"Did you ever hear Lynn say that she had to get the h-e-l-l out of there?" Parker spelled it out.

"Yes, sir, something to that effect after the funeral and the graveside service. Lynn was not in the best of sorts, and she said she needed to get the hell out of there," he confirmed.

"As she was leaving, did she holler over at you to ask if you were coming over tonight?" asked Parker.

"No, sir," said Rushing.

Parker gave it another try. Would he have taken Melinda with him to Lynn's that night?

"If she was with me, she would have gone to Lynn's."

Next he turned to Lynn's boat.

"Have you been up on Lake Lanier with her?"

"Yes, sir, we've been skiing a few times."

"Was your wife along?" asked Parker.

"She came a few times, yes, sir."

"Other times she was not with you while you were with Lynn?"

"That's correct," admitted Rushing. "If schedules didn't allow. I'd get off morning watch. My wife would be at work that day."

He also admitted having dinner with Lynn and without his wife at her favorite LongHorn Steakhouse while the GBI investigation was ongoing.

Before he stepped down, Parker asked Rushing if he thought that two people associated with the same woman dying under the same circumstances was an oddity.

"Yes, sir, that's quite an oddity."

After eleven days, during which the prosecution presented sixty-eight witnesses, the defense rested its case having called on just five. Lynn, who was expected to take the stand in her own defense, remained silent. Watching her intently, James Turner felt that remaining mute was not her choice.

"I think she was itching to get up there and testify, but her attorneys wouldn't let her, because she'd be found guilty because her attitude—everything with her is an act or a show. I don't think Lynn really knows who Lynn is. She was very uppity," he says.

In the break before both sides summed up, a brief conversation with the defense lawyers underlined the decency of the family dragged into this nightmare.

James made a point of seeking out Jimmy Berry. "We, me and my family, we really appreciate you defending Lynn, because whatever the jury comes back with, it's a loss for everybody, nobody is really winning," he told him. But at least I know if the jury says she's guilty, that no one will come back and say it's unfair because you defended her. You are an excellent attorney and she had every opportunity. I don't hold anything against you, you were just doing your job." Berry, visibly moved, said, "James, I really appreciate it, you don't know how much it means."

Facing the jury for the last time, Berry began his closing argument by throwing his eggs all in one basket. He cited his expert, Dr. Palmer, who had asked why Glenn's kidney hadn't been tested. They'd tested the liquid in the bottom of the casket and in the liver.

"I can't tell you how ethylene glycol got in his system," he said, talking directly to the jurors. "I can't tell you that it got into his system before or after death. They brought nobody in to rebut his testimony. I asked, 'From your data and from what you've seen of the Glenn Turner case, can you tell us whether ethylene glycol contributed to the death of Glenn Turner?' His opinion was it did not.

"He said, 'How in the world can somebody drink enough of that stuff to kill 'em and not know that they're drinking it?' They never brought one person in here who says, 'You know, I tried to kill myself one time and I certainly knew that I was drinking something nasty.' They never brought anybody in here to testify about any extensive tasting of this who has survived. We don't know what it tastes like. We don't know what it would taste like in soup, in Gatorade or tea, and we don't even know, the state hasn't even shown to you, exactly what was used.

"The bottom line is, according to Mr. Palmer, there's not enough there for you to be able to say if Glenn died of ethylene glycol poisoning, number one; number two, they did a terrible job of investigating the case.

"It doesn't matter whether you don't like Lynn Turner. It doesn't matter whether you don't like us," he went on. "None of those things matter. What matters is that you follow the rule of law. The judge is going to give you the rule of law, and I hope and pray that you can follow that.

"I'll leave you with this," he concluded. "If you go back into that jury room and you have questions that are unanswered, then the state of Georgia has not proven this case to you beyond reasonable doubt. And I hope and pray that you will find Lynn Turner not guilty of this indictment. Thank you, ladies and gentlemen."

District Attorney Pat Head strode over to the jury box, shaking his head. "You have a better chance of winning the lottery tonight," he said. "The simplest solution is correct: two men died of ethylene glycol poisoning, two men were having a relationship with Lynn Turner.

"Mr. Berry is a master of smoke and mirrors. Don't be fooled by him. Glenn Turner's murder was all about greed, a desperate woman whose financial obligations were threatening to drown her. She had had thirty-five thousand dollars in credit card debts, she's borrowed twenty-four thousand dollars on her home, her debts amounted to one hundred and forty thousand dollars. When she looked at Glenn and Randy, she saw the answer to her problems: an easy three hundred thousand dollars in insurance policies would save her neck. Don't let her get away with it, with murder."

He read aloud a poem written by a famed toxicologist, Dr. John H. Trestrail III. As he recited the words, they flashed across a large screen above a picture of Lynn, her face staring like a deer caught in the headlights, over the

top of a coral pink turtleneck sweater. Above her head
was the title of the work, "The Poisoner."

> *The Borgias, DeMedicis and all those past—*
> *You may have thought you had seen the last.*
>
> *But we poisoners are still around today,*
> *And if you miss my crime, I'll get away.*
>
> *The body lies there neat and clean,*
> *as the cause of death is seldom seen.*
>
> *And the coroner may take time to pause—*
> *is the death due to natural cause?*
>
> *An autopsy or tox screen many reveal death's why,*
> *but I hope the case will just slip by.*
>
> *My crime is quiet and well thought through.*
> *For you're used to violence—can I fool you?*
>
> *The event's rarity is on my side,*
> *For I count on you burying my homicide.*
>
> *And though I roam free 'round the nation,*
> *I live in fear of an exhumation.*
>
> *The clues I leave may be hard to find,*
> *you see, to me, I have a superior mind.*
>
> *My weapons are there before your eyes,*
> *But they are so very small—of molecular size.*
>
> *I don't think you'll have a notion,*
> *For mine is murder in slow motion.*

It gives me time to just slip by,
And create my perfect alibi.

Where to look for me isn't clear.
I may be far, or I may be near.

I could be a stranger, though it is quite rare,
for I'm probably related to the victim there.

I choose the place, the means and time,
for poisoning is usually a household crime.

The knowledge gained by my living close,
made it so very easy to deliver the dose.

Seeing it as poisoning would be profound,
but I think you'll miss it as you look around.

I'm a different kind of killer as you can see.
I am a POISONER—can you catch me?

It took the jury less than five hours to make up their minds.

They had filed into the jury room to begin their deliberation after lunch on Friday, May 14. At 7:30 P.M. they were back in the courtroom, listening to their foreman John Glover say they had found Julia Lynn Turner "guilty of malice murder." Lynn, who moments before had told a Court TV reporter that she was "thinking positively and prepared for any outcome," didn't even blink. She turned to the men and women who'd decided her fate, gave them a look of utter contempt and calmly removed her earrings.

Then just for a fleeting moment, she betrayed her first flicker of emotion, says Donald Cawthon, who had kept his gaze fixed on her. "The only time she batted an eye was on that last day. I was in the back. She walked over to the other side of the courtroom, up the aisle past the mother, and the mother's jaw dropped. You could see she thought, I'm going to jail, and that was it, end of the expression."

As Lynn was led out, her mother's shoulders slumped, her friends and family looked down at the floor in silence. Across the aisle Kathy Turner sat with her arm around Linda. Outside, as the Turners and Thompsons assembled on the courthouse steps, Kathy and Nita fell weeping into each other's arms. When she regained her composure, Kathy told the press, "I was scared of my feelings. Whether she would go down or not. It has been a hard nine years and two months for us. But we feel justice has been served."

She wasn't surprised by her daughter-in-law's lack of remorse. "I expected that from her. She never showed emotion. She is a cold-hearted person. I wish she could have done differently and let Glenn go on and let him be."

Despite their grief, these two bereaved families showed compassion for the woman whose daughter had caused them such pain and who was now about to lose her. "Our thoughts and prayers go out to Lynn's family. They don't want this either. It's a bittersweet day for all of us," said Perry Thompson, adding that he hoped that Lynn would soon face trial in the death of Randy. "That's what we owe our son. He's not here to speak for himself, just as Glenn is not."

The verdict didn't bring any relief to Glenn's best buddy. Particularly galling was the knowledge that, under Georgia law, although she'd been sentenced automatically to life in prison, in just fourteen years, this woman who had killed Glenn could be considered for parole. He was mad that she wasn't going to get a needle stuck in her arm. "It's not going to bring any closure," said Donald. "I'm just sad they didn't go after the death penalty. She deserves it."

CHAPTER SIXTEEN:
The End of the Line

Despite the relative speed of the verdict in what had been a complicated case, initially, it hadn't been unanimous, according to jury foreman John Glover. The first vote was nine to three against Lynn, but as they hammered out all the evidence, the holdouts changed their minds one by one. After several more votes, they were agreed. It hadn't been Lynn Turner's flawed personality, her coldness, her reckless extravagance or even her adulterous affair that had sealed her fate: it was the scientists. They had convinced the jurors that there was only one way antifreeze could be in those men's kidneys and livers—they had to have swallowed it. They didn't believe either victim had drunk it on purpose. The other stuff? "They were all just pieces that fit together," Glover said.

Jimmy Berry immediately cried foul. Though his client may have looked as if ice ran in her veins, he said, "I know she feels it on the inside, but she can't express it very well on the outside." He was still seething over the decision to let details of Randy Thompson's death be introduced into evidence. "We heard more evidence on the Thompson case than the Turner case. If we had tried the Glenn Turner case alone, in my heart I believe the verdict would have been different." He also railed against the decision to allow the poem to hang over Lynn's head as the district attorney made his closing arguments. "We felt it was like she's saying it," he said. It seemed set up to look as if she had written those words.

As the jurors left to begin their weekend, Lynn was removed in handcuffs to begin the first night of her new life as a convicted murderess at the Houston County Detention Center just up the road from the courthouse. Ringing in her ears was prosecutor Jack Mallard's remark that plans for a Forsyth County grand jury to hear testimony against her in the death of Randy were already in the works. "She's not going anywhere," he cautioned ominously.

However, to the disgust of both families, Lynn would continue to profit from Glenn and Randy's deaths. Glenn's pension, now $790, was still paid into her bank account every month. She would also continue getting monthly checks for $1,500 from Social Security for her and Randy's two children. "It's blood money, and she'll get it until the day she dies," said Pat Head. By his estimation, she had already raked in $150,000 since the day she murdered her husband.

The trial may have been over, but it had taken its toll on the families who'd sat through it. James felt they had been so wronged on the case that he quit the bail bond business to become a private investigator. "The trial was an emotional roller coaster," he says. "Even if you have a slamdunk case, you just never know what these twelve jurors are going to say. It was heartbreaking to sit and listen to different things, but the most disheartening thing was the fact that when the actual officers took the stand—they didn't do anything.

"The first responding officer on the scene, he left shortly after the paramedics and all got there. Because he was so upset that they were not handling it as a crime scene, he left, and was ordered to come back. He said then he went to the homicide investigators and he said, 'You got to look into this,' and they told him, 'You're wrong, she didn't do nothing.'"

It seemed to James that Glenn's colleagues on the CCPD failed him, just as had the other professionals who could have done something to save him or at the very least solve his murder. James says he was staggered by the testimony of the hospital personnel. "It's just amazing that so many people could make so many mistakes and not actually be involved together. The RN at the hospital testified that she had said, 'Do not let this man go. You need to admit him: there's something wrong.'" James also wonders what happened at the medical examiner's office. "If I was [the M.E.] and was told there's nothing wrong by the police department, who are not medical people, and we got a thirty-one-year-old healthy man with no medical issues, he's a police officer, in good physical condition and he's dead, I'd think, There's something wrong," he says.

But what really sticks in his craw is that everyone had been okay with Lynn's story. "I've studied the autopsy report, the police report, I was at the trial. And it don't make no sense," he says. "She said he attempted to drink what appeared to be gasoline out of a glass container in the basement. Well, for a start, what is an open glass container of gasoline doing there? Then she works for nine-one-one, she's got someone delirious and she has no medical training, she knows the first thing she should do is to call nine-one-one. Then she told the investigators he's attempting to jump off the balcony and the only reason she knows this is because he woke her up. Yet she puts him back to sleep and she goes back to sleep. What if he does it again and it doesn't wake her up?"

Instead of treating her like any other member of the public, the authorities allowed their sympathy for her to cloud their judgment. "If they had done just one interview, it would have opened up a can of worms. They never interviewed her—they didn't do shit to her. That's what really irritated me. I raised hell on the phone that night. I said she had done something, and they didn't interview her or check one of her damn stories out—that's what threw red flags up to me."

He wonders if she had some pull with somebody in authority, if she knew a guilty secret. There were rumors about her being entangled with some high-ranking officers. "If she had some dirt like that, Lynn would have screamed it in a heartbeat if they had tried to do something. All they had to do was interview her formally. Her story was shot full of holes, she was seeing other people and he was leaving her. And there was financial gain. It was all about money. If they had done their job, Randy would still be alive."

Five days after being found guilty, 35-year-old Lynn encountered maximum security Metro State Prison for women in Atlanta. As she was being processed into the system, Cobb County officials were looking for a way to stop her receiving another dime from Glenn's pension—an amount by then totaling $85,000—and came up with the "slayer statute," a state law that forbids pension payments to anyone convicted of killing a state employee even though they had been named as a beneficiary. They also were discussing forcing her to make full restitution to the taxpayers.

After being strip-searched she was handed a shapeless beige shirt and ill-fitting pants. The jail once made news when *Primetime*'s Diane Sawyer climbed into similar scrubs to spend a day and night there for a TV story about life behind bars. The program noted that the facility harbors some of the most violent female criminals in Georgia. Used to twisting men around her finger, Lynn would have to learn how to survive in a world where lesbian relationships are the norm. If she joined in the fun she'd be a "stud" or a "femme." If she didn't, she'd be left out. Up to ninety percent of the inmates are reckoned to have had sex with another woman while in prison.

According to the show, in such a hormonally charged environment, much of the conflict is fueled by jealousy. On *Primetime*, prisoners showed Sawyer how to make lighters, weapons and sex toys from whatever they find lying around. They can have visits from their children twice a month. There are classes in anger management, dog training, cosmetology and computers. There are none on chemistry.

Ironically the woman who once quizzed a Humane Society employee about drugs used to euthanize animals, might be a candidate for pet therapy, a program that has been operating for nearly two decades since a friendly St. Bernard named Geraldine was brought by to say hi. The thinking is that the dogs provide an outlet for emotion. "Animals show unconditional love. The inmates are able to finally hug something and love it back," Ceola West, Metro State Prison Activity Therapist, told Sawyer.

The following Tuesday, May 18, Cobb County commissioners showed Lynn no love whatsoever, cutting off her financial lifeline. Spokesman Robert Quigley said that steps were being taken to recoup the $85,000 they had already paid out and that the private insurance company that paid her over $100,000 on her husband's death had been told of her conviction and might also seek its money back.

By Tuesday, June 29, 2004, Jimmy Berry and Vic Reynolds were back in court. They had rounded up over a dozen supporters of Lynn to persuade a judge that pending an appeal, she should be released. Judge Bodiford was not swayed. She would stay locked up, he decided. The Turners were dismayed that she could even ask. "My brother has not had a second chance, why should she?" said Linda. But Bodiford allowed that his decision to let the jury hear about the similarities in Randy Thompson's death could be cause for an appeal. It was the most important decision he'd taken on the bench. He believed it was the right one, but he said that it would be up to the Georgia Supreme Court to uphold it or strike it down.

In June, Lynn's mother and stepfather took action against her in civil court. Since she had no need for income, and as they were retired and living on Social Security and limited investments, they asked for the balance from the sale of the house at Tallantworth Crossing, her 1998 Jeep Grand Cherokee and what was left in her Bank of America account to be signed over to them to raise her children. They put the figure at $50,000. On the 17th their request was granted by Judge Jeffrey Bagley.

That summer, while her parents were struggling with the new reality, they would be solely responsible for 8-year-old Amber and Blake, 5, Lynn embarked on a writing campaign to obtain all the paperwork pertaining to an appeal. From her new digs, utilizing her familiarity with legal procedures, and using the name Julia Lynn Womack Turner, she wrote to the clerk of the Cobb County Superior Court:

Jay C. Stephenson
Clerk Superior Court
P.O. Box 3370
Marietta, Georgia 30061

Please provide me with a copy of my entire file, to include, but not limited to any and all documents filed by the Judge, State, Defense and any other party. I am currently incarcerated at the Cobb County Adult Detention Center. Thanking you for your assistance in this matter.

Sincerely,
Lynn Turner.

The letter contained her prisoner number, 775433 and her new address, cellblock 6. Deputy Clerk Chris Plummer acknowledged receipt of the letter and told her that he would need a signed order from the judge unsealing the transcripts, warning her that these were the only free copies she would get and that if she needed them replaced, it would be at a cost of 25 cents a page.

On October 1, 2004, Lynn was back in court, this time claiming she was broke. The public defender's office had declared her indigent and said they would provide a Marietta lawyer for her appeal. It was an argument she soon wished she had never made. At a hearing to decide whether she was entitled to free legal aid, Pat Head produced six witnesses to testify that she was nowhere near penniless. A loan coordinator from Ameriquest Mortgage Company told the court that she had been granted a refinancing loan just one month before the trial and when she'd sent in her application, she had enclosed recent pay stubs. Jimmy Berry tried to quash the evidence. "The public defender made the ruling and it ought to stand," he argued.

Judge Bodiford allowed the paperwork to be submitted, and an agreement was reached. Lynn would have to pay for attorneys if she decided to appeal her conviction, but transcripts of the trial would be provided free, saving her almost $20,000. Even if the house still had an outstanding mortgage, the balance of her assets amounted to some $50,000 and Head believed that she had a lot more stashed elsewhere. Despite losing Glenn's pension, she was racking up $1,500 every month from Randy's death. The judge had no idea what she had done with that money, he added.

Berry said Lynn was in the process of ceding custody of Amber and Blake to her mother and stepfather, and the checks would then go directly to them. Linda Hardy couldn't believe her sister-in-law's latest barefaced audacity. "Here she is again, trying to get away with something," she said.

All told, that first week in October was not a good one for Lynn. Four days later, on Monday, October 4, she was indicted by a Forsyth County grand jury in the death of Randy. His parents wept. "It's been a long road, but we never wanted to take it in the first place," his father told reporters outside the court. "We'll see what happens. We're relieved it's gotten to this point. It's just that we don't know how long the road is going to be, it's a long, long time before it's over with. The fact is, he's never going to come back. Maybe we can get some kind of closure some day and this is a step in the right direction. Randy can't speak for himself and neither can Glenn Turner. So we'll do what we have to do." Nita added, "I want the person who did it to be brought to justice, I want that for my son."

The news was transmitted to Lynn in the Cobb County Adult Detention Center, where she'd been brought to wait out the results of her appeal. There was more: Gwinnett County District Attorney Danny Porter announced that he was asking yet another grand jury to indict her on three counts of forgery. Cobb County prosecutors had tipped him off to the allegedly phony tax returns she'd given to Ameriquest when refinancing her home. She'd used the money to pay her lawyers. It didn't surprise Porter. "This is consistent with the personality described during the trial. Here is this person facing these murder charges, and she goes out and commits another crime in an attempt to defend herself in a murder-for-profit case," he told the *Marietta Daily Journal*. She could be looking at a further 10 years on each charge in prison, he said.

With only the welcome odd outing to the court to break the monotony she faced daily in the newly renovated and expanded center, Lynn hit the law books, asked for pencil and paper and busied herself with more letters to Cobb County's Superior Court.

"I have made several requests for documents that were filed but I have not received, this being my second request direct to you. There are approximately 5500-6000 pages of documents that I did not receive. I do need them so I can continue to work on my appeal," she complained to the clerk.

On December 8, Lynn got an early lump of coal for Christmas when Jack Mallard confirmed that he would seek the death sentence at her upcoming trial. If ultimately carried out, it would make her the first woman put to death by the state of Georgia since 1945. Mallard's appointment as special prosecutor for the second trial was dismaying to the defense. Not only would they be up against the evidence that was allowed through similar transactions in the first case, Mallard had been privy to everything that had gone on inside the courtroom and in the Cobb County district attorney's office.

As he spoke, the eyes of the Turner and Thompson families, separated only by the aisle, were riveted on him. Lynn, in a navy pantsuit and with her hands cuffed, answered clearly, "Not guilty" when asked to enter a plea. She did not react when Mallard stated that he wanted her to pay with her life. After the ten-minute hearing was over, she was led off to the Forsyth County Jail in Cumming, where she would remain until a jury in Randy's murder trial decided whether she would live or die.

Jimmy Berry claimed his client was taking it in stride. "She knew it was coming," he said gloomily and acknowledged that defending her in the second trial would be an uphill battle. Nita Thompson declared that she didn't care what happened to Lynn Turner "as long as she is where she can't hurt anybody else. I want her to stay [in jail] forever."

The New Year started just as badly. On January 30, 2005, the Georgia Supreme Court decided that Lynn was stuck with Judge Bagley, whom she'd tried unsuccessfully to have recused, claiming he'd talked to both her and her mother when they worked in the Forsyth County Courthouse.

On Monday, February 7, 2005, Lynn was back in court looking for money. At a hearing in Marietta, Vic Reynolds asked that the public pick up an estimated $20,000 tab for experts to testify at her upcoming trial. Once again, her lawyers would argue that Randy had been suicidal; he had tried to take his own life before, and this time he'd succeeded. That was to be the crux of their case.

Lynn's attorneys calculated that when a new jury heard Melanie Harper testify that she feared Randy had swallowed a fistful of pills the night before he died, and that his painkillers had been flushed down the toilet, it would introduce an element of serious doubt into their minds. The tactic had Nita Thompson shaking her head in disbelief. Her son was no martyr, he had a low threshold for pain; he would never have killed himself in such an agonizing way.

On November 13, 2005, Lynn was back in court demanding a new trial. Once more Jimmy Berry and Vic Reynolds complained that Judge Bodiford had erred when he allowed the prosecutors to introduce the "similar transaction." The request was denied. Much to her fury, he declined to explain why, a decision that brought some consolation to Glenn's mother. To her it was vindication that Lynn knew what she had done and didn't need the judge to spell it out to her again.

Lynn's next appearance was Friday, March 17, 2006, after being reindicted in the death of Randy Thompson. In an unusual move, Mallard had impaneled a grand jury to indict her again on Randy's murder, but this time had thrown in "aggravating circumstances," which upped the ante and would allow him to seek the death penalty. The grand jury granted his wish. For the hearing, Lynn was smartened up and wearing a dark blue dress with a matching jacket, and ankle shackles. She shuffled to the table, where she sat with her lawyers. When asked to stand and enter a plea, she said clearly, "Not guilty." The new case had now dragged on for over a year and a half, and showed no signs of coming to trial quickly. Her defense team had filed more than 100 motions.

Lynn was back in court in March. This time she was grumbling about her living quarters. Donald Cawthon was there and happily observed that Glenn's murderous wife now looked pretty rough. "It's getting to Lynn, she's all wrinkled and pale-faced," he says with a grin. "Her lawyer got up and said, 'We are going to call Ms. Turner,' and I'm like, 'What?' She got on the stand that day and I couldn't believe it. She was complaining about the 'inhumane conditions.' I'm thinking, You've got to be kidding me. It was a damn joke. In this whiny voice she's saying, 'I can't get my tennis shoes. The doctor says I can get them.'

To Donald it was a sickening list of grievances from the woman who'd snuffed out the life of his buddy.

"Her lawyer asks, 'How often do you have access to a computer, Miss Turner?' She says, 'I've had twenty minutes for the whole year,' then she's complaining 'The cell's cold' and she's not getting her prescription drugs. 'Oh no, they don't give me the right doses. I'm not sleeping well, I have anxieties.' She wants to go back to Metro. It's better than Forsyth County. She's also the jailhouse lawyer up in Cumming—she's giving the other prisoners advice on how to handle their cases."

Although there's been one guilty verdict, Donald says he won't rest until he sees the second trial through to the end. "I am not stopping with one case. I may not live long enough to see her get the needle. Even if she gets death in Randy's case, death penalty cases drag on for twenty years. But I'll live with the thought that she will have to endure twenty years on death row, knowing she'll die at the end of it."

No matter what happens to Lynn Turner, the loved ones of the men whose lives she destroyed will never be the same. The Thompson family has been torn apart: Nita and Perry divorced after more than thirty years together; Nita's health has deteriorated—she had a heart attack a couple of years after Randy died—and she and Angie no longer speak. These days, Nita devotes herself to her daughters, Kimberly and Brandie, and their children, whom she so plainly adores. She is still close to Nicholas, who is now a strapping teenager, and hopes that when the nightmare is finally over, she can reestablish contact with Amber and Blake.

Their tragedy made the Turners circle the wagons. On January 8, 2007, members of both families faced Lynn across a courtroom once more. "She does not look good," said Linda. "She's lost a lot of weight, her eyes are sunk back in her head a little bit and she looks a little worried. The last time she would stare at me. She only did that [a] couple of times. The sad part for her, and I was shocked, is that not one person was there for her." Linda said she's looking for Lynn to show some sign of remorse, but so far, she hasn't seen so much as a glimmer. "I wish she would, because I would feel better if she did, but I don't think I am ever going see it."

Eight days after potential jury selection began, Judge Jeffrey Bagley bowed to the inevitable and ruled to move the trial out of Forsyth County, saving the taxpayers the $150,000 that had been budgeted for it. Most of the potential jurors knew all about Lynn Turner and several admitted they could not be impartial. He said he would not divulge the new location until days before the proceedings were due to begin.

Kathy Turner chose not to stay home. The last twelve years have taken their toll, and this feisty and deeply reli-

Stacey Messex is still trying to forgive. "I just had to pray that God would take away my anger and allow me to et it go and be at peace that Glenn is in Heaven and watching me every day. I miss him terribly, but also believe I will see him again. I still catch myself, after all these years, looking at Cobb County police cars to see if it is him. My children and husband know all about him. They know he was someone special that was taken away way too early. I still cry when I think about him. I still stop by his grave to say hi. I still look at our pictures and smile. I will always miss him, always love him."

gious woman is tired. She still has the cleaning b
she began when her children were small, but she's
to slow down. She volunteers at a school in the
noons and is active in her church. "People still gi
clippings. One week one ended up in the offering
Someone fished it out and gave it to me, saying, 'I
this is meant for you.' I don't read about it [the case]
more, but I do want to keep track of what's going on

Each year she returns to Jacksonville for her far
reunion. The week after, she and her children keep
other important date—the private memorial gathering
Glenn's graveside. Donald started what's also become
annual event. "He calls all the guys to make sure they
going to be there, and he orders the flowers—he's l
another son to me," said Kathy. She clings to what Gle
told her shortly before he died: "He said, 'Mom, I
changing my life.' God gave me that and it is very co
forting." Each Christmas, with Linda and Margie at h
side, she writes a message to Glenn on a cutout paper a
gel and hangs it on the Angel Tree at the cemetery.

Glenn's former sergeant, Mike Archer, after a temp
rary stint in auto sales, went back to being a cop. Dav
Dunkerton is no longer at the 4th Precinct. "I transferr
out. We were together over two years, and I didn't ha
another partner after that because of the pain it cau
me when I lost him," he said.

To Donald, Glenn's death left an unfillable hole ir
life. "There is not a week goes by that I don't genui
genuinely, think what it would have been like fo
family and my family to get together. He would hav
somebody different, he would have had a family a
would have seen my boys and my wife and I woul
met his new family. Every day I feel very fortu
have the kind of love I had for my best friend," he
enjoyed being with him more than I did being v
first wife. It was a special bond."